Sacrificing Soldiers on the National Mall

The publisher gratefully acknowledges the generous support of the Ahmanson Foundation Humanities Endowment Fund of the University of California Press Foundation.

Sacrificing Soldiers on the National Mall

Kristin Ann Hass

UNIVERSITY OF CALIFORNIA PRESS
BERKELEY LOS ANGELES LONDON

Parts of chapter 1 were published in a different form as "Remembering
the 'Forgotten War' and Containing the 'Remembered War': Insistent
Nationalism and the Transnational Memory of the Korean War," in
Transnational American Memories, ed. Udo J. Hebel (Berlin: Walter de
Gruyter, 2009). Parts of chapter 2 were published previously as a book review,
"Peggy Pascoe's *What Comes Naturally: Miscegenation Law and the Making
of Race in America* and the Use of Legal History to Police Social Boundaries,"
Michigan State Law Review 2011, no. 1 (2011): 255–61.

University of California Press, one of the most distinguished university
presses in the United States, enriches lives around the world by advancing
scholarship in the humanities, social sciences, and natural sciences. Its
activities are supported by the UC Press Foundation and by philanthropic
contributions from individuals and institutions. For more information,
visit www.ucpress.edu.

University of California Press
Berkeley and Los Angeles, California

University of California Press, Ltd.
London, England

Library of Congress Cataloging-in-Publication Data

Hass, Kristin Ann, 1965–.
    Sacrificing soldiers on the National Mall / Kristin Ann Hass.
        p.   cm.
    Includes bibliographical references and index.
    ISBN 978-0-520-27410-5 (cloth : alk. paper)
    ISBN 978-0-520-27411-2 (pbk. : alk. paper)
    ISBN 978-0-520-95475-5 (ebook)
        1. Mall, The (Washington, D.C.).   2. War memorials—Washington
(D.C.).   3. World War II Memorial (Washington, D.C.).   4. Korean War
Veterans Memorial (Washington, D.C.).   5. National Japanese American
Memorial to Patriotism (Washington, D.C.).   6. Memorialization—United
States.   7. Collective memory—United States.   I. Title.
    F203.5.M2H377   2013
    975.3—dc23   2012044182

Manufactured in the United States of America

21   20   19   18   17   16   15   14   13
10   9   8   7   6   5   4   3   2   1

In keeping with a commitment to support environmentally responsible and
sustainable printing practices, UC Press has printed this book on Rolland
Enviro100, a 100% postconsumer fiber paper that is FSC certified, deinked,
processed chlorine-free, and manufactured with renewable biogas energy.
It is acid-free and EcoLogo certified.

For Cameron, Finn, Cole, and Hazel

CONTENTS

List of Illustrations ix

Acknowledgments xi

Introduction 1

1. · Forgetting the Remembered War at
the Korean War Veterans Memorial 21

2. · Legitimating the National Family with
the Black Revolutionary War Patriots Memorial 59

3. · The Nearly Invisible Women in
Military Service for America Memorial 96

4. · Impossible Soldiers and the National Japanese American
Memorial to Patriotism during World War II 122

5. · "We Leave You Our Deaths, Give Them Their Meaning":
Triumph and Tragedy at the National World War II Memorial 152

Epilogue 196

Notes 199
Selected Bibliography 229
Index 243

ILLUSTRATIONS

1. Charles L'Enfant's 1791 plan of Washington. 11
2. McMillan plan. 13
3. Korean War Veterans Memorial. 25
4. Korean War Veterans Memorial. 28
5. Korean War Veterans Memorial figures chart. 50
6. Korean War Veterans Memorial. 55
7. Black Revolutionary War Patriots Memorial design with Ed Dwight. 84
8. Black Revolutionary War Patriots Memorial figures. 85
9. National Liberty Memorial rendering. 93
10. Strom Thurmond Memorial. 94
11. Women in Military Service for America Memorial, before restoration. 107
12. Women in Military Service for America Memorial. 116
13. Women in Military Service for America Memorial with sign. 117
14. Women in Military Service for America Memorial entrance. 119
15. National Japanese American Memorial to Patriotism during World War II. 123
16. National Japanese American Memorial to Patriotism during World War II. 124
17. National Japanese American Memorial to Patriotism during World War II. 139
18. Friedrich St. Florian's initial design for the National World War II Memorial. 169

19. National World War II Memorial. 181

20. National World War II Memorial. 183

21. National World War II Memorial. 192

22. National World War II Memorial. 193

ACKNOWLEDGMENTS

The first person I want to thank for helping me to write this book is Susan Raposa, the information specialist for the Commission of Fine Arts. At the very start of this process she was helpful and thorough, and she encouraged me to believe that there was indeed a book worth writing in the neatly stacked boxes in the quiet CFA offices. Marcella Brown, the information resources specialist at the National Capital Planning Commission, also aided early on by opening up her files. Shelly Jacobs at the Ronald Reagan Presidential Library worked diligently on my FOIA requests, and Jennifer Mandel helped me sift through the newly opened material. The staff at the National Park Service National Capital Region offices generously gave me access to material in their files. Martha Sell at the American Battle Monuments Commission helped me negotiate every researcher's nightmare—a fire in the archives. Archivists at the George Bush, George W. Bush, and William J. Clinton Presidential Libraries graciously helped me determine that their collections held little for me. The same is true for Kim Nusco at the John Carter Brown Library. I am indebted to all of them.

I am also incredibly grateful for the time key actors took to talk to me and respond to my arguments about the memorials. Maurice Barboza, Marilla Cushman, Don De Leon, Ed Dwight, Frank Gaylord, Jan Scruggs, Friedrich St. Florian, Jan Scruggs, and General Wilma Vaught are all remarkable and remarkably busy people. I couldn't have written this book without their help. And though I know they don't all share my conclusions, I hope they find a profound respect for them in these pages.

My dear friend and favorite photographer, Hank Savage, took nearly all the photographs in the book. This is the second book he has illustrated for me, and I couldn't be more grateful. Thank you, Hank.

Scholars Beth Bailey, Pete Daniel, Ed Linenthal, George Sanchez, and Dell Upton each stepped up to provide crucial support at some point in the project. I am grateful for their kindness and their scholarship.

The Program in American Culture at the University of Michigan has been my intellectual and institutional home for a very long time. I am lucky and proud to be part of this community of scholars. I want to thank the AC staff—Judy Gray, Mary Freiman, Marlene Moore, Brook Posler, and Tabby Rohn—for being so good at what they do. Graduate students Aimee Von Bokel and Paul Farber were able assistants as I wrote. And, of course, I am indebted to my friends and colleagues here, past and present, for the time they have given in reading drafts, asking hard questions, and pushing me in unexpected and productive ways. This is especially true of Paul Anderson, Sara Blair, Jay Cook, Julie Ellison, Jonathan Freedman, Joe Gone, Sandra Gunning, June Howard, Mary Kelley, Tiya Miles, Damon Salesa, Xiomara Santamarina, Carroll Smith-Rosenberg, Amy Stillman, Alan Wald, Penny Von Eschen, and Magdalena Zaborowski. Julie, June, and Mary have also been important mentors for me. Phil Deloria and Greg Dowd both helped me think through this book and saw me through the tenure process with kindness and grace; I will always be grateful to them. Michael Witgen was my closest reader and most focused critic. I am much obliged for his help; he made this a better book.

Niels Hooper at the University of California Press has shepherded this book across what feels like, to both of us I am sure, vast expanses of time and space. Thank you for all the weak coffee in bad conference hotels across the country and for your perseverance. Thanks also to all involved parties at the press, especially the patient and efficient Kim Hogeland and the eagled-eyed Elizabeth Berg.

I cannot thank my friends enough. Marybeth Lewis proofread the whole manuscript. Ann Stevenson kept me going on innumerable occasions; Curt Catallo fed me on innumerable occasions. Deirdre, John, Hugh, and Guy Cross took great care of me when I was in Washington. Heidi and Vincenzo Binetti shared the chaos and the fun of the life of a scholar with a house full of kids. The teachers at Bach Elementary School, Slauson Middle School, and Pioneer High School took fabulous care of these kids. Jean Mandel, Dahlia Petrus, and Sioban Scanlon inspired me to want to do this right. And Frank Mitchell helped because he is Frank.

I have had an unending supply of unconditional love from my parents—Earlene Hass and Robert Hass. Anything I have ever done well comes from them. My family—Leif, Luke, Tommy, Margaret, Sahai, Tom, Brenda, Marilynn, Duncan, Molly, Jenny, Duncan, Josephine, Ella, Fiona, Louisa, Charlie, Leon, Co Co, Bill, Karin and family, Libby and family—have supported me in a million ways, big and small. Of course, Cameron Magoon has been my partner in this and in all things. Thank you for every little thing, really. Finally, I want to thank Finn and Cole and Hazel for being Finn and Cole and Hazel. You guys gave me a reason to write this book.

Introduction

> They say, We leave you our deaths: give them their meanings: give
> them an end to the war and a true peace: give them a victory that
> ends the war and a peace afterwards: give them their meaning.
> We were young, they say. We have died. Remember us.

ARCHIBALD MACLEISH

IN 1943 THE TREASURY DEPARTMENT asked librarian of Congress
Archibald MacLeish to write a statement to help sell war bonds.[1] This is
from the poem he wrote. It is just a few lines, but it evokes a pact between
the soldier and the nation in no uncertain terms: "We leave you our deaths;
give them their meaning." The life of the soldier is traded for a memory that
makes a shared meaning of the death. MacLeish understood the work of
remembering soldiers for what it is—grave and consequential. The endless
parade of visitors to the war memorials on the National Mall in Washington,
D.C., seem to make their pilgrimages with a sense of this gravity. Middle
school students who don't quite get it are hushed by impatient chaperones,
and the resulting silence feels something like reverence. Millions of people
(these school groups, families on vacation, and visiting dignitaries) go to the
war memorials on the Mall every year—and likely will for perpetuity—to
witness history and to see for themselves what it means and what it has meant
to be an American.

From 1791, when the capital was designed, to 1982, the story told on the
National Mall was the story of great American leaders and their triumphant
ideas about democracy. There were no national war memorials on the Mall.[2]
Since 1982, when the Vietnam Veterans Memorial was dedicated, the story
told on the Mall has shifted to emphasize American wars and soldiers. In
fact, in the last thirty years five significant war memorials have been built
on, or very nearly on, the Mall. The Vietnam Veterans Memorial, the Korean
War Veterans Memorial, the Women in Military Service for America Memorial, the National Japanese American Memorial to Patriotism during World

War II, and the National World War II Memorial not only have transformed the physical space of the Mall but have also dramatically rewritten the ideas expressed there about the United States. (The Black Revolutionary War Patriots Memorial was also approved by Congress in this period but has not yet been built.) This book is about this war memorial boom, the debates that surrounded each memorial project, the memorials these debates produced, and the new narratives they created about what it means to be an American. This book asks, in Archibald MacLeish's terms, what meanings we have made in exchange for the lives of the young, dead soldiers. It also asks if we have made good on our enormous responsibility to them.

This sense of responsibility has, of course, a history. In the United States before the Civil War, many Americans were hostile to the idea of a standing federal army and its soldiers. Most soldiers were volunteers in local militias, and many, though certainly not all, soldiers in Washington's federal army were "hirelings" to whom little ceremonial attention was paid.[3] (Surely there were heroes of the Revolutionary War, but foot soldiers were relatively neglected and there was a continued wariness of the federal army.) During the Civil War the white citizen soldier emerged as a heroic figure and became an important character in the construction of American nationalism. As historian Drew Gilpin Faust describes it, "They came to belong to the nation, and the nation came to belong to them."[4] This link was reflected in the burial of foot soldiers in marked graves for the first time at Gettysburg and Lincoln's reimaging of the nation in terms of the sacrifice of those soldiers in his address there.[5] ("But, in a larger sense, we can not dedicate—we can not consecrate—we can not hallow—this ground. The brave men, living and dead, who struggled here, have hallowed it, far above our poor power to add or detract.")[6] As historian Thomas Laqueur puts it, the Gettysburg Address was "an occasion for redefining of a polity on the bodies of those who gave their lives for it."[7]

This emphasis on the fallen soldier as central to the life of the nation led in World War I to dog tags, service flags, and repatriation policies, because the soldier that belonged to the nation required recognition and celebration. The ascension of the figure of the soldier continued through the Second World War, when "our boys" from Brooklyn and Biloxi "saved a world in flames." It has, however, been complicated in the post–World War II period. The Vietnam War, in particular, tarnished the figure of the American citizen soldier, brought an end to the draft in the United States, and led to a professionalized, although not necessarily egalitarian, all-volunteer military; it changed both the actual terms of service and the terms in which service was understood.

Indeed, Cold War and post–Cold War conflicts have proved challenging to a consistent understanding of American wars as virtuous, and this has complicated the revered social position of the soldier. The Civil War and World War II have been mostly understood—despite the ways in which they were complicated and the contradictory nature of the phrase—as "good wars" fought in the name of freedom and democracy. This framing, which has gained considerable strength through popular histories and films in the last thirty years, has allowed for a post-Vietnam reclaiming of "our boys" as heroic.[8] But there continues to be a tension between the wars the United States is fighting and the ideal of the "good war." This tension has raised high-stakes questions about the soldiers fighting in these wars and has fueled the war memorial boom on the National Mall.

Nearly all the advocates for the new memorials on the Mall are quite explicit about wanting to build their memorials in response to the problematic memory of the Vietnam War. For many, the crisis of patriotism produced by the Vietnam War created a need to reassert U.S. nationalism in particular terms, and for all of them, honoring the memory of American soldiers who served in Vietnam inspired a desire to produce more memory of more soldiers. War memorials on the Mall emerged as important sites at which to do just this. These memorial advocates were probably not studying scholarly theories of nationalism, but they may as well have been. The most pervasive theme in scholarly thinking about nations and nationalism is that memories of dead soldiers are central to the construction of nationalism.[9] Nineteenth- and twentieth-century theorists of nations return again and again to the creation of shared pasts, particularly shared memories of soldiers. These shared pasts, or memories, are not merely expressions of nationalism; they are constitutive of it. Nations and memories, in fact, exist in mutual dependence—a "memory-nation nexus."[10] In this formulation, nation and memory are inextricably bound; memories constitute nations, and as sociologist Jeffery Olick writes, memory is "the handmaiden of nationalist zeal."[11]

In 1882, one of the first theorists of nationalism, Ernest Renan, described the nation as an essentially *cognitive* construction: "A nation is a spiritual principle, the outcome of the profound complications of history; it is a spiritual family not a group determined by the shape of the earth."[12] Emphasizing the importance of a shared past in creating the nation, he argued, "More valuable by far than common customs posts and frontiers conforming to strategic ideas is the fact of sharing, in the past, a glorious heritage and regrets." Renan understood these shared pasts as dynamic rather than fixed: "Forgetting, I would even go so far as to say historical error is a crucial factor in the creation of a nation."[13] Nations, then, are constructed by, among other things, the daily willful forgetting or misremembering of shared grief. Later theorists complicate this, but Renan's formulation of how nations operate has had remarkable staying power and suggests that war memorials serve multiple, powerful social purposes.

Historian Benedict Anderson, the most influential of recent theorists of nationalism, builds on Renan's thinking: "Ultimately it is this fraternity that makes it possible, over the past two centuries, for so many millions of people, not so much to kill, as willingly to die for such limited imaginings."[14] He continues, "These deaths bring us abruptly face to face with the central problem posed by nationalism: What makes the shrunken imaginings of recent history (scarcely more than two centuries) generate such colossal sacrifices?" Invented pasts, in this formulation, are so potent that they produce nations for which millions willingly die. In other words, the idea of the nation produced by a past invented by war memorials, for instance, is no trifling matter. In the thinking of these theorists, the stakes in the memorial process could, in fact, hardly be higher. This is also true for recent practitioners in the United States—it is what drove the individuals and agencies who fought to get their war memorials on the Mall built.

In *The Invention of Tradition,* historian Eric Hobsbawm gives specific form to the process of constructing these crucial pasts. In his formulation, nations are shaped by practices that "imply a continuity with the past" but don't necessarily involve recalling objects or affects of the past.[15] In other words, the memorial does not actually remember a discrete object, but invents a version of the past to be remembered for the purposes of the present and in so doing creates nationalism for its moment. Historian Anne McClintock echoes this point when she argues, crucially, that the past that gets invented is not random but serves social needs of the moment. She pushes for thoughtful, thorough parsing of these invented pasts: "Nationalisms are not simply phantasmagoria of the mind; as systems of cultural representation whereby people come to imagine a shared experience of identification with an extended community, they are historical practices through which social difference is both invented and performed."[16] In the U.S. context, race and gender are key social differences at play in the reconstruction of U.S. nationalism. In fact, the gendering and racialization of national imagery are essential points of entry into thinking about how nations work. Race and gender appear everywhere in the debates about the memorials on the Mall, sometimes in quite unexpected ways. And they require moving beyond the potentially too loose framing of the "phantasmagoria" of a nebulous, invented shared past—or memory—into the hard particularities of these "shared imaginings."[17] The remembered past, then, is not just *any* past, reproduced and misremembered. Rather, particular pasts are put to particular uses in particular moments. We need to address these particularities to understand the nationalism of any particular moment.[18] This is crucial framing for thinking about the nation and nationalism in the United States in the last thirty years. It is crucial, but not particularly *precise* framing, and it requires some further thinking about memory and remembering.

We are, as scholar after scholar has proclaimed, in the midst of a memory boom.[19] According to historian Jay Winter, we are experiencing an "efflorescence of interest in the subject of memory inside the academy and beyond it."[20] In the academy, this boom has produced a rich body of literature. A good deal of energy in the literature on memory is devoted to developing terminologies and mechanisms for understanding and holding onto processes of memory, however fleetingly. Collective memory, countermemory, narrative memory, habitual memory, prosthetic memory, vernacular memory, official memory, and postmemory are just a few of the useful ways of thinking about memory that scholars have developed. Postmemory and prosthetic memory relate to the interest in memories of previous generations, for example.[21] Collective memory tries to understand the broad social dynamics of memory. Vernacular memory tries to understand shared memory produced by individual actors, rather than by the state. Perhaps the two most productive areas in memory studies have been the relationship between history and memory and the links between memory and trauma.[22] Historian David Blight gets quite productively at the history/memory problem when he writes, "History and memory must be treated as unsteady, conflicted companions in our quest to understand humankind's consciousness of the past."[23] Perhaps most usefully, Jenny Edkins evokes trauma to get at the uses to which memory is put when she argues that states produce trauma, and then "by rewriting these traumas into a linear narrative of national heroism . . . [the] state conceals the trauma it has . . . produced."[24] Both ideas need to be present in thinking about memory on the Mall. Most of this sprawling literature on memory is compelling, but it also threatens to make *memory* so loaded a term as to be nearly meaningless and vulnerable to trivialization, as Winter describes it, "through inclusion of any and every facet of our contact with the past, personal or collective."[25]

To bring some measure of precision, if this is possible, to thinking about memory, Winter suggests the term *remembrance* as a substitute for *memory*. He likes *remembrance* because it implies agency, locating memory with the *act* of remembering and therefore the context of remembering. This is useful not only because it implies agency—memory doesn't occur in a vacuum but is the work of actors in contexts—but also because it shifts thinking about memory and, with it, the memory-nation nexus, away from actually remembering in the most common sense. Memory, in the memory-nation nexus, seems not to be about recalling an event but rather about producing a past and recollecting for the sake of the future, with a fluctuating sense of obligation to historical detail.

This flexibility of memory is certainly part of the story of war memorials in the United States. The history of American war memorials can be told in two ways. In the first version, it is a story of the democratization of memory shaped by increased interest in the sacrifices of individual citizen soldiers. In the second version, it is a story of the sacrifices of individual soldiers used to define racial difference and a highly racialized nation, despite the historical particularities of the war in which they fought.

The democratization narrative begins in Gettysburg, where the bodies of soldiers were buried in individual graves for the first time. Starting in the 1860s, the local war memorial of choice across the country was the figure of the common soldier in the town center.[26] Soldiers in the First World War were issued dog tags so that they might be more efficiently identified in death, buried, and insistently named on headstones and in memorials. Building on this focus on the individual soldier, the Second World War was remembered with infrastructure (parks, highways, auditoriums) for the victorious GIs and families of the fallen. At the Vietnam Veterans Memorial—surely a distinctive memorial—the dead are named, and ordinary people bring unsolicited offerings to the site. This intensification of the attention paid to individual loss—from the grave, to the name, to the spoils of victory, to the bottle of aftershave left at the Wall—makes sense as a democratization narrative: the common man (if not the common woman) is honored, rather than the state for which he fought. This is just what Lincoln asked for at Gettysburg: that the soldier be honored above all else. As historian Ed Linenthal describes it, American memorial culture in this period was "characterized by the democratization of memorials and memorial process."[27]

My first book, *Carried to the Wall: American Memory and the Vietnam Veterans Memorial*, contributes to this democratization narrative. There I argue that African Americans, Mexican Americans, Puerto Ricans, American Indians, and working-class Irish and Italian Catholic Americans transformed public memorial practices in the United States by bringing their private practices of grief to the Wall. These rituals, especially the leaving of personal objects, introduced ways of negotiating the liminal position of the dead into national spaces. That some of the least politically and socially powerful people in the United States rewrote nation-forging memorial practices to demand that attention be paid to increasingly personalized individual losses is potentially democratizing. As Linenthal suggests, in this moment, "memorialization had become a significant form of cultural expression.... [M]uch more than a gesture of remembrance, memorialization was a way to stake one's claim to visible presence in the culture," which often "became a strategy of excavation and preservation of long hidden ethnic American voices and grievances."[28] These elements of the democratization narrative get played out in dramatic terms at the Vietnam Memorial.

There is much to celebrate in this democratization narrative. Honoring citizen soldiers seems laudable, as does public speech from the ground up. The emergence of a powerful, multiracial, multiethnic public memorial form, which demands that attention be paid to the individual bodies of fallen soldiers, also seems worth celebrating. But the democratization narrative is not the only story to be told about the building of war memorials in the United States. Especially since the Civil War, U.S. war memorials have also worked to imagine a white nation. The Civil War has been remembered in Gettysburg, Washington, and beyond in terms of a racialized reconciliation—expressing white unity, repressing the memory of slavery, and erasing race from the memory of the war. Kirk Savage writes, "The commemoration of the Civil War in physical memorials is ultimately a story of systematic cultural repression, carried out in the guise of reconciliation and harmony."[29] Cecelia O'Leary sees this "racialized reconciliation"—of white northern veterans and white southern veterans—expressed in war memorials, battlefield celebrations, soldiers' reunions, and the emergence of Memorial Day in this period.[30] As Blight describes it, "The problem of 'reunion' and the problem of 'race' were trapped in a tragic, mutual dependence" that defined memorial practice well into the twentieth century.[31] This whitening of the memory of war deeply complicates the democratization narrative.

The long period of relative disinterest in war memorials that stretched from the end of the Civil War memorial-building boom in the 1920s into the post–World War II period allowed the visual tension between the democratization narrative and the whitening of the memory of soldiers to lie dormant. It is important to note, however, that the whitening of memory did not disappear in the postwar period. It can be traced in quite dramatic terms to the living memorials that were built after the war. Memorial highways were often constructed over African American neighborhoods bulldozed to create space for them, and memorial pools were often built in suburbs to which African Americans were denied access by the Federal Housing Authority's redlining practices, which sharply restricted African American access to mortgage loans, and by restricted covenants.[32] The *representational* problem of the tradition of "the white soldier who gets remembered" and the actual populations that served in wars waged by the United States, however, did not return until the 1980s, when interest in memorials was renewed.

This representational problem for memorials needs to be understood in terms of broad shifts in the thinking about race in American culture as well as specific public understandings of race and the military. Further, the specific question of race and military service was, and continues to be, important to debates about the all-volunteer military. The draft ended with the Vietnam War in 1973 in part because of public protests about the racial and economic inequality of the Selective Service System. There were, however, other reasons. As historian Beth Bailey explains it, "A group of free-market economists who gained influence in the presidential campaign and administration of Richard M. Nixon provided the initial and determining structure for the all-volunteer force," ending the draft as a political liability and turning over military service to the free-market arena.[33] Still, a major concern about the all-volunteer military was that it would be predominantly filled by poor African Americans. Bailey describes this concern as cutting across the political spectrum: "Some worried about the exploitation of black Americans, in part because of a powerful and persistent belief that African Americans had been treated as cannon fodder in the Vietnam War and in part because of a belief that volunteers drawn heavily from the nation's most disadvantaged group would not be true volunteers." She adds, "Others feared an army composed of poor—and thus presumably angry, degenerate, or unskilled—black men."[34] Both anxieties were in play for the individuals and agencies working to build war memorials, and the memorials they built reflect the difficulties in negotiating the histories of racialized memory and democratized memory.

So while "remember the soldiers, remember the soldiers, remember the soldiers" is a mantra of the memorial conversations on the Mall, the *content* to be recalled, or recollected, is sometimes only minimally present and is often misconstrued for the purposes of the present. The fact of remembering—or, as Winter would have it, the remembrance—seems to be more important than what happened in the past. James Young comments, "It is as if once we assign monumental form to memory, we have to some degree divested ourselves of the obligation to remember."[35] In fact, on the Mall in the recent past it is almost as if once we *gesture* toward memory, we divest ourselves of the obligation to remember what actually happened.

Writing about scholarship on commemoration, historian Kirk Savage begins with a reminder that commemoration is defined as a "call to remembrance."[36] He understands this to mean that commemorations "prod collective memory in some conspicuous way." And though he is thoughtfully skeptical about what collective memory might actually be, his simple definition is salient for contemporary commemoration in the United States. A will for memory to be evoked—the call to remembrance—is expressed unequivocally, but the evocation of memory trumps remembrance itself.[37] Memory, in the common use of the word, is both a faculty and an object. Memorializing has as one of its effects linking the faculty of memory with the experience of connecting to the meaning and value of the nation, quite apart from that other meaning, the particular thing remembered. As a result, in thinking about the memorials on the Mall, historian Joanna Bourke's pithy observation that remembering "operates in the service of social power" is more pressing than tracking the myriad processes of memory.[38]

For this reason, I stick closely to the conversations about the memorials as they were planned and debated. Witnessing is a methodological imperative for this book. It witnesses the process through which social power is expressed in the minutes of meetings and published reports and stories in the press; it observes and reports on the operation of social power in the details of the process of remembrance.[39] Each chapter takes up a specific memorial project and systematically tracks the conversations and debates that surrounded the memorial from the first suggestions for a memorial through always tumultuous site and design debates to the memorial's dedication. Each chapter studies these debates as they have been preserved in the papers of key organizations, the memories of key participants, and the newspapers reporting on the memorials in progress.[40] This allows us to observe the process through which the past is invented to serve the social needs of the present. It reveals complicated, confounding, uneven, and often extraordinary processes of constructing nationalism. Blight has called for studies of memory that are "rooted in deep research, sensitive to contexts and to the varieties of memory at play in any given epoch."[41] Witnessing the memorial process in this way enables us to reveal the way nationalism is constructed.

Today, Washington, Lincoln, and Jefferson all occupy the Mall with such gravity that it is hard to imagine this national memorial space without them.[42] But, in fact, the story of the Mall is one of periods of great investment in and anxiety about its symbolic potential alternating with periods of neglect and indifference. In the periods of neglect, it has been home to slave pens, untamed gardens, Civil War deserters, "the flotsam of the war," Army hospitals, brothels, public markets, grazing cattle, the city's railway station, and temporary military buildings. In periods of great interest, Washington, Lincoln, Jefferson, and now a parade of twentieth-century wars have been reworked to define the nationalism of their moment.

In 1791 Washington charged Pierre L'Enfant with the design of the new capital. L'Enfant wanted the U.S. capital to look like the center of the mighty empire he hoped it would become. As his map shows, the symbolic center of his city was an "immense T-shaped public park"—which would eventually become the Mall.[43] L'Enfant and his plan have been much celebrated since 1791, but these celebrations often neglect to mention that, before his plan was realized, he was forced to resign because he had "difficulty in subordinating himself," and his grandiosity was not fully realized as the capital city was built.[44] The Mall as a site of explicit national symbolic speech was largely neglected into the 1830s.[45] In fact, to accommodate the slave trade that had become so central to American life, the early nineteenth-century Mall was home to sprawling slave pens. The brutal reality of slave pens was hardly what L'Enfant had imagined for this grand public space, but it does say something quite pointed about national life in the United States in the early 1830s.

Dramatic changes on the Mall later in the nineteenth century made it more explicitly a national symbolic space, but it was transformed in fits and starts—and with difficulty. The Washington Monument, the beginnings of the Smithsonian Institution, and the development of elaborate gardens shaped the Mall, while sectionalism, the Civil War, and its costs shook the nation. The Washington Monument Society was formed in 1833. Its members planned to spend no less than $1 million and vowed to build "the highest edifice in the world and the most stupendous and magnificent monument ever erected to man."[46] In 1848, when ground was broken, the speeches reflected

FIGURE 1. Charles L'Enfant's 1791 plan of Washington. (Courtesy of the Library of Congress.)

the anxieties of the moment, suggesting that the size of the memorial spoke to the enormity of the project of holding the nation together.[47]

As the monument was being built, other long-lasting changes were taking place on the Mall. An 1846 act of Congress gave the newly formed Smithsonian Institution the land on the Mall from Ninth to Twelfth Streets, and in 1855, the first Smithsonian building went up on the Mall. The Smithsonian Institute Building, known as "the Castle" because of its twelfth-century Gothic-style architecture, was the first of twelve museum buildings that would line the Mall from the Capitol to the Washington Monument. Built at a rate of roughly one every twenty years, these museums eventually defined the eastern half of the Mall. These institutions established the Mall as a site of pilgrimage for the linked receipt of knowledge and the celebration of national achievements.[48]

Despite the great height of the Washington Monument and the potency of the artifacts on display on the Mall by the 1880s, a plan for fully developing the national monumental core was not put into place until the turn of the century, when the success of the 1893 World Columbian Exposition in Chicago inspired a Michigan senator to reclaim and redesign the Mall. The success of the "White City" at the Chicago World's Fair in articulating a vision of a civilized, contained, vaulted, white nation is well known. Less has been made of the fact that the success of the Chicago fair inspired a revitalization of the real national capital.[49] In 1900, Senator James McMillan set out to remake the National Mall in the shape of the White City. With presidential and congressional support, McMillan formed the McMillan Commission and asked the fair's architect, Daniel Burnham, to lead the effort to realize the symbolic potential of the long-neglected national landscape in Washington.

The commission published its plan in 1902. Its principal elements involved shifting the Mall to realign the Capitol and the Washington Monument; moving the train station off the Mall; placing the Lincoln Memorial at the west end of the Mall facing east; building a Jefferson Memorial on the north-south axis of the Mall facing the White House and the Washington Monument; and building a memorial bridge, lined up behind the Lincoln Memorial, that would connect the Mall to Arlington National Cemetery. The effect of the plan was to create a clean, clearly delineated ceremonial federal space that was removed from the city itself. (This separated it from the local space, allowing for a literal whitening of the most heavily black city in the United States at the turn of the century.) The plan also added two "great men of ideas" to the Mall: Lincoln and Jefferson.

With this plan, Burnham and his associates were able to reproduce some of the successes of Chicago's 1893 Columbian Exposition. They achieved this on a grand scale. They made order out of chaos, expressed insistent national pride, and most importantly, drew sharp lines around highly charged national symbolic space. Though this space would continue to be refigured and fought over, the McMillan Mall would become, in the minds of many, *the* Mall—a finished work of art that defined a finished nation, a high point of democratic civilization embodied by Lincoln and Jefferson and their enormous Doric columns.

The early twentieth century on the Mall was also marked by a much less compelling, but not unimportant, centralization and federalization of patriotic practices and productions of the past in national space. A slew of federal agencies were established to oversee the Mall. It makes sense that as the Mall took on greater significance, the mechanism for maintaining and controlling

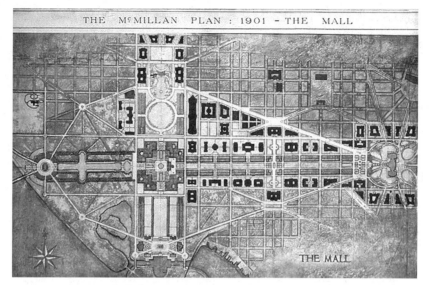

THE MALL

FIGURE 2. McMillan plan. (Courtesy of the National Capital Planning Commission.)

it tightened. In 1916, the National Parks Service was formed as part of the executive branch of the federal government to "conserve natural and historic objects." The National Parks Service assumed responsibility for oversight of national monuments, historic parks, national memorials, historic trails, heritage areas, battlefields, and cemeteries. The U.S. Commission of Fine Arts was established in 1910 by an act of Congress, and the National Capital Park Commission was established by an act of Congress in 1924 to maintain and oversee District of Columbia parks.[50] In varying degrees, these agencies were created for and charged with the protection of the Mall that had emerged from the McMillan Commission Report. The Commission of Fine Arts was, in fact, a direct response to the controversies surrounding the Lincoln Memorial.[51] Clearly, the Mall remade by the McMillan Commission represented a triumph of the national that Congress and others deemed worth protecting.[52]

The intense interest in building on the Mall dissipated after the major elements of the McMillan plan were completed. Between 1935 and 1979, there was another long period of relative neglect and disinterest in adding to the McMillan plan. Museums filled out the center of the Mall, and there were impassioned debates over their architectural forms, but little attention was paid to the memorial core. In fact, the western end of the Mall, between the Washington Monument and the Lincoln Memorial, was crammed with temporary military buildings during World War I that were not removed until the 1970s. Nixon, who flew over them in his helicopter almost daily, complained that they were eyesores.[53] He wanted them to be replaced with "Tivoli-like" gardens. Although the agencies responsible for the Mall found Nixon's plans to be too elaborate, his request resulted in the creation of Constitution Gardens. Stretching from the Lincoln Memorial to the Washington Monument, just north of the Reflecting Pool, which runs between the memorials, these gardens were dedicated in 1976 as a modest bicentennial tribute. In 1982, a few months before the dedication of the Vietnam Veterans Memorial, the humble Signers Memorial for the fifty-six signers of the Declaration of Independence was dedicated in Constitution Gardens.[54]

Also in the period 1935–79, however, interest in *using* the symbolic space of the Mall intensified dramatically. During these years, in moments of crisis or rupture in the national narrative of a triumphant, virtuous, free American republic, people used the Mall to seize the national stage and rewrite national narratives. This process gave the Mall new potency as sacred national ground. Starting in 1939, civil rights activists claimed the Lincoln Memorial and the Mall, and therefore the nation, as their own. They claimed the Lincoln Memorial and the Mall as sites that could lend moral authority and national sanction to their movements.[55] For example, in 1939, the Daughters of the American Revolution refused to allow contralto Marian Anderson to perform in their Constitution Hall because she was African American. First Lady Eleanor Roosevelt resigned her membership in protest, and the concert was brilliantly rescheduled for Easter Sunday on the steps of the Lincoln Memorial. Anderson sang and the Mall was changed.[56] Her performance quickly became famous. Scott Sandage quotes civil rights activist Mary McLeod Bethune as declaring the day after the concert, "We are on the right track, and through the Marian Anderson protest concert we made our triumphant entry into the democratic spirit of American life."[57] Arguing that black protesters "refined a politics of memory at the Lincoln Memorial," Sandage examines the reclaiming of Lincoln at this site through "a formula civil rights activists and other protesters would repeat at the Lincoln Memorial in more than one hundred big and small rallies in subsequent decades."[58] In Sandage's formulation: "It was the unrelenting nationalism that finally offered black activists a cultural language to speak to white America and to elicit support.... [T]he famous picket sign, 'I AM A MAN,' may have been morally compelling, but winning political and legal rights for blacks required a more focused message: I AM AN AMERICAN. Nowhere was this idea dramatized more vividly than in the Lincoln Memorial protests held from 1939 to 1963."[59] Most famously, Martin Luther King Jr. delivered his "I Have a Dream" speech—arguing that equality for black Americans would be the ultimate expression of American nationalism—with Lincoln at his back and the Capitol in his sights.

Anderson, King, and thousands of other civil rights activists in these decades managed, without inscribing a single slab of granite, to refigure the Mall.[60] They successfully staked a claim in the memory-nation nexus. They used the best of the "ideas of great men" on the Mall to make an argument about who Americans have always been and to call on the nation to live up to the ideals of the great men on the Mall. Lincoln may have been figured in his memorial as the savior rather than the emancipator, but Anderson and King, standing before Lincoln, evoked him as the agent of their freedom and asked the nation to grant them the rights that he had promised.[61]

Following this lead, protesters opposed to the Vietnam War also seized the Mall. In November 1969, more than 500,000 protesters sought to use the moral authority of Lincoln to argue against a war that they understood as immoral and as a threat to freedom in Vietnam and at home. Years later, the gay rights movement also turned to Lincoln on the Mall. Activist Paul Monette recalls standing on the steps of the memorial during the April 1993 March on Washington and thinking, "We need a Lincoln to stand for equal justice and bind us together again."[62] This repeated use of the Mall for protests spoke to the curious success of the McMillan plan. The Mall had achieved the status of sacred national ground. The uses to which it was put may not have been just what McMillan envisioned, but these activists and others who followed sought to refigure the national by claiming and, in some cases, reinscribing the symbolic landscape that Burnham and his associates had charged so highly.

In 1979, Vietnam veteran Jan Scruggs initiated a new era for the Mall when he proposed building a Vietnam War memorial there. This memorial set off a decades-long argument about how the nation should be imagined. This debate has changed the Mall and the argument it makes about the nation.[63] It is possible to tell the story of the Mall from 1791 to 1979 without mentioning war memorials because, until 1979, there were no national war memorials on the Mall.[64] Whereas previously all the memorials on the Mall had commemorated great men and their ideas, Scruggs changed that with the initially controversial, then much beloved and Mall-altering Vietnam Veterans Memorial.

Scruggs, a Vietnam veteran who was reading Carl Jung and thinking about the collective unconscious, set out quite explicitly to change the collective consciousness in the United States regarding Vietnam veterans.[65] The title of his book about building the memorial, *To Heal a Nation,* expresses his intentions accurately: he sought a collective recovery from the personal and national traumas of the Vietnam War. He was particularly interested in recovering the social position of the soldier, and the war memorial he built to do this was successful beyond his wildest dreams. Designed by Maya Lin, the memorial is distinct from anything else on the Mall. It is conspicuously modern, the antithesis of the neoclassical style that pervades the rest of the Mall. Located just northeast of the Lincoln Memorial, it is a black granite *V* set into the earth and inscribed with the names of all American KIAs, POWs, and MIAs from the Vietnam War. It is not Beaux-Arts triumphalism or a figural assertion of heroism. It is mournful and complicated. It asks its audience to think about the loss of life in the war, and it does not celebrate that loss.

So much has been written about the Wall by others, and by myself, that I will not rehearse the long arguments about it here, except to say that it was hated for its lack of interest in figurative representation of the heroism of the soldier and loved for its insistent naming of those soldiers. The war is intentionally effaced; it is a veterans' memorial, not a war memorial. The veterans who fought to get the memorial built made this crucial decision. They wanted a memorial that would "heal the nation" and that would recognize the sacrifices of those who served and died. Lin's design sought to remember the dead without celebrating the war. Her impulses were antiwar. Scruggs's impulses were, I think, mixed; he was deeply prosoldier but agnostic about the war. In the end, Scruggs's vision and Lin's design (and the heroic figures, the *Three Fighting Men,* that the Reagan administration required them to add) managed to celebrate the soldiers without celebrating the war. The memorial enables the soldiers to regain their social position because they sacrificed in spite of the deeply troubling nature of the war.

Architectural historian Dell Upton has claimed that the Vietnam Veterans Memorial made memorials matter again after a more than sixty years of dormancy.[66] There are two reasons for this. The first and most obvious is that the memorial was an enormous success. After a boisterous period of public debate, people from every possible political position on the war embraced the memorial. Visitors have flocked to the memorial in unprecedented numbers. A new, highly contagious practice of public mourning was born there, which involves the public in the memorial process through leaving objects. It became a kind of national wailing wall, unlike any other memorial in American history. It really mattered to millions of people. The second reason is less immediately obvious but might have more potent long-term consequences. The memorial, despite its crucial contribution to reviving the status of the soldier, produced much anxiety about possible antiheroic, antiwar, antinational interpretations of the memorial, the soldier, and the nation, and this led to a rash of war memorials on the Mall.

This book is structured chronologically. The memorials appear in the order in which they were debated and (with the exception of the Black Revolutionary War Patriots Memorial) built. The first chapter deals with the Korean War Veterans Memorial, which was dedicated in 1995. The hulking, blank-eyed, stainless steel figures marching across the Mall produce an ideological contortionism around the figure of the soldier. The builders of this memorial were determined to respond to the Vietnam Veterans Memorial—as well as the nation and the figure of the citizen soldier it imagined—with a not-tragic representation of war and soldiering. The memorial process confronted questions about representing a complicated Cold War conflict in the context of U.S. wars that promise freedom, about representing pre-Vietnam era American soldiers in a post-Vietnam context, and about representing a multiracial fighting force in the context of figurations of the soldier as white and male. Answering these questions in memorial form—refiguring the soldier as not always white; representing armed African Americans, Mexican Americans, American Indians, and Asian Americans on the Mall; glorifying the ideal of blind devotion; and celebrating the heroism of these figures in the context of a Cold War conflict proved to be contradictory and vexing challenges for the veterans and the federal bureaucracies involved. This chapter traces the process through which they shaped the memorial. Here a new cultural logic about soldiers and the nation begins to emerge on the Mall.

Chapter 2 examines the unbuilt Black Revolutionary War Patriots Memorial. The idea for this memorial did not come from veterans' organizations or military lobbies. Its principal proponent sought, and still seeks, to use the exalted position of the sacrificing soldier to stake a claim for inclusion of African Americans in literal and figurative narratives of nation formation. This memorial project is quite bluntly a legitimation project: it seeks to make visible and unassailable the contributions of African Americans to U.S. nationalism. Inspired by Alex Haley's *Roots,* Washington lawyer Maurice Barboza sought to uncover his own genealogy. He discovered that he was, like many African Americans, descended from black and white soldiers who fought in the Civil War and the Revolutionary War. Barboza was determined to use his claim to the revered, sacrificing dead to stake a claim for African Americans in national narratives. The story of the memorial moves through a dense thicket of anxiety about racial purity, miscegenation, the not-white soldier, masculinity, and linked ideas about the nation. Though this unbuilt memorial clearly does not change the Mall, it does demonstrate what was speakable on the Mall in this moment and what was not.

Chapter 3 takes up the Women in Military Service for America Memorial and so must again take up the question of what was speakable on the Mall in this moment and what was not. Approved with some difficulty by the same Congress that approved the Korean War Veterans Memorial and the Black Revolutionary War Patriots Memorial, the Women's Memorial sought to make visible the contributions of women to the U.S. military. The memorial's proponents were insistent and explicit about their desire to make these contributions seen. They were not explicit about challenging the male gendering of the figure of the soldier and the nation, but their project required just this. The memorial was built, and with great effort, it was built on the Mall—at the very far reach of the Mall, but still officially on the Mall. The resistance encountered by this project and the accommodations it was forced to make reveal the national investment in figuring the soldier as male. The memorial is underground and without permanent signage. Shaped by the gendering of the soldier and the nation, as well as by the kinds of wars the United States has waged in the last fifty years, this memorial sought to challenge common understandings of who the troops to be supported are and what that support might look like.

Chapter 4 engages the National Japanese American Memorial to Patriotism during World War II. Like the Black Revolutionary War Patriots Memorial, this memorial works to claim a place in the monumental core and in the national family for Americans denied access to full citizenship by a crippling racial logic. It uses the moral authority of the World War II veterans to denounce the internment of Japanese Americans. Its advocates also conflated patriotism and military service and, in doing so, not only created deep divisions among Japanese Americans but created a troubling memorial. It is the only memorial in Washington to read, "Here We Remember a Wrong," but the wrong admitted and the terms of the admission are more complicated than this bold statement might suggest. The process of building this memorial raised compelling questions about the figuring of the Japanese American soldier, about blind devotion, and about the possibilities for anti-racist nationalism in the United States.

The final chapter returns to the center of the Mall, where the National World War II Memorial was dedicated in 2004. This "complete architectural rendering of the war" also sought to be a complete architectural rendering of the struggle to define the soldier and the nation on the Mall. A sprawling and determined expression of American exceptionalism and federal power, the memorial began with a Capraesque story about recognizing the greatest generation. However, the competing visions of the Mall, war, and soldiering quickly got complicated. In the memorial process, there was a constant tension between the arguments made for building the memorial—always about honoring our soldiers—and the argument about these soldiers that the memorial itself might make. This chapter traces the epic, seventeen-year struggle to get the memorial built and reveals much about the social position soldiers have attained in the United States.

Throughout the book I explore two key, and linked, uses to which the memory of the soldier is put in these memorials. First, the soldier is used to overcome the problems of war and military service raised by the Vietnam War, enabling and encouraging an unfettered celebration of military service. Second, and this is not a secondary argument, the soldier is used, with mixed results, to legitimate African Americans, women, and Japanese Americans as fully equal national subjects. These legitimation projects use the soldier to redraw primary boundaries of national inclusion. The Black Revolutionary War Patriots Memorial, the Women in Military Service for America Memorial, and the National Japanese American Memorial to Patriotism during World War II use the elevated status of the soldier, despite what the soldier is doing in the world, to make claims of national belonging based on military service, and the results are revealing. The memorial to black patriots has not been built. The memorial for women was built underground with no permanent signage. And the Japanese American memorial foregrounds the apology for the internment.

The key uses to which the figure of the soldier is put in these memorials require an articulation of the centrality of soldiering to U.S. nationalism and serve to minimize the accounting of loss. Both uses participate in making the argument that national belonging and military service, even under the most profoundly contradictory and discriminatory circumstances, are inextricably bound. Military service becomes the ultimate expression of national belonging, regardless of the terms of that service or what that military service does in the world.

The book begins and ends with the two largest and most central memorials: the Korean War Veterans Memorials and the National World War II Memorial. These projects are the most preoccupied with celebrating sacrificing soldiers, and they are ultimately the ones that most powerfully rewrite the meaning of the National Mall. The memorials in the three middle chapters participate in elements of this celebratory logic. They are crucial to the story of the Mall and U.S. nationalism because they reveal a powerful but less successful drive to use the elevated social position of the soldier to refigure U.S. nationalism as not always white and male. In so doing they mark the maintenance of seemingly outdated boundaries of national inclusion. It is important to understand the impulses of these two kinds of memorials as linked and as producing together the story of what happened on the Mall. The ascension of the figure of the soldier is linked to the maintenance of boundaries of inclusion *and* shapes thinking about war and soldiering in ways that have real consequences for the endless parade of pilgrims to the memorials. This is how we have remembered our young dead soldiers who do not speak.

ONE

Forgetting the Remembered War
at the Korean War Veterans Memorial

THE KOREAN WAR VETERANS MEMORIAL was dedicated in July 1995, forty-two years after a tense stalemate was reached in Korea, twenty-two years into the period of the all-volunteer military in the United States, twenty years after the fall of Saigon, and just a few years after the collapse of the Soviet Union and the end of the Cold War. It is the first of many memorials built on the Mall in response to the Vietnam Veterans Memorial. It began with a fairly straightforward, not unreasonable desire for acknowledgement of service in the Korean War. However, in a long, fraught process, the American Battle Monuments Commission, the Korean War Memorial Advisory Board, and various commissions in Washington charged with getting the memorial built sought to use what they understood as the "blind devotion" of soldiers from a "simpler time" in a national recovery project.[1] The veterans who wanted a memorial sought to see their service valued; the builders of the memorial wanted to rewrite the social position of soldiers and soldiering in quite specific terms: they wanted to foreground the service of manly, heroic soldiers. They were not interested in the details of the war in which these soldiers had fought; they were, in fact, invested in obscuring the details of the war with larger-than-life figures of soldiers. These desires played out in a complicated memorial process and produced looming gunmetal gray figures that haunt the landscape of the National Mall.

THE WAR

The war waged on the Korean peninsula from June 1950 through July 1953 has come to be called "the Forgotten War" in the United States. In this usage *forgotten* means "not remembered" in a domestic context.[2] It is a war to which people in the U.S. have paid little attention since it ended. This is different from a war not remembered in terms of why it was fought and what happened in the world as a result. Both kinds of forgetting are relevant in the United States, but only the former is a cause of concern. In the discussions about building a Korean War memorial on the National Mall, the term *forgotten war* appeared everywhere. It was often used with the unselfconscious implication that the sacrifice of American soldiers was what had been forgotten and should be remembered. There was a remarkable silence, however, on the question of why the war was waged. Remembering "the Forgotten War," in fact, involved vigorous forgetting of the details of the war itself. Instead, the conversations turned on the problem of how the sacrificing soldier should be remembered. For this reason, it is important to begin this exploration of the Korean War Veterans Memorial with a few details about the war and what the war meant in the world.

South Koreans often call this "the 6/25 War" because it started on June 25, 1950. This makes sense in the context of Korean history; it marks the war as another event in a long series of struggles against colonial rule. The 6/25 War grew out of the problem posed by former Japanese colonies in the post–World War II period. Korea had been essentially under Japanese rule since the Sino-Japanese War ended in 1895. When the Japanese surrendered in 1945, both the United States and the USSR had troops and interests in Korea. Following Japan's surrender, Korea was hastily split in two at the thirty-eighth parallel. The United States stayed in the south and the Soviet Union stayed in the north. The country was to be run by a joint U.S.-USSR commission for four years, at the end of which Korea would reunify and govern itself independently.[3]

Not surprisingly, this plan was not popular with Koreans. Political agitation emerged in both North Korea and South Korea. Eventually, the United States and the Soviets backed competing reunification efforts, as both countries came to see the thirty-eighth parallel as a significant front in the Cold War. In 1950, an odd sort of civil war broke out when the Soviet-supported North Korean Army crossed the thirty-eighth parallel into South Korea. President Truman expressed anxiety about a new phase in the spread of communism. In a June 27 statement, he claimed, "The attack upon Korea makes it plain beyond all doubt that communism has passed beyond the use of subversion to conquer independent nations and will now use armed invasion and war."[4] Truman, significantly, did not respond by asking the U.S. Congress for a declaration of war. Instead, he turned to the United Nations. He continued, "I know that all members of the United Nations will consider carefully the consequences of this latest aggression in Korea in defiance of the Charter of the United Nations. A return to the rule of force in international affairs would have far-reaching effects. The United States will continue to uphold the rule of law."[5] Truman understood the war as a response to communist aggression, and he turned to the UN to fight for the rule of law rather than the rule of force. It was a Cold War conflict.

Truman's framing of the war was accurate to an extent, but it crucially neglected the colonial origins of the conflict and therefore oversimplified the status of South Korea as an independent nation seeking freedom from communist rule of force. This enabled an oversimplified understanding of the war as an attempt to bring freedom to people threatened by communist aggression. This is important to note because the war's memorializers would look back with nostalgia on what they wanted to see as a simpler time, but the Cold War was not simple. Historian Penny Von Eschen's description of the Cold War as "a far more tangled, and far more violent, jockeying for power and control of global resources than that glimpsed through the lens of the U.S.-Soviet conflict" makes this point.[6] Both the problematic details of Korean history and the violence of this Cold War conflict disappear in the memorial process.

United Nations Security Council Resolution 82 called for North Korea to withdraw and supported a UN effort to defend the South. U.S. and South Korean troops did most of the fighting and dying. They were, however, joined over the course of the war by soldiers from Canada, Australia, New Zealand, England, France, the Philippines, Turkey, the Netherlands, Thailand, Ethiopia, Greece, Colombia, Belgium, South Africa, and Luxembourg. When the mostly U.S. and South Korean forces crossed the thirty-eighth parallel into North Korea in October 1950, the Chinese entered the war to support the North Koreans and their interest in maintaining communism in Korea. The war lasted three years, during which 273,127 South Korean soldiers and an estimated 520,000 North Korean soldiers were killed. A total of 114,000 Chinese soldiers and 54,246 American soldiers were killed.[7] Roughly three million Korean civilians lost their lives. The war ended in a stalemate that has lasted fifty-five years. A demilitarized zone—2.5 miles wide and 155 miles long—was established at the thirty-eighth parallel. Uninhabited by humans for so long, the DMZ now holds interest for wildlife biologists. (Species of birds struggling in other parts of Korea—ruddy kingfishers, watercocks, and von Shrenck's bitterns—thrive in the DMZ.)[8] But it is not abandoned. The length of the DMZ is vigilantly policed on both sides, keeping the war on the Korean peninsula very much alive. This gives the term *forgotten war* an awkward resonance. It was the first hot front in the Cold War. It was the first proxy war of the Cold War, the first war in which the superpowers used the bodies and territories of others to wage war. Given the way that the tensions in Korea have heightened rather than abated in the post–Cold War era, "the war that stays alive" might be a more accurate description. But this is not what is remembered at the Korean War Veterans Memorial.

ON THE MALL

At the foot of the Lincoln Memorial, directly across the Reflecting Pool from the Vietnam Veterans Memorial, in Ash Woods, hulking figures stand on the National Mall. These figures are surrounded by a quiet body of still water and broad expanses of granite carved with aphorisms and images. The Korean War Veterans Memorial is a tangle of competing design elements that are not easy to describe or decipher.

The memorial has three central design elements, each with multiple dimensions. The largest and most striking element is the triangular Field of Service, which slopes slightly upward and is populated by nineteen statues of seven-foot-tall soldiers clad in ponchos and helmets. Made of stainless steel with a rough, deeply textured, unfinished patina, they have exaggerated, over-sized facial features with great, hollow, empty eyes. Like a battle-ready combat troop, they appear to be marching up a gentle incline on the Mall. They are armed, but their weapons, which are not raised, are partially obscured by the bulky ponchos. The soldiers seem to move forward by steady plodding, rather than with speed or determination. The field through which they walk is planted with low shrubs and divided by nineteen long, low, black granite slabs, which carve up the field and mark it as off-limits to visitors. Although their attention is scattered—some face forward, some turn to engage another figure, others look wearily over their shoulders—they appear to be marching together toward the enormous American flag at the top of the incline.

The second major design element of the memorial is the black granite Mural Wall that runs parallel to the Field of Service. It resembles the wall of the Vietnam Veterans Memorial in that both are long, black, reflective

FIGURE 3. Korean War Veterans Memorial. (Photo by Hank Savage.)

expanses similarly situated at the base of the Lincoln Memorial. But, in several crucial ways, the wall of the Korean War Veterans Memorial is quite different. It is not carved with the names of those killed in the war, but etched with images of more than 2,400 soldiers and military workers. Photographs from the National Archives emerge from the dark stone in varying sizes and degrees of clarity. Crowded together in some places and separated by expanses of black in others, they seemed to be placed randomly. They are, in fact, placed in a pattern designed to evoke the mountainous terrain of Korea, but this is nearly impossible to see. The images themselves also are not clearly visible, but must always be deciphered through the reflections of the nineteen figures and the reflection of the viewer looking into the granite. It is a murky wall, but also a living wall—its figures are very much alive and engaged in the business of war; they are not inert, tragic, named dead.

The final major design element is the Pool of Remembrance, which sits beyond the flagpole at the top of the incline. This pool of still water is penetrated by an extension of the Mural Wall. Above the pool, this thick wall is carved with striking white letters that read, "Freedom Is Not Free." The pool is surrounded by benches useful for contemplating this claim and its context. This inscription is suggestive, asserting that the war was fought for freedom, that a price was paid, and that this is what needs to be remembered. Obliquely, this refers to what the war was supposed to be about but, in the same breath, turns that meaning inward. It implies that what the United States does in the world is to bring freedom and that the importance of this is not the success, the terms, or the context of the effort, but the price paid in the name of this freedom by the figures marching toward the flag.

The memorial also includes other design elements. Just in front of the lead soldier in the Field of Service is a flagpole, at the base of which is an eight-ton triangular stone inlaid with the following text: "Our Nation Honors Her Uniformed Sons and Daughters Who Answered Their Country's Call to Defend a Country They Did Not Know and a People They Had Never Met." This language also requires contemplation. The nation is feminized. The soldier is uniformed, and referred to as the child of the state. "Sons and daughters" answered the call, but only sons are represented in the memorial. Most strikingly, these sons were asked to sacrifice their lives in a situation of which they had no knowledge. The country and the people remain unnamed and therefore unknown. This language is oblique. The words *Korea, communism, containment,* and *Cold War* are not used. This is odd, given the history of the war and the fact that the Cold War had so recently been won. The memorial seems a logical place for celebrating that triumph. But as memorial scholars Barry Schwartz and Todd Bayma write, "The Korean War Memorial's slogan reasserts idealism by leaving vital interests undefined."[9]

U.S. vital interests in Korea were certainly complicated, but leaving them undefined leads to further complication. Writing about the Cold War in Asia, Christina Klein contends that "the political and cultural problem for Americans was, how can we define our nation as a nonimperial world power in the age of decolonization?"[10] The language of the memorial is stunningly generic; the only substance it offers is the soldiers' service. Domesticating the war in this way—focusing on the soldier rather than what he or she did in the world—avoids the problem posed by Klein. At the same time, it provides the answer to her question. Emphasizing the soldier and evading the war's context allow the nation to be defined as a "nonimperial world power in the age of decolonization." This strategy is used throughout the memorial. Shifting the emphasis from the war to the soldier also speaks to the needs of the military of the moment—the thorny problem of recruiting for an all-volunteer military. More information about the Korean War might have complicated the memorial's statement that "Freedom Is Not Free." The shift to the soldier avoids the vital interests of the past to address the vital interests of the present.

There is more. The north side of the path on the north side of the Field of Service is marked by low granite panels bearing the names of the nations that made up the United Nations force in Korea. And a granite panel at the edge of the Pool of Remembrance is carved with the death tolls ("USA 54,246, UN 628,833") and numbers of MIAs and POWs.[11] (The millions of Korean civilians killed are not explicitly remembered here or anywhere else in the memorial.) Finally, at the entrance to the memorial, a kiosk provides an interactive computer that displays photographs and allows visitors to search for names and service records of those who served.

This is an awful lot for visitors to contend with as they move through the memorial. It marks the remembering as both fraught and resolute; after all, the memorial occupies a great deal of the most sacred symbolic real estate in the United States, and it does so in a manner that seems determined to fill the space as densely as possible. It asserts quite clearly that no single symbolic gesture would suffice for those wanting to remember. Most crucially, it insistently foregrounds the service of larger-than-life soldiers to deal with the problem of the kind of war being remembered.

If you are not too distracted by the confusingly competing elements of the design, if you simply stand still before the figures of the soldiers and look at their faces for a while, the commemoration of the soldier is further complicated. The figures' faces are not uniform, like the language of the inscriptions, and they are not generic. They are hollow-eyed, tense, and often contorted. They are, in fact, painful to look at. The rough finish, the blank eyes, the sheer bulk of them, the distracted scatter of their postures—all make the figures both powerfully present and hard to read. Their ghostly, sometimes twisted faces are remarkably moving—they seem to express not platitudes but something of the anguish of the soldier's experience.

The Korean War Veterans Memorial (KWVM) is one of many memorials built and debated in the memorial-building frenzy of late twentieth-century United States. It is the product of a time in which the desire for memory in a national context was intense. The Ninety-Ninth Congress, which initially approved the KWVM in 1985, also approved two other major memorial projects: the Black Revolutionary War Patriots Memorial and the Women in Military Service for America Memorial. Before the Vietnam Veterans Memorial was approved in 1979, more than forty years had elapsed since the last major memorial was built on the Mall, and no national war memorial

FIGURE 4. Korean War Veterans Memorial. (Photo by Hank Savage.)

had ever been built on the Mall. In the twenty years after the Vietnam Veterans Memorial was completed, four major war memorials were built on the Mall. At least nineteen others were vying for space.[12]

These memorials are explicitly and determinedly part of a struggle to rebuild American nationalism in the wake of the Vietnam War. The way the Vietnam War was waged, the logic that drove the war, and the kind of nation the war imagined were profoundly disruptive of U.S. nationalism in this period. The problem was not simply that the war was unpopular or that the draft was unfair or that rebellious youth did not want to serve. All this was compounded by the powerful voices in the United States who wanted to see Americans as the people who brought the world freedom in the Second World War rather than as the wagers of an unwinnable, unpopular, complicated war in Southeast Asia. Many Americans seemed to want to understand themselves as a nonimperial world power in the age of decolonization, rather than an imperial global power waging the Cold War in newly claimed former French, British, and Japanese colonies. This desire drove the push to build these memorials.

The problem of military service in this period was also pertinent and pressing for these memorial projects. The all-volunteer military had, much to the surprise of many, a very successful beginning. In 1973, 1974, and 1975, the army's modest recruiting goals were easily met.[13] But by 1976 recruitment had clearly slowed, and by 1979 there was a 16,000-person shortfall that inspired army chief of staff General Edward Myer to tell Congress that the nation had a "hollow Army."[14] The army responded with increased salaries, increased incentives, and the "Be All You Can Be" advertising campaign. The Vietnam Veterans Memorial was hardly helpful in this context; the Wall wasn't an appealing companion to these campaigns. When the Korean War Memorial process began, Selective Service registration had recently been reinstated in response to the Soviet invasion of Afghanistan. The Department of Defense was worried about what would happen if some political incident required a sudden increase in volunteers; there was a lot of anxiety about the feasibility of an all-volunteer military in a wartime situation. As a result, even though in the late 1980s and early 1990s the military reduced its size, dramatically contracting the need for new recruits, the Department of Defense continued to need to raise pay and improve educational benefits in an effort to meet recruiting goals.[15] These recruitment issues would certainly have been on the minds of some of the memorializers.

The story of the building of the KWVM, the debates it engendered, the debates it did not engender, the questions the memorial process raised about the nation, and the figure of the soldier are all linked to difficulties in reconciling old ideas about the nation and the new kinds of wars it was waging. The looming, pained soldiers at the center of this memorial are celebrated and sacrificed. The war in which they served is obscured in the memorial process. The rough, raw faces of the statues emerged from the battle over the figure of the soldier, embodying the struggle to move from the real, complicated experience of soldiers to a positive representation of the willingness to serve that might act as a corrective to the abstraction, the ambiguity, and the grief represented at the Vietnam Veterans Memorial. The Korean War Veterans Memorial is not simple, but it strives to simplify and domesticate war and military service.

ORIGINS

Where is the Korean War memorial?
Somehow I never can find that.

E. G. WINDCHY

Both the Vietnam Veterans Memorial and the National World War II Memorial have well-worn origins stories. Jan Scruggs came home from seeing *The Deer Hunter* determined to heal his national community. A constituent approached his congresswoman at a pancake supper in Ohio to ask her why there wasn't a World War II memorial, and the lawmaker, stunned by the realization that there wasn't one, embarked on a great crusade. In the case of the Korean War Veterans Memorial, the impetus is probably also best traced to Jan Scruggs and *The Deer Hunter*. In newspapers, congressional arguments, and presidential speeches, the answer to the question, "Where did the drive to build the Korean War Memorial come from?" was almost always linked to the Vietnam Veterans Memorial. Crucially, there were two parts to these references to the Wall. The first was essentially that Korean War veterans should have a memorial because the Vietnam veterans have one. The second was that there should be a war memorial on the Mall that is *not* the Vietnam Veterans Memorial—not abstract, not about grief, not about loss, not about tragedy, not about the nation imagined by the Vietnam Memorial.

In 1955 the *Washington Post and Times Herald* published a short, lonely letter to the editor on the subject of a possible Korean War memorial. It read:

> Each day I admire the altogether fitting and proper memorial statue honoring the courageous lads of America who planted the flag on Iwo Jima during World War II.
>
> Now I'm wondering if there is a memorial somewhere for the equally courageous boys of United Nations who fought under many flags, including our own and that of the United Nations, to stop the aggression of the North Korean and Red China communists on the Korean peninsula.
>
> That was a notable landmark in world history, when a number of nations joined together to stop an aggression which touched them only indirectly.
>
> Men of all races and creeds died for freedom there. Should not there be a monument showing the heterogeneous qualities of those united forces? Would not that serve to remind us and others that even the "little wars" against free people (or even against unfree people) are important today?
>
> G. Holcomb
> Falls Church[16]

Borrowing Lincoln's language at Gettysburg—"it is altogether fitting and proper that we should do this"—G. Holcomb offers a complicated vision of what could be remembered about the Korean War. He foregrounds the "courageous boys" but suggests that what should be marked about the Korean War is that it was waged by the United Nations and fought by men of "all races and creeds." When he asks, "Should not there be a monument showing the heterogeneous qualities of those united forces?" he asks a powerful question.

In 1955, memorials were not of much interest to most people in the United States. World War II was remembered mostly by local, living memorials, and renewed interest in memorialization was still at least twenty-five years away. In the immediate post–Korean War years, there were precious few letters to editors about Korean War memorials, and Holcomb's cause was not taken up. But what he suggests should be remembered—a newly heterogeneous military (or, perhaps more accurately, a newly *desegregated* U.S. military) and a UN fighting force—are worth noting because these striking, logical, obvious terms for remembering the Korean War in the 1950s were absent when the memorial process began in the early 1980s. They had been replaced by the memorial needs and desires of the 1980s. In the conversations about the memorial, responding to the Vietnam Veterans Memorial was far more pressing than remembering desegregated forces or a UN-waged war. Of course, remembrance on the National Mall of either race or a U.S. war fought multilaterally was thorny business, and these challenges did shape the memorial that was built. But, in the final design, both race and the United Nations are present only as traces.[17]

G. Holcomb was not entirely alone in his desire to see a memorial built. The American Battle Monuments Commission made some noise about raising funds in the mid-1960s. And in the preceding years, a few individuals tried to stir interest in a memorial. In Marlboro, New York, Eli Belil started pushing for a memorial in the late 1970s. Belil, a Korean War veteran and research director for *Penthouse* magazine, wrote letters to state and federal authorities, various veteran's agencies, and the American Battle Monuments Commission, but got nowhere. He encountered "official roadblocks, ignorance, and apathy when it comes to recognizing the sacrifices of those of us who so long ago fought and paid the ultimate price for freedom in a faraway land."[18] It wasn't until the Vietnam Veterans Memorial (VVM) was built that any serious momentum was gained for a Korean War memorial. In 1987, Belil expressed a common sentiment when he said, "I'm not knocking the

Vietnam veterans and the fact that their memorial is finally a reality, but like Vietnam, Korea was a battleground in which almost as many men lost their lives over a shorter period of time. . . . [A]ll they have to show for it are a few fading pictures . . . and the scars that neither time nor the Government's apathy will heal."[19] Belil attributes the pre-VVM lack of interest to the Korean War veterans' unwillingness to "make waves," indicating a generational difference between the Vietnam and Korean veterans but also implying that, before 1982, getting a war memorial built required making special, disruptive demands that the proud (and maybe more compliant?) Korean War veterans were unwilling to make. Holcomb was interested in remembering the war in the context of world history. Belil and the voices that emerged after the Vietnam Veterans Memorial was completed were interested in something else: recognition for individual sacrificing soldiers and the need to heal.

The closest the KWVM gets to an origins story of its own dates to 1981, when Chayon Kim, a Korean-born naturalized U.S. citizen, formed the National Committee for the Korean War Memorial.[20] Kim's life had been saved by American troops during the war. She would later recount hours of "huddling in a bunker while American B-29s dropped bombs on North Korean troops all around her hiding place."[21] Inspired by a meeting with Mrs. Douglas MacArthur, Kim established a memorial committee comprising a few self-appointed individuals without governmental affiliations. Just one month after the spectacularly successful dedication of the Vietnam Veterans Memorial, in December 1982, Kim was removed from the committee.[22] Two years later, the committee dissolved in the face of serious financial improprieties.[23] One-time committee member Myron McKee had taken advantage of veterans' desire to see the memorial built as a way to line his own pockets, paying himself $650,000 to raise $600,000. Before this happened, however, Kim's committee did make a couple of key contributions to the memorial process.

According to the *Journal of the American Institute of Architects,* in November 1982, at the dedication of the Vietnam Veterans Memorial, members of Kim's committee distributed six thousand questionnaires that read: "If you are a veteran, we value your advice and participation in the building of the Korean War Memorial. (1) Above ground, visible, or below ground; (2) modern art or traditional art; (3) decisions by veterans or decisions by architects."[24] Only 350 questionnaires were returned, but the verdict was clear: above ground, traditional, and dictated by veterans. (This is almost but not quite what they got.) The questionnaire and its response clearly defined the Korean War Memorial principally as a response to the VVM. It set the terms of the debate explicitly around rewriting the Vietnam Memorial rather than the particular history of the Korean War. In the memorial process, rewriting "traditional art," privileging the decisions of veterans, and lifting the memorial form above ground (resurrecting it, if you will) were of central importance to the memorial's advocates. But each of these elements turns out to be more complicated, more slippery, than the questionnaire's emphatic concision suggested.

"Traditional art," for instance, used in juxtaposition to "modern art" in the survey, would have had a particular and quite pointed resonance in 1982. In the early Cold War era, U.S. federal agencies had embraced modernism to represent "American-style freedom of expression" in contrast to "Soviet-style repression." However, by the 1980s popular rejection of modernism paved the way for a return to traditionalism. For historian Casey Nelson Blake, the 1993 *Knoxville Flag* outside of the General Services Administration building in Knoxville signaled "the replacement of modernism as an official style by a new patriotic realism, dressed up in the rhetoric of conservative identity politics."[25] When Blake worries that "the ascendancy of neotraditionalist public monuments" will "imagine a public life with no surprises—no surprises from artists, no surprises from racial and ethnic minorities, no surprises from crime and violence, and no surprises, above all, from public protests and civil unrest," he describes exactly what many of the questionnaire respondents and the veterans and agencies seeking to build the Korean War Memorial wanted: an explicit rejection of the possible ambiguities of modernism.[26] Kim's questionnaire, in the shadow of the decidedly modern and not clearly patriotic Vietnam Memorial, posited traditional art in the terms Blake describes, as "an official style of new patriotic realism."

An October 1982 letter to the editor of the *Washington Post* written by E. G. Windchy of Alexandria captured the initial gentle push for a memorial for Korean War veterans: "Where is the Korean War memorial? Somehow I never can find that."[27] The tone of this letter—wry, gentle humor, not entitled outrage—is interesting. In 1982, with the buildup to the dedication of the VVM underway, it expressed a sense that if the Vietnam veterans were getting a memorial, the Korean War veterans should get one too. A few years later, the lack of a memorial would become a source of righteous anger for many. By 1985, the gentle chiding was gone; when Virginia representative Stan Parris, a Korean War veteran, introduced a bill calling for the building of a memorial to honor Korean War veterans in Washington, the congressional record was full of indignation.

This new indignation is reflected in the headlines that followed passage of the Korean War Veteran Act of 1985. The *Christian Science Monitor* headline "Giving Korean War Vets Their Due" captures the mood. The refrain in newspapers—"They don't have one . . . and they should"—was repeated again and again. In the fall of 1985, a *New York Times* article begins, "Almost as many (54,259) died in the Korean War as in the Vietnam War (58,022) but there is no Korean War memorial in the Washington area,"[28] and a *Los Angeles Times* editorial begins, "At least two decades late, a bill is moving through Congress to erect a Korean War memorial."[29] Remembering the forgotten war in these conversations had remarkably little to do with the war to be remembered. And, between G. Holcomb in 1955 and E. G. Windchy in 1982, a significant shift in logic is evident. Holcomb turned to Lincoln at Gettysburg to justify his interest in a memorial about the particular details of the war, while Windchy assumed that a memorial should be built because it was appropriate and the Vietnam veterans had one.

Kim's committee, which successfully initiated the push for the memorial, lobbied at the Vietnam Veterans Memorial dedication not only for a Korean War memorial but also for the particular shape it should take. The committee explicitly marked the emergent Korean War Memorial as a response to the VVM both in the need to remember the soldiers who served in these Cold War conflicts and also in the need to correct the anticelebratory, antiheroic design of the VVM.[30] These terms were neither inevitable nor universally desired. They were, however, the terms that would triumph in the struggle over the memorial design. And it is important to note that these terms did not come from the veterans.

Before 1985 there was no active national organization of Korean War veterans. In 1984 Korean War veteran Bill Norris was dismayed by the poor turnout of Korean War veterans at a Twenty-Fifth Infantry Division Association reunion and set out to connect with his fellow veterans. He had trouble generating interest at first, but his persistence led to the formation of the Korean War Veterans Association. Their modest first meeting was a memorial service at Arlington National Cemetery in July 1985. On that day each veteran carried a single mum—a flower symbolizing both sorrow and the silence of the memory of the war.[31] At this meeting they produced a statement of principles for their fledgling organization: "To support the ideals this Great Country was founded on; To maintain the dignity and pride of the Korean War veterans who served this country when asked to; To work towards the recognition of those who did not return from the Korean War; To maintain and foster the comradeship between the men and women who served during the Korean War; To perpetuate the memory and reason which required our service during the Korean War."[32]

This statement is straightforward and moving, especially the final principle. They were not just asking to be remembered; they were seeking to "perpetuate the memory and *reason*" for their service. And although they were not writing about a war memorial and did not form the organization with a war memorial in mind, they became key advocates for the memorial, and their terms for remembering the war could have been useful as the process moved forward.

THE LEGISLATION AND THE TERMS OF THE DEBATE

This brave group has been leapfrogged by time and it is up to
those of us serving in Congress to rectify the situation.

REP. STAN PARRIS

In October 1985, the Ninety-Ninth Congress passed the Korean War Veterans Act authorizing $1 million for the design, planning, and construction of a Korean War memorial. This was the third time the memorial had been proposed in Congress. In 1982, Representative John Hammerschmidt sponsored "a joint resolution to authorize the erection of a memorial on public grounds in the District of Columbia, or its environs, in honor and commemoration of members of the Armed Forces of the United States who served in the Korean War."[33] In 1983, Claude Pepper introduced a different bill. Adding "Allied Forces," this one read, "A joint resolution to authorize the erection of a memorial on public grounds in the District of Columbia, or its environs, in honor and commemoration of members of the Armed Forces of the United States and the Allied Forces who served in the Korean War."[34] Both bills died in committee. A 1985 version, which was approved, dropped the allied forces; the logic behind this deletion is not made explicit in the congressional record, but the debate about the 1985 bill is revealing. The war to be remembered was an American war fought by American troops, and the role of the United Nations got precious little mention. Korea, communism, the millions of Koreans killed, and the Cold War also received hardly a passing mention.

The terms of the discussion in Congress echo the sentiments expressed in newspapers. Over and over again, the memorial is described as long overdue. The reason for building a memorial is universally assumed: to recognize the sacrifices of those who served. The war itself is described only in the most generic terms, as a quest for freedom, and the numbers of Americans who served and died are repeatedly emphasized. The service and sacrifice of the American soldiers are the central concerns. Representative Stan Parris was a sponsor of the bill; his language reflects the tenor of sentiments expressed in Congress.[35] In May 1985 he stated, "A great disservice has been done to a very large segment of our population—a group of 5.7 million American Citizens who served during the Korean War." He continued, "54,236 Americans made the ultimate sacrifice for their country and the ideals of freedom ... ideals which form the foundation upon which this nation rests." To him it was "incredible to note that there is not a memorial in the nation's capital." He concluded, "[T]his brave group has been leapfrogged by time and it is up to those of us serving in Congress to rectify the situation."[36]

The final legislation is fairly straightforward. Public Law 99–572 was signed by Ronald Reagan on October 28, 1986, and calls for a memorial "in honor and commemoration of members of the Armed Forces of the United States who served in the Korean War." It guarantees space on the Mall and puts the American Battle Monuments Commission in charge of overseeing the building of the memorial. It calls for the establishment of an *all-veteran* Korean War Memorial Advisory Board (KWMAB) to do two things. First, it was to select the design—subject, as is the case with all memorials built on federal lands in Washington, to the approval of American Battle Monuments Commission, the Commission of Fine Arts, and the National Capital Planning Commission. Second, it was to oversee fundraising for the memorial, or, in the language of the bill—"encourage private donations for the memorial."[37]

The precedent had been set in this period for memorials on the National Mall to be built with private donations, when the Vietnam Veterans Memorial Fund rejected federal funds for their memorial for explicit political reasons.[38] And though advocates for the Korean War Veterans Memorial did not seem to share this political position, they were required to raise the money to pay for their memorial from private sources. The Ninety-Ninth Congress also approved the building of a memorial for black Revolutionary War veterans and for women who have served in the U.S. military. These memorials also were required to be paid for with nonfederal monies.

In the end, the Korean War Veterans Memorial cost more than $18 million.[39] Hyundai Motors of America gave the largest corporate donation, $1.2 million. Samsung Information Systems and a handful of other Korean corporations also gave generously, but most of the donations came from individuals. A Dear Abby letter in 1988 raised more than $400,000; a congressionally approved Korean War Memorial coin raised over $8 million; and the Korean War Veterans Association worked tirelessly to raise funds for the memorial. The pages of its aptly named newsletter, *The Graybeards,* were preoccupied with fundraising for the memorial from January 1986 through the dedication in 1995.[40] Even as they expressed frustration about the pace of progress and the ever-increasing costs, the *Graybeards* editors pushed constantly for donations. In fact, they dedicated much more space to fundraising than to other issues related to the memorial, most notably the design. They spent precious little ink on the details of the design. The only design-related issue that came up with any regularity was concern about fair representation across military branches. Mostly what the editors and letter writers expressed over and over again was the desire to see the memorial completed on the Mall. And as successful as they were as fundraisers for the memorial, their power to influence the design of the memorial, had they been interested, seems likely to have been quite limited. In 1991 when they pushed for more progress and more accountability in the memorial process, the memorial board chair publicly berated them, and their representative on the advisory board resigned from the organization with an angry letter.[41]

Congress's stipulation that veterans select the design was crucial to the memorial process and perhaps more consequential for the memorial than the stipulation that private monies be used. A jury of well-known architects, landscape architects, artists, and critics had selected the Vietnam Veterans Memorial; the fact that the VVM board did not include any veterans had been the subject of some controversy. This likely inspired the desire for an all-veteran board. Certainly, in its own unscientific way, the survey conducted at the dedication of the VVM made clear the desire for an all-veteran jury. And those who responded got their wish.

Given that 5.7 million people served in the Korean War–era military, President Reagan had a good pool from which to form his committee. Reagan had disliked Maya Lin's design for the Vietnam Memorial from the start. His secretary of the interior, James Watt, had threatened to delay groundbreaking for the memorial unless modifications were made to her design. The Frederick Hart sculpture of three Vietnam War era soldiers was a last-minute, controversial addition because Reagan and Watt insisted on the addition of heroic figures. In selecting veterans to serve on this board, Reagan had a chance to set the record straight on the Mall. Not surprisingly, the veterans he chose were not the kind of veterans who made up the membership of the Korean War Veterans Association (KWVA) but the highest ranking and highest achieving Korean War veterans. He appointed eleven men and one woman, including one African American and one Latino, four colonels and three generals, five CEOs (most notably, the CEO of Occidental International Corporation, a petroleum company with more than $22 billion in annual profits), and representatives of selected veterans organizations, including the KWVA.[42] The board chair was General Richard Stilwell, a four-star general and the son of a four-star general who had earned his nickname, "Vinegar Joe," through toughness and acidity.[43] These folks were charged with building the memorial, but, like all memorials on the Mall, it would need the approval of the Commission of Fine Arts and the National Capital Planning Commission.

In response to the McMillan Plan for the Mall, the U.S. Commission of Fine Arts was established in 1910 by an act of Congress. The commission is charged with "giving expert advice to the President, Congress and the heads of departments and agencies of the Federal and District of Columbia governments on matters of design and aesthetics, as they affect the Federal interest and preserve the dignity of the nation's capital."[44] The commission is composed of "well qualified judges of the fine arts" who are appointed by the president to a term of four years. Recent chairs of the commission include William Walton and J. Carter Brown, who served from 1971 to 2002. Brown, from the socially important—and once slave-trading—family that endowed Brown University, was among the most prominent forces in the American art world in the second half of the twentieth century. He served as the director of the National Gallery for twenty-three years, during which time he tripled its endowment and added the modern I.M. Pei addition. He also led the Commission of Fine Arts for more than thirty years, serving under seven presidents. Described as "America's unofficial culture minister," he had a great deal of influence in Washington. Brown was one of the strongest advocates for Maya Lin's VVM design and, as such, had pushed for a particular, modern commemorative aesthetic on the Mall.

Also building on the logic of the McMillan Plan, the National Capital Park Commission was established by an act of Congress in 1924. In 1926, it was reestablished as the National Capital Park and Planning Commission, and Congress gave it comprehensive planning responsibilities for the national capital. The twelve-member commission now "includes five citizens with experience in city or regional planning, three of whom are appointed by the President of the United States and two by the mayor of the District of Columbia."[45] The commission has long been made up of architects, designers, and planners with extensive cultural capital, that is, Washington's cultural elites interested in the capital as a grand national and international stage. This commission had also vigorously supported Maya Lin's design.

As if all these players did not sufficiently complicate the memorial process for the Mall, Congress passed the Commemorative Works Act in 1986. Congress had recently approved three full-scale memorial projects, and demand for many more was on the rise; besieged by the demand for new memorials, Congress sought to quell the memorial fever, or at least rein it in, with specific guidelines. The act stipulates that "an event or individual cannot be memorialized prior to the twenty-fifth anniversary of the event or the death of the individual" and that "military monuments and memorials may only commemorate a war or similar major military conflict or a branch of the Armed Forces. . . . [M]onuments and memorials commemorating lesser conflicts or a unit of the Armed Forces are not permitted."[46] Thus, for the Korean War Veterans Memorial, the stage was set for a showdown between Reagan-era military elites and Kennedy-era cultural elites. President Reagan's twelve-member KWMAB, the Commission of Fine Arts, and the National Capital Planning Commission were required to approve a design together.

THE FIRST DESIGN

In 1988, an open design competition was held. The American Battle Monuments Commission produced, in consultation with the KWMAB, an elaborate document that specified the conditions of the competition and provided guidelines for submission, a statement of purpose, and a statement of philosophy of the memorial. Building on the language of the legislation, this statement of purpose read in part, "The memorial will express the enduring gratitude of the American people for all who took part in that conflict under our flag. It will honor those who survived no less than those who gave their lives, and will project in a most positive fashion, the spirit of service, the willingness to sacrifice and the dedication to the cause of freedom that characterized all participants."[47] Giving lives, serving, willingness to sacrifice, and dedication to freedom—this language reflects the conversation around the legislation, that service and sacrifice trump the war itself. The "cause of freedom" is as close as the language gets to specifics about the war, but "freedom" hangs as something of a free-floating signifier. Freedom for whom? Freedom from what? Freedom in what sense? Where are the specifics about freedom and this war? None of these questions are raised or addressed in the competition guidelines or the conversations that would follow about what the memorial might be.

In describing the memorial to potential designers, the American Battle Monuments Commission (ABMC) and the KWMAB included language that added an additional purpose for the memorial: "These patriotic virtues have been common to those who served their country in other times of national crisis—and must not be lacking in the instance of future emergencies. Therefore, the Memorial must radiate a message that is at once inspirational in content and timeless in meaning." This memorial, then, was to honor the sacrifices soldiers had made and to ensure the willingness of future soldiers to give their lives in the era of the all-volunteer military. It also needed to exist out of time—to be timeless—and by implication, not be too tightly wedded to historical specificity. The statement reads like the ABMC and the KWMAB had been studying the work of Renan, Hobsbawm, and Anderson on nationalism; it requires the design to use the memory of lost soldiers to maintain the nation in particular terms. It also requires soldiers for the future. The statement ends, "The Memorial must be unique in concept, and one that will present a renewable living aspect of hope, honor, and service."[48] In a period in which the military was struggling for recruits, this language about a "renewable aspect" would have had a particular, pointed resonance.

The language of this call is determinative and also stylistically prescriptive.[49] They wanted a memorial that would be "reflective," "uplifting," "respectful," and an expression of "pride."[50] They also wanted it to express "hope," "honor," "service," and "gratitude." They further required that all military details—weapons and uniforms—be portrayed in "exquisite detail." This alone not only ruled out abstraction but dramatically limited the range of aesthetic possibilities. Further, the statement required that the American flag be featured as a central design element. And the call was explicit about the role of grief: "Any design which has inherent in it an essence of grief is not acceptable." The statement called for attention to sacrifice without grief, without even "an essence of grief."

The call for designs could not have been more clear about the board's position on the VVM and the consequences of this position for the KWVM. They did not want to list names of the dead because they didn't want "the emotional reaction characteristic of the Vietnam wall."[51] They wanted to honor sacrificing without getting into the details of sacrifice. In fact, they didn't want *anything* characteristic of the VVM to be present in Ash Woods. They sought an anti-Wall. Like the conversations around the memorial legislation, the design competition was not shaped by particular questions about the war itself. G. Holcomb's thinking about a possible memorial to a heterogeneous, internationally summoned fighting force—or any other concept reflecting the Cold War or the United Nations or other ideas about Korea between 1950 and 1953—was strikingly absent. Only a vague notion of freedom remained. The need to inspire future sacrifice was much more pressing for the AMBC and the KWMAB; it would determine the shape of the memorial. In the statement, the only specifics about the war refer to an uncomplaining willingness to defend "a nation they never knew and a people they never met. . . . [Our troops] fought brilliantly and tirelessly and enabled our nation to achieve its aims—and to prove to ourselves, and the world, that America comes to the aid of its friends, defends it principles, and never retreats from freedom's fight." This statement does not include any direct reference to Korea, Koreans, the Cold War, stalemates, demilitarized zones, or even communism.[52]

Despite the complexities of this call, the winning design—one of 543 entries—was remarkable. It was an intriguing, complicated symbolic expression. It aspired to speak to the "dualities and paradoxes of war and truth" and to "contribute to an historical understanding of the Korean conflict."[53] And it took very seriously the mandate to foreground the soldier. It sought to reflect on the particular experience of those who fought in Korea in a powerful gesture about what it *felt* like to be a soldier in the Korean War. Responding to interviews with veterans, the designers developed an interest in the Korean War as a walking war. One veteran's observation that "we knew the war through our feet. . . . [W]e walked every inch of that country" became an organizing principal for the design.[54] It was a line of thirty-eight nine-foot-tall, fully armed, "ethereally" rendered granite figures that stretched 350 feet toward an American flag.[55] The flag was set at the center of a plaza defined on its western edge by a seven-foot-high wall carved with bas-reliefs and inscriptions. A thin red line of granite was to move through the line of soldiers to the flag to create the sense of a journey through war. There was an awful lot going on in this design: the soldiers, the soldiers, the soldiers; the desire to emphasize the walking war; the spectacular scale; the centrality of the flag; the use of the number thirty-eight; the narrative of a journey; and finally, the ethereal rendering of the figures. All these elements are worth teasing out a little, but it was the last—the figuring of the soldier—that would determine the shape of the memorial that was built on the Mall.

Veronica Burns Lucas, of the winning four-member design team from Pennsylvania State University, told the press at the unveiling that the team connected with the idea of a war known through the soldiers' feet. She said that they were drawn to this, in part, by a famous David Douglas Duncan photograph.[56] Duncan took the photograph in August 1950. In it, the soldiers, newly arrived in Korea, are making their way north to defend the Pusan Perimeter along the Naktong River.[57] Looking at the photograph now and knowing something about the war, one sees the march as tense. They are going into battles that many of them won't survive. They will eventually push the North Koreans and Chinese back over the thirty-eighth parallel, and then the North Koreans and Chinese will push back again before they reach a stalemate. The proposed design echoed elements of both the Duncan photograph and the memories of veterans of the walking war.

The black-and-white photograph of soldiers walking a dirt road through a deep valley is fascinating. The soldiers, in the foreground, are walking toward the camera on a dusty white road. The thin dotted black line they form on the road immediately draws the eye. More soldiers are standing and sitting by jeeps on the side of the road, also looking at the moving line of soldiers and emphasizing the centrality of the line. But the background of the photograph—the dark, looming mountain range—also draws the eye. A striking landscape of black and gray mountains under building gray clouds competes with the line of soldiers for the viewer's attention. The tension between foreground and background and the relative emptiness of the middle ground seem to speak to the problems of remembering the soldier rather than the war; the soldier is literally foregrounded in bold terms, and the photograph, as a result, seems hollowed out, empty despite its dramatic elements.

There is, however, an important distinction between the way the photograph represents the soldiers and the way the design proposed to represent them. In the photograph, the figures are foregrounded, but they are also tiny, dwarfed by the dramatic landscape. In the memorial design, the scale is reversed. In fact, the scale of the design bordered on the outrageous: thirty-eight figures, nine feet tall, 350 feet long. This scale made the soldiers literally monumental, ensuring that they would dominate the landscape of

Ash Woods and shift the focus away from anything beyond their presence. Depicting the soldiers as bigger than the landscape through which they move has serious implications: it represents them as bigger than what they were doing in the world.

This is what enabled designer John Paul Lucas to tell the press that "patriotism is the primary narrative theme of the memorial." He added, "We hope that visitors will be stimulated by the symbolism to think about the nature of the war itself."[58] It is significant that, for him, patriotism came first, then the nature of the war. And it is perhaps more significant that he speaks of the nature of the war in terms of the experience of the individual soldier—*this is what this war felt like.* Lucas and his fellow designers did not take up questions about why the war was waged or what it meant or what the outcome was. The designers, working within the perimeters of the design competition, were interested in the specificity of the experience of the soldier. A specific memory of the war, as they understood it, was a memory of what it felt like for the soldier rather than what it did in the world. If they had embraced Duncan's scale, they would have created a very different sense of what the war felt like; figuring the soldiers as dramatically oversized is a powerful shift away from the photograph and the war.

The symbolic vocabulary used by Burns Lucas, Leon, Lucas, and Pennypacker Oberholtzen is at once literal and oblique. The design contest did not explicitly require figures of soldiers, but it would be hard to satisfy the contest's explicit stipulations—and nearly impossible to meet the implied requirements around celebrating heroism and honoring soldiers—without representing them. The Burns Lucas, Leon, Lucas, Pennypacker Oberholtzen design used thirty-eight soldiers because the line between the North Korea and South Korea held at the thirty-eighth parallel and the war lasted thirty-eight months. This makes sense in a very literal way but also requires that the soldier's bodies serve not to represent soldier's bodies so much as lines on a map and days on a calendar. This seems especially problematic when the strong desire to remember a heroic war runs up against the realities of a stalemate that has lasted more than fifty years. The looming bodies of the soldiers are refigured as markers of how long it took them not to win, or as markers of a line that has been wrapped in barbed wire for fifty years, a demilitarized zone long devoid of any human presence. Does it work against the rhetoric of foregrounding the soldiers and their sacrifices to use the figures in this way? Certainly it complicates the figure of the soldier in the proposed memorial; it dehumanizes them even as it sacralizes them.

Another element—this one required by the contest—is the flag. The designers describe the march to the flag as a march "towards a goal, an end . . . the experience of moving into and through war, of release from war into the embrace of peace and the reflection upon war."[59] The flag, in this description, is a symbol of the peace for which the soldiers fought. Another central feature of the original design, as the designers saw it, was an embedded narrative about this movement through war:

> In the first third of the line, the figures would be placed so as to convey caution, uncertainty, and causalities in the first part of the war; the second third would begin with the figure of a platoon leader, the only figure not facing the flag. He would symbolize the achievement of order and purpose, and the figures would take on highly ordered, forward moving configuration. In the third section the order would continue, but the figures would be placed farther apart, symbolizing the decreased frequency of combat and the negotiation of truce. The last soldier would be in a posture of reflection; he has achieved success in military action.[60]

This is a fairly complicated narrative and would have been a challenge to convey in physical form. The designers compounded this challenge with their ideas about the figures themselves.

The Burns Lucas, Leon, Lucas, and Pennypacker Oberholtzen design requirements for the figures were vague, and they wanted the figures themselves to be vague. They describe the soldiers as "ghostly," "ethereal," "impressionistic," and "utterly lacking detail."[61] The designers did not produce sketches of what this might look like; without sketches, all parties in all the agencies involved seem to have imagined the figures as they thought they should be. And what they imagined was all over the map. The ideas proved impossible to reconcile. If the design had been more specific, the boards and agencies might well have rejected it. And so, in a memorial intended to represent soldiers in a way that might inspire sacrifice in future conflicts, there was an enormous struggle over the literal representation of the body of the soldier.

On June 14, 1989, in his remarks at the official unveiling ceremony for the design, President George H. W. Bush, never beloved as a rhetorician, stumbled through his speech on liberty, honor, Lincoln, and sacrificing soldiers. His uncertainty was both understandable and revealing. The initial design for the memorial was confusing in its efforts to represent sacrifice and the war. It was an evocative if sometimes perplexing mix, but, in the end, its nonrepresentational figures were not nearly specific enough. The memorial that needed to be built because the soldiers need to be remembered in terms different from those used at the Vietnam Memorial required remembering heroic figures above all else.

THE SUBSEQUENT DESIGNS: GI JOE ON THE MALL

Drawn to the simplicity of the line of figures, the reviewing agencies—the Commission of Fine Arts (CFA) and the National Capital Planning Commission (NCPC)—had provisionally approved the Burns Lucas, Leon, Lucas design. But the design approval process imploded over disagreements about the physical details of the representation of the soldiers. Shortly after the design was unveiled, each of the agencies involved—the ABMC, the CFA, and the NCPC—began to express misgivings about how the other agencies were thinking about the figures. There were concerns about scale. Thirty-eight armed figures stretching the length of a football field would certainly put the forgotten war on the map, but were these appropriate dimensions? The approving agencies were sure from the start that they were not. The agencies also began pushing the design to be more responsive to its highly charged site. This debate was quickly trumped by more specific concerns about what the figures would look like.

From the start, the CFA and the NCPC wanted the memorial to be more "inclusive."[62] Although neither race nor ethnicity was mentioned anywhere in the design competition instructions, the prospect of thirty-eight white figures representing the first desegregated American fighting force was recognized as a problem. J. Carter Brown insisted that the figures be raced.[63] At the same time, the KWMAB and the ABMC were pushing for crisp military detail. Neither crisp detail nor racial specificity formed part of the original design. Burns Lucas, Leon, Lucas team member Don Leon is emphatic that racial and military designations were absolutely not part of the designers' thinking. They envisioned "non-representational" figures. Race was "not at all" part of their vision; what they had in mind could not support that level of detail.[64]

The importance for the ABMC of a high level of detail in the figures was made clear in the spring of 1990 at a meeting held at the Corcoran Gallery of Art in Washington to choose the sculptor for the memorial. Three finalists had been selected: Frank Gaylord, Rolf Kirken, and Lawrence Ludtke. As architect Kent Cooper recounts, "Gaylord, a WWII combat veteran, made a

riveting oral presentation and his emotion-packed, three-dimensional studies captured everyone's attention. He was clearly the winner."[65] As Don Leon
describes the meeting, Ludtke went first, and his realistic but casually rendered figures infuriated General Stilwell, the chair of the KWMAB. The
open collars of their shirts, their lack of fitness, and their state of disarray
enraged him. Ludtke told Stilwell, "With all due respect, Sir, I was in that
army, I was on that march, and this is what it looked like." Stilwell replied,
"That may be what it looked like but that is not how we are going to remember it." Leon describes this remarkably candid exchange about forging the
nation with an invented past as the beginning of the end for his design.[66] Not
only was Stilwell clear that his invented past was the one to be remembered,
but his vision required far more detail than the designers had ever wanted.

Even if they had envisioned realistically rendered figures, the problem of
who to represent would likely have trumped the problem of *how* to represent
the soldiers. A few months before the meeting at the Corcoran, architects
from Cooper-Lecky, the architect of record for the VVM, were called in to
oversee this memorial. They were soon making revisions for all the agencies.
The initial revisions focused on "commemorative quotas"—service distribution and ethnic distribution. Four statues were designated as KATUSAs
(Korean Augment to the U.S. Army, Korean soldiers who serve with the
U.S. military). The remaining thirty-four statues were given racial and ethnic
designations: nineteen Caucasians, six Hispanics, five African Americans,
two American Indians, and two Asian Americans. This distribution, which
was not easily reached, was problematic from the start. According to Barry
Schwartz, "Designers noted that African Americans made up 10% of the
troops, mainly in the 'non-technical skills areas,' which implies that their
service was less valuable."[67] The number of Korean War veterans who were
Puerto Rican, and therefore not seen as fully legitimate U.S. citizens by some
of the parties involved, complicated the number of Hispanics to represent.
A compromise reduced the number of Hispanics from six to five to avoid
including more Hispanics than African Americans.[68]

Although the sterile language of "commemorative quotas" kept the focus
on numbers, the problem was not just about figural specificity or numbers
per race; it was a profound problem of refiguring the soldier in the United
States. In the national context, representing soldiers who are not white has
been tricky. The figures at the Vietnam Memorial, the first to do this on the
Mall, are complicated figures. *The Three Servicemen* represents the Vietnam
veteran as not always white, but it follows a familiar, well-worn racial hierar-

chy. The figure in the center is white and is the tallest. He is a half step ahead of the other figures and holds out his arms to protect them.[69] Another figure is clearly African American. The third figure, the machine gunner, is an "ethnic mix."[70] Sculptor Frederick Hart used some Latino models because he wanted to include Latinos, but he also included "features that could also be Slavic, Eastern European, or Near Eastern." Figures during the last period of interest in memorials, the post–Civil War memory boom, are almost entirely white, and they quite explicitly define soldiering in white terms. For the Korean War Veterans Memorial, this was a loaded problem with a complicated history.

Even as color guards started to be consistently multiracial and the composition of the military was more heavily nonwhite than the population at large, the problem of figuring the soldier as something other than white was difficult. Ralph Ellison's famous insight that white paint requires a few drops of black to be truly white has been carefully complicated in the last ten years by work in the study of whiteness. The central tenet of this work is that whiteness in the United States has, from the nation's inception, depended upon an Indian or African or Asian "other" with and against which whiteness could be constructed. The idea is that race is a social rather than biological fact, and this is true whether people are "raced" white or black or Indian. This premise, despite its limitations, is useful for thinking about the ways in which soldiers have been represented. Civil War memorials, with the possible complicated exception of Saint-Gaudens's Shaw Memorial in Boston, have famously whitened the war and the soldiers who fought in it.[71] In the nineteenth century, Custer's blond curls glowed on barroom walls everywhere, rewriting his death at the hands of Indians as a triumph of white power.[72] As David Blight, Cecilia O'Leary, Kirk Savage, and others have argued, the nation-building work accomplished by the memorial boom of the nineteenth century was highly racialized and produced a North-South reconciliation around the celebration of the white soldier. The lack of interest in war memorials for the last three quarters of the twentieth century allowed this problem to lie fallow, but because the commissions involved were determined to avoid the embarrassment of ignoring race in the memorial to the first desegregated war, these complicated questions of representation were raised.[73] It is worth noting here that the question of representing women was only barely raised, and when it was, Stilwell was adamant that it was out of the question.[74] A full 120,000 women served in a range of positions in the war, but no women are included in the final design—or in earlier iterations, for that matter.[75]

The problems of representing race and avoiding women were not the only issues inspiring redesigns. In the first set of significant suggested revisions, these questions inspired another dramatic set of changes. Stilwell was clearly not taken with the first design's narrative of moving through war into peace. At the board's request, the figures were redrawn to represent soldiers actively engaged in battle, as if they were under fire with a man down.[76] Instead of marching steadily, the soldiers were shown "kneeling, some pulling pins out of grenades, some holding bazookas ready to fire."[77] Asked by a CFA commissioner to explain the line of the march in this new context, to clarify its "tactical function," Cooper replied, "This is an undefined mission.... [T]hey are subject to hostile action.... [T]hey are alert ... caught in a moment in time."[78] General Stilwell's explanation was that the oversized soldiers simply marching on the Mall might be "boring" and that they had wanted to "introduce a narrative story of soldiers responding to unexpected unfriendly fire."[79] This was referred to as the "Delta Scheme."

The pressure to add military specificity and ethnic and racial designations—if not women—to the design can be easily understood in the context of the steadily increasing expectation that war memorials remember soldiers as specifically as possible in the context of the evolving makeup of the military: remember bodies, remember sacrifice, remember names, remember the racial composition of the military, remember the women who served, and so on. These are complicated propositions, though the logic that requires them is fairly straightforward. But adding a narrative element—a real attack, frozen in time—is something else. The fear that the thirty-eight giants might be boring implies other expectations for the memorial and what it was supposed to accomplish. Introducing a narrative of soldiers responding to unfriendly fire allows the figures to enact a particular kind of heroism. The scale of the figures and the number of figures were not, in Stilwell's estimation, enough to do what he wanted the memorial to do. As they struggled with the limitations of the symbolic vocabularies required of the memorial, Stilwell and the board turned to a more familiar visual vocabulary for representing war heroism and war heroes: the movies. Stilwell and the KWMAB imagined a war movie on the Mall.[80] But translating filmic images into a memorial in stone is tricky at best. Responding to an attack requires raising weapons, which specifically memorializes violence in a way that memorials in the United States have long sought to avoid. For example, if an enormous soldier is to pull a pin from a grenade on the Mall, in what direction will he face to hurl the explosive? Toward Lincoln? Washington? The Vietnam Memorial? Across the

Tidal Basin to Jefferson? Or toward Arlington National Cemetery? There was a problem of containing the violence that the Stilwell narrative would have brought to the Mall.

This was all too much for the original design team. They described the revisions as turning their fluidly marching figures into a "GI Joe battle scene."[81] They claimed that the revisions "decapitated" the memorial concept and transformed their process of moving through war to peace and reflection to "make the scene convey battle and victory."[82] Frustrated and shut out of the Cooper-Lecky revisions, Burns Lucas, Leon, Lucas hired a lawyer and sued for the right to control the fate of their design. They went to court but were never able to convince a federal judge that they had any rights to the design after having collected the prize money.

THE FINAL DESIGN

In January 1991, after another set of extensive revisions, the Commission of Fine Arts had a change of heart. After having granted provisional approval to the second KWVM design, the CFA withdrew its support and sent Cooper-Lecky back to the drawing board. Praising the Vietnam Memorial, J. Carter Brown reminded the designers that there was value in simplicity: "One reason it is so effective is that it doesn't wave its hand at you."[83] Certainly, a 350-foot oversized stainless steel live action battle scene on the Mall might constitute hand-waving. As Brown described it, the memorial as designed was "overbearing to the point of bombast."

At this point, the United States was engaged in the first Iraq War and, as they describe it, the war changed the commissioners' thinking about how to remember the Korean War. Robert Peck of the CFA told the *New York Times*, "Given what is happening in the Middle East, I think about this in a different context." He saw more war memorials coming and was concerned about precedent. Peck was worried about the fussiness of the murals, the narrative, all the information. "Our memorials are turning into outdoor museums," he complained. In this light, the original design was more appealing because it "had at least a bold single idea."[84]

Six months later, Brown and the CFA had had it. They recommended that the figures and the drama they were to enact be eliminated entirely. This inspired a furious response from the KWVMA and the ABMC. For these agencies, the figures were the reason to build the memorial, and there would

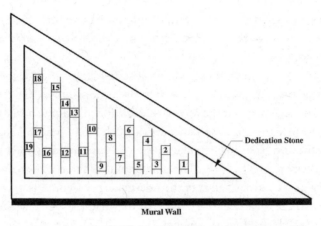

FIGURE 5. American Battle Monuments Commission Korean War Veterans Memorial figures chart. (Courtesy of the American Battle Monuments Commission.)

be no memorial without them. Letters poured in from Korean War veterans across the country. In August 1991, the ABMC sent Brown an angry letter offering a "last compromise." Nineteen freestanding seven-foot-tall statues reflected in a mural wall to make thirty-eight slightly smaller figures on the Mall. (Why cling to thirty-eight with such tenacity?) This letter referred to the VVM design process and the addition of the statue as a compromise that saved the memorial.[85] In the end, the CFA agreed to the modifications, and the compromise held.

However, stylistic concerns had yet to be addressed. William Lecky told interviewers, "There is no question that there was a healthy conflict between what the client wanted, which was something very realistic and militarily accurate and what the reviewing commissions—the artistic side if you will—preferred, which was something more abstract. . . . [T]he final solution was what we like to call 'impressionistic styling,' which makes it very clear what is being portrayed, but diminishes the sense of an actual collection of ground troops moving across the Mall."[86] This is a polite way of saying that what they did stylistically was to fudge it. This impressionistic styling allowed the designers to avoid a whole series of problems. In the memorial as it stands, the military details are roughed in at best. The ponchos were added to cover weaponry and obscure uniforms, making the figures less threatening and more generic.[87] Although the racial designations were never officially scrapped, a walk through the memorial with a map of these designations in

TABLE 1 ABMC Chart

Position	Service	Duty	Race	Weapon
1.	Army	Lead Scout	Caucasian	M-1
2.	Army	Scout	Caucasion	M-1
3.	Army	Squad Leader	Caucasion	M-1
4.	Army	BAR Man	Afro-American	Browning Automatic Rifle (BAR)
5.	Army	BAR Assistant	Caucasian	Carbine
6.	Army	Rifleman	Afro-American	M-1
7.	Army	Group Leader	Caucasian	Carbine
8.	Army	Radio Operator	Caucasian	Carbine
9.	Army	Army Medic	Hispanic	None
10.	Army	Forward Observer	Caucasian	Carbine
11.	Air Force	Air-Ground Controller	Caucasian	Carbine
12.	Marine Corps	Assistant Gunner	Caucasian	Tripod
13.	Marine Corps	Gunner	Caucasian	Machine Gun
14.	Navy	Corpsman	Afro-American	None
15.	Marine Corps	Rifleman	Asian American	M-1
16.	Army	Rifleman	Caucasian	M-1
17.	Army	Rifleman	Hispanic	M-1
18.	Army	Assistant Group Leader	Caucasian	M-1
19.	Army	Rifleman	Native American	M-1

hand makes clear the extent to which race dropped out of the design in the design process. According to the U.S. Army Corps of Engineers, the final designations are "12 Caucasians, 3 African Americans, 2 Hispanic, 1 Oriental, 1 Indian (Native American)," as Table 1 illustrates.[88] The first three figures are white, while the last is American Indian, but none of this is entirely clear in looking at the figures.[89] Some of the responsibility for representing "diversity" fell to the photo engravings on the wall. Lecky assured the commissions that "we have been working hard with the client to make sure that we are politically correct and that all the necessary people are being shown."[90] But this effort did not resolve the problem of how to represent the soldiers.

The figures have rough, exaggerated facial features; it is tricky to identify any particular racial type. This is problematic because of the expectations that people bring to memorials. Because nearly all war memorials in the United States have represented soldiers as white, it is possible that these figures all become white by default. Kent Cooper claims that the figures are brushed with "traces of race." He says this quite plainly, as if it was a category of representation or experience of race that would make sense to people in the United States and be commonly understood. But "traces of race," in the history of race and racialization, has often meant whiteness. Just enough race heightens the masculinity of the figures in this logic, while too much race would make them too specifically not-white. Cooper was trying to say that race did not disappear in the memorial process, but his language tripped him up, and he ended up speaking a perhaps unintentional truth. The impression-istic stylistics return the memorial to its original white-by-default iteration—a rough, exaggerated, familiarly borrowing whiteness. Which is not to say that the figures are intended to be seen as white, but rather that incorporat-ing "traces of race" avoids representing the heroic armed soldiers as absolutely African American, Mexican American, Asian American, or Indian. Literary critic Walter Benn Michaels has written, partly as a push back against white-ness studies, "Either race is an essence or there is no such thing as race." He claims that "our actual racial practice can be understood only as the expres-sion of our commitment to the idea that race is not a social construction."[91] Traces of race in the figures express this tension; they give the figures the lux-ury of racial mobility that the soldiers themselves did not have. This approach avoids the problem of either too much or too little race on the Mall, but even this avoidance was not easy to achieve.

The fight over the details of these representations was so intense that both the ABMC and the CFA were involved in a level of review that sculptor Frank Gaylord thought extremely unusual.[92] In 1992, new constraints were established: "The troopers are to be treated as a unit, on an undefined mis-sion, caught in a moment in time; all figures are wearing ponchos which are blown from behind with increasing velocity at the apex; the figures are alert, wary, and are in various kinds of communication with each other. . . . [A]ny articulation of the figures for purposes of portraying communication should not interfere with the general forward movement of the unit; the figures will be treated as a single composition."[93]

As the figures developed, the CFA, the ABMC, and Cooper-Lecky kept close watch. In 1994, an ad hoc committee they had formed made regular reviews. In July and November, members of the committee went to see the figures in progress in Gaylord's Vermont studio. A November 15, 1994, Lecky memo on one of these visits conveys the level of involvement with the design details. A statement of the committee specifies, "The ad hoc design com-mittee has always described these statues as *young gallant warriors* having embarked on a *successful* mission. Emphasis on *young, gallant, and success-*

ful. . . [G]enerally speaking the committee felt that the faces were older than our directions. If mention is made in the remarks below, about mouth adjustments, it means that the mouth should be either, a) closed, or b) open, but doing something—talking, breathing heavily, in any case determined and focused, as opposed to being open and unfocused."[94]

This statement is followed by a list of changes for the statues. The first change for the lead statue, #1, reads, "Bridge of nose too broad." Gaylord reacts strongly to this, calling #1 the "runt of the litter" and saying, "He is Caucasian, his nose is not too broad."[95] But this was not the only concern about #1. Cooper wrote, "It was agreed to modify the facial expression to be less soulful and 'more intensely searching.'" Less soulful? Why would the lead soldier need to be less soulful? And since when are soulful and searching at odds? This is baffling. Another item on the list reads, "Left arm and hand too limp." Lecky wrote, "The bent wrist holding the rifle on many figures seems contrived and more appropriate to a ballet than a military situation."[96] Ballet? Since when are bent wrists part of the line of a dancer? Gaylord called this concern ridiculous and added that he didn't do limp wrists. The comments on figure #3 include, "Face looks too *sweet,* adjust mouth/lips." Figure #5 is "too tired, dead in the water, totally panicked, ok to be stressed out but show more determination." Figure #6 is "not acceptable, looks like he is sleeping, also looks like has he has a disdainful expression." Figure #12 is "too pregnant." Too pregnant?

Brown generated his own list in response to the visit. His list of required changes included the following: "The fatness of the lips to be reduced"; "the eyes often seem unfocused, drugged"; "the number of open mouths needs to be drastically reduced"; and perhaps most striking, "there is an excess of novelty in the faces." In this context, what exactly is an excess of novelty? He also complained that #1's lips were "too pouty." Kent Cooper summarized the responses: "There was a lack of alertness and purpose in most of the faces. There was a minimum sense of being in a place of potential danger."[97] Noses too broad? Lips too fat? Wrists too limp? Too pregnant? The figuring of the soldier here is remarkable. It seems impossible not to conclude that standards of masculinity, heroism, and whiteness were being articulated—indeed, mandated.[98] The wrists of the figures as they stand on the Mall are not limp, but the noses are broad and the lips remain fat on nearly all the figures. They are fascinatingly racially indistinct and racialized at the same time, which must be what Cooper means by "traces of race."

Frank Gaylord still bristles at this language. More than ten years after the memorial was completed, his frustration with the committees' involvement in shaping the figures is still palpable. Gaylord saw the figures as elements in a single composition. He understood each figure as part of something else, moving together in complicated unison. He sought to render expressive figures that reflected his own experience of war; he wanted something real. But the fussing of the committee, for whom what the individuals looked like was paramount, thwarted this vision.[99]

For the committee, getting the racing and gendering of the figures right trumped Gaylord's composition and his desire to express something particular about the war. Pregnant, limp-wristed soldiers on the Mall would apparently not inspire the kind of future sacrifice they wanted. Further, this gendering of the soldiers seems linked to bigger questions about the Cold War. Historian Robert Dean has written about an "imperial brotherhood" of Cold War political elites powerfully shaped by a "ideology of masculinity."[100] He claims, in fact, that the wagers of the Cold War were blinded by the demands of the masculinist ideologies of their moment. He contends that waging and losing the Cold War conflicts, which simple logic and elite educations might have kept these empirically minded people out of, were linked to ideas about masculinity that have not been adequately explored. The criticisms of these figures are certainly suggestive in this context. They suggest that the anxieties about masculinity that propelled the war also shaped the memorial.

The impressionistic stylistics do something significant to the figures that the ad hoc committee did not address: it blinds them, in a sense. The soldiers have enormous eyes—enormous but hollow eyes. The impression of a pupil is created by just that, an impression. Thus the soldiers, to be honored, to be finally remembered, have no capacity to *look*. In thinking about the visual and visuality, the idea of the gaze, the power to look and see is central. Representation of the gaze is connected to giving and wielding power. The most powerless in the realm of visual representation are those without the gaze. Gaylord clearly did not intend the figures to be blind; they are, in fact, looking. And he thought a good deal about where and how they are looking. But when you notice the hollowed eyes, it is hard not to see this tension. It is hard not to notice that the enormous, looming soldiers intended to be celebrated and honored by this memorial are represented as empty-eyed. Gaylord may not agree, but this seems like a successful strategy for him. He managed to find a way to humanize his composition despite all the pressure to produce generic masculine heroes. His figures "without the gaze," in fact, seem to have the "thousand-yard stare." They are, despite the interference, remark-

FIGURE 6. Korean War Veterans Memorial. (Photo by Hank Savage.)

able. They save the memorial from being devoid of meaning beyond the most obvious patriotic pomp.[101]

These elements in the battle to figure the soldier in this war memorial make painfully clear both the importance of representing the soldier in particular terms—heroic, manly, gallant, not-too-not-white, virile, successful, and so on—and the difficulties of constructing memory in these terms. Barry Schwartz argues that the "dignity of the veteran is affirmed by representing his identification with the state."[102] This seems right but was not enough for the builders of this memorial. The veterans sought straightforward acknowledgment of their service and sacrifice. The ABMC and the eventual architects required identifying with the state *and* defining the soldier in very particular terms.

SERVICE AND DISSERVICE IN THE MEMORIAL

In 1969, a young Bill Clinton wrote a now infamous letter explaining his position on the Vietnam War draft. In it he raised questions about the legitimacy of the draft system: "No government really rooted in limited, parliamentary democracy should have the power to make its citizens fight and kill and die in a war they may oppose, a war which even possibly may be wrong, a war which, in any case, does not involve immediately the peace and freedom of the nation."[103] He continued, "The draft was justified in World War II because the life of the people collectively was at stake. Individuals had to fight if the nation was to survive, for the lives of their countrymen and their way of life. Vietnam is no such case. . . . Nor was Korea, an example where, in my opinion, certain military action was justified but the draft was not, for the reasons stated above."[104] He ends the letter, "I am writing too in the hope that my telling this one story will help you to understand more clearly how so many fine people have come to find themselves still loving their country but loathing the military, to which you and other good men have devoted years, lifetimes, of the best service you could give. To many of us it is no longer clear what is service and what is disservice."

It is just this fissure that the Korean War Veterans Memorial sought to breach. The men and women pushed by the Vietnam War to loathe the military could see in the determined grief of the Vietnam Veterans Memorial an expression of their sense of loss and disconnection. The Memorial Advisory Board and the American Battle Monuments Commission explicitly sought, early in the era of the all-volunteer military, to rewrite that logic for understanding military service. They wanted to equate service with honor and to express pride and gratitude. To do this, they avoided the problem that had so vexed the young Clinton: what the soldiers were doing in the world. They inscribed the insistently generic words, "Our Nation Honors Her Uniformed Sons and Daughters Who Answered Their Country's Call to Defend a Country They Did Not Know and a People They Had Never Met," at the feet of a line of nineteen marching figures because more detail about the war or the vital interests at stake would muddy the waters, would get in the way of the great marching men.

In 1995, President Bill Clinton stood before the crowd gathered for the dedication of the Korean War Veterans Memorial and hailed the memorial as "a magnificent reminder of what is best about the United States."[105] What Clinton celebrated in the memorial was the diversity of those who served, the traces of race that barely survived the memorial process: "In this impressive monument we can see the figures and faces that recall their heroism. . . . [T]he creators of this memorial have brought to life the courage and sacrifice of those who served in all branches of the Armed Forces from every racial and ethnic group and background in America. They represent, once more, the enduring American truth: From many we are one." This is a very generous, perhaps aspirational reading of the memorial that celebrates a nationalism justified by diversity in a moment when diversity was becoming an important trope. But without Clinton's framing, this diversity is hard to see in the memorial. As the notes of the ad hoc committee make clear, the kind of diversity the memorializers could tolerate was quite limited. Clinton's 1969 letter does a much better job of representing the problem that drove the building of the memorial than this 1995 speech does of representing the memorial itself.

In the end, though, the memorial is not unintelligible. Kent Cooper says of the memorial, "We have tried to give the veterans here what we could not give them with the Vietnam memorial."[106] He continues, "We are not glorifying war, but esteeming the honor of service to country. That is what the vets cried out for. . . . [T]he Korean War Veterans Memorial is in some way a tribute to simpler times. This is a monument to blind devotion."[107] What Cooper misses here is that simpler times would not have required blind devotion, and that the terms of the memory that became so determinative for this memorial were not what the veterans had cried out for. The Korean War and the Vietnam War were different in important and consequential ways. The memory of a UN-waged war with broad international support should not be used as a corrective to the memory of a war broadly criticized by the United Nations and by nations around the world.

Simpler times would have made for an easier memorial, but the problem of how to remember ultimately cannot be disconnected from the war itself. The problem of the "nation as a nonimperial world power in the age of decolonization" or of the racial and gender composition of that imagined nation did not disappear in the memorial process; rather, it *drove* the memorial process.[108]

What is just under the surface here, what Kent Cooper assumes will be logical, is that honoring service in this context requires avoiding all that the builders of the KWVM sought to correct in the Wall—especially the presence of loss and the implication of tragedy. The blind devotion of soldiers can only be celebrated when their deaths are honorable rather than tragic. Otherwise, cannon fodder is just cannon fodder. To ensure honorable deaths, the soldiers needed to be understood in terms of the sacrifice they made, with only the most oblique references to what they did in the world. The memorial, by celebrating the soldier in this context, allows the soldier to represent war and allows the work that the war might have done in the world, the global implications of the war and the challenges that it might have presented to U.S. nationalism, to recede out of sight and therefore out of both the past and the present that the memorial constructs.

The Korean War Veterans Memorial is a complicated, multidimensional response to the Vietnam Veterans Memorial and the questions it raised on the Mall about remembering American wars and remembering American soldiers. The need for a particular kind of nationalism, manifest—militarized and domesticated—in the Korean War Memorial process, gains momentum, gets complicated, and is refigured in the monuments that follow it on the Mall. During the time the Korean War Memorial was fought over and built, three attempts were made to *use* the ascension of the figure of the soldier to challenge the figuring of that soldier and the figuring of the nation. The problem of sacrificing soldiers as "traced with race" and that of the insistent figuring of the soldier as not only male but masculine in particular heroic, virile terms were taken up and fought over in the Black Revolutionary War Patriots Memorial, the Women in Military Service for America Memorial, and the National Japanese American Memorial to Patriotism during World War II. The chapters that follow take up the stories of these memorials.

TWO

Legitimating the National Family with the Black Revolutionary War Patriots Memorial

My own great grandfather, John Curtis, a white man from Maine, gave his life for the cause of freedom during the Civil War when he was gunned down at Cold Harbor, Virginia. But for the photograph he took days before, and which was passed down to me, there would be no memorial.

MAURICE BARBOZA

THE STORY OF THE BLACK Revolutionary War Patriots Memorial recounts a failed attempt to use the revival of the status of the sacrificing soldier to redraw primary boundaries of national inclusion. The story of the memorial reveals the tenacity with which the Daughters of the American Revolution, who are central to this story, fought to maintain these boundaries, and the less tenacious but still successful maintenance of these boundaries by the various individuals and federal agencies involved in the memorial process. It also reveals the limits of the revival of the sacrificing soldier. Finally, it reveals how an obvious but, for some, untenable truth—that African Americans served in the Revolutionary War and that they are both figurative and biological creators of the nation—is repressed in the maintenance of these boundaries and remains outside the scope of soldiers celebrated on the Mall in this moment.

A few years ago, Reverend Al Sharpton described the genealogical discovery that he is descended from slaves owned by the family of the late Senator Strom Thurmond as "probably the most shocking thing of my life."[1] While Sharpton's shock is entirely understandable, it is also useful for understanding the struggle over the Black Revolutionary War Patriots Memorial. Removed from the personal circumstance of two larger-than-life public figures with radically different worldviews, the possibility that a Thurmond might have been owned a Sharpton, given where they come from in South Carolina, isn't all that remote. Further, given the nature of the relationship, it is not at all surprising that it was unrevealed for generations. Of course, Sharpton knows this, and he is still shocked.

A cousin of the late Senator Thurmond, Doris Strom Costner, responded to news of the connection to Sharpton by saying, "He's in a mighty good family."[2] There is a fascinating elision in Ms. Costner's comment and, in this elision, a riot of U.S. histories. She moves immediately from "owned by" to "in the family" without contending with the ways in which these descriptions might and might not be distinct. The question of the Thurmond family genealogy is linked to the story of the still unbuilt Black Revolutionary War Patriots Memorial by the large questions it raises about race, legitimation, and nationalism in the United States. (The memorial is also linked in more specific terms to the not-white genealogy of the family of one of the twentieth century's most ardent segregationists, whose mixed-race daughter would become an advocate.)

Thurmond would likely have been shocked as well, despite his intimate knowledge of miscegenation and his lifelong (and failed) struggle to keep both his own family and the national family white. This shock is linked to the senator's efforts to keep the Thurmonds and the Sharptons distinct despite what was actually happening between them. It is surprising that the famously white man and the famously black man are possibly kin because so much energy has been put into distinguishing between black and white, repressing the long formative history of miscegenation in the United States. The Black Patriots Memorial is an attempt to use the figure of the soldier to rewrite this history. The Sharpton-Thurmond story illustrates the ideological enormity of the project.

The term *miscegenation,* as historian Peggy Pascoe explains, first appeared during the Civil War in response to the specter of free African Americans. Pascoe argues that the term "provided the rhetorical means of channeling the belief that interracial marriage was unnatural into the foundation of post-Civil War white supremacy."[3] These post–Civil War concerns draw, of course, on two hundred years of anxiety and a long history of legal and cultural responses to black-white sexual relations.[4] Pascoe's framing is particularly useful here because it speaks to the challenge at the heart of the Black Revolutionary War Patriots Memorial: not simply to make the fact of black military service known but to refigure miscegenation as both natural and nationally constitutive in the United States.

The Korean War Veterans Memorial is a national legitimation project for war and heroic male soldiering in a post–Vietnam War context. Sprawling over a large track of real estate on the National Mall, it celebrates and reifies the sacrificing soldier to encourage blind devotion and obedience to the nation in the context of the new kinds of wars the United States was waging. The Black Revolutionary War Patriots Memorial aspires to put the celebrated soldier to a different use. Whereas the builders of the Korean War Veterans Memorial struggled with the problem of "racing" the soldiers it remembers, the builders of the Black Revolutionary War Patriots Memorial were trying to get black *soldiers* on the Mall as a way of getting black *faces* on the Mall. The veterans to be celebrated in this memorial have been gone for nearly two hundred years, and so were not active agents in the memorial process. The ABMC had no role in the memorial process. The memorializers were a small, complicated band of advocates for rewriting the origins story of the nation. They wanted black faces on the Mall, at the national memorial core, because they wanted to rewrite the figuring of the nation as white-from-its-inception. The Black Revolutionary War Patriots Memorial was, and continues to be, a legitimation project that requires some thinking about—or rethinking of— the language of legitimation.

The story of the memorial begins in 1978 with the photographic portrait of a Civil War soldier on the wall of Maurice Barboza's family home. The photograph had been a curiosity to Barboza for "years and years," and some months after watching Alex Haley's *Roots* on television, he was inspired to look into his own genealogy.[5] Who was this white soldier on the wall, and what connection did he have to Barboza, an African American with a Portuguese surname?[6] What he found surprised him. He discovered that he was properly a son of the American Revolution. He describes himself as "an eleventh generation American through my maternal great grandfather, who arrived from England ten years after the Mayflower."[7] He discovered that in his "family line, there are Gays, Baldwins, Haweses, Nuttings, Wellingtons, Thomases, Curtises, and Stinsons, among others." He has two maternal great-great-grandfathers who were Union soldiers, "one from Virginia, the other from Maine. . . . [O]ne was black . . . the other was white."[8] And his eighth maternal great-grandfather removed, Jonah Gay, fought in the Revolutionary War.[9]

At the time, Barboza was an attorney and lobbyist in Washington. A friend who heard this story recommended that he go to an event at work, a Black History Month lecture by black genealogist Charles Blockson. Blockson had been working on problems of African American genealogy for more than a decade and had published *Black Genealogy* in 1977. Blockson listened to Barboza's story and suggested he join the Sons of the American Revolution. Barboza applied for membership in 1980 and, after producing the required genealogical documentation, was accepted into the society. "No organization," he writes, "had ever welcomed me so sincerely or made me feel so beloved."[10] Inspired by this experience, he suggested that his aunt, Lena Santos Ferguson, join the Daughters of the American Revolution. Her experience was quite different and ultimately led to the campaign for the Black Revolutionary War Patriots Memorial.

DAUGHTERS OF THE AMERICAN REVOLUTION

Being black is not the only reason why some people have not been accepted into chapters.

SARAH KING, DAR PRESIDENT GENERAL

In 1980, Lena Santos Ferguson first sought membership in one of the thirty-nine Washington chapters of the Daughters of the American Revolution (DAR). After three years of significant struggle, Santos Ferguson was begrudgingly granted a limited membership-at-large. This meant that she was not a voting member and did not belong to any local chapter—the center of DAR activity. Despite having the same genealogical documentation that granted her nephew easy entry to the Sons of the American Revolution, Santos Ferguson met fierce resistance from local and national DAR bodies.

A few years earlier, in 1977, Karen Farmer had apparently broken the racial barrier of the DAR when she became the first African American to be accepted for membership in the organization.[11] But Farmer's acceptance in a Detroit chapter did not help Santos Ferguson. It probably hurt; together Farmer and Santos Ferguson may have looked like a trend. Santos Ferguson was unable to find the required two members to sponsor her for a local chapter. The one sponsor she did find was Margaret Johnston, a member of the Mary Washington chapter and the wife of a General Motors executive. Johnston understood what was happening to Santos Ferguson and didn't like it. She told the *Washington Post*, "It was made clear to me that she was not welcome because she is black."[12] When DAR member Elizabeth Thompson considered seconding Johnston's nomination, her friends reacted with shock and disdain. Thompson was told that if she helped Santos Ferguson, the chapter would "probably fall apart."[13] Despite this threat, she left the Mary Washington chapter to join the Elizabeth Jackson chapter, where she sponsored Santos Ferguson.[14] (Interestingly, the Elizabeth Jackson chapter survived but the Mary Washington did not.)

In 1984, the organization's president general, Sarah King, had three revealing responses to the problem of Lena Santos Ferguson's membership, as reported on the front page of the *Washington Post* under the headline "Black Unable to Join Local DAR." First King said, "Being black is not the only reason why some people have not been accepted into chapters.... [T]here are other reasons: divorce, spite, neighbors' dislike.... I would say being black is very [far] down the line." King does not deny that being black is a reason for blocking admission to the DAR; she just claims that it might not be the most pressing reason. For King, the distance between a reasonable request and Santos Ferguson's attempt to join "the society" is indicated by her insistence that "being black isn't the only reason." It is as if she failed to understand that this statement still assumes that being black was reasonable grounds for barring someone from membership. King then said, "There are a lot of people who are troublemakers. You wouldn't want them in because they could cause some problems." King did not explicitly state that Santos Ferguson was a troublemaker. She did not make reference in print to any specific problems with Santos Ferguson's membership. What she did say, repeatedly, was, "If you give a dinner party, and someone insists on coming and you don't want them, what do you do?"[15]

King did not deny that African Americans had served in the Revolutionary War. In fact, in the first *Post* story, she mentioned the Rhode Island Reds and told the reporter, "See, if you can find me one, we want them [blacks], but I do think the lines should have integrity and legitimate descent. I don't think you can have it any other way."[16] King's language was charged; "integrity and legitimate descent" did not refer to high-quality genealogical research. In 1979, two years after Karen Farmer successfully joined the DAR, the society revised its application process to include an added requirement: proof of marriage for each generation. In 1984, the DAR National Congress proposed amending the bylaws to include the language that only "legitimate" descendants were eligible for membership.[17] This would have serious consequences for African Americans wanting to join.

The DAR's interest in rules—and in this intense policing of the boundaries of its membership—was new. From its founding in 1892, at the start of the first great memory boom in the United States, until the 1940s, the greatest obstacle to membership was the invitation of two sponsors. The rules about establishing a paper trail for *direct* (not "legitimate") lineage were far looser. There was some pride associated with taking the word of potential members, the assumption being that a lady would never lie. Rules tightened somewhat in the post–World War II period, when membership in the society was increasingly sought after. But the most dramatic tightening of the rules coincided with the effort of black women to join the organization.

It is also worth noting that the DAR requirements for membership interpret "service in the Revolutionary War" rather broadly. Their definition includes civil service, political service, and what they call patriotic service, which includes "Members of the Boston Tea Party; Defenders of Forts and Frontiers; Doctors, nurses, and others rendering aid to the wounded (other than their immediate families); Ministers who gave patriotic sermons and encouraged patriotic activity" and among other things, "Furnishing a substitute for military service."[18] Under the 1984 rules, then, you could join the DAR because your relative sent a slave to fight in his place, but you could not join the DAR if you were a descendant of that slave, because he would have been unable to legally marry and therefore unable to produce "legitimate descendants."

Language about "legitimate" births and marriages had serious implications for people whose ancestors had been, in large part, legally barred from marrying for centuries. Though King insisted that the changes had "nothing to do with black people," her claim is hard to believe. She argued that the changes "had to do with the modern trends of society."[19] She added, "We're trying to guarantee the integrity of the society." King's language here is worth consideration. When she claims that the DAR wanted to move to "legitimate" members only to "guarantee the integrity of the society," she seems to be talking about both the DAR and the society at large.

The DAR's insistence that the only women worthy of membership in either society were the products of legally sanctioned marriages rules out a huge number of white and black women, given the history of reproduction in the United States. If the past had been as they wished it to be, the DAR would not have had to negotiate with this strange logic.

In the past, sexual mixing of the races, or amalgamation or miscegenation, was not a topic of polite conversation; in fact, it was a subject of great anxiety. In this past, it was unthinkable for someone like Lena Santos Ferguson to ask for membership, and shame was the only imaginable response to the kind of relationships that would lead a person like Santos Ferguson to think she deserved to be recognized as part of the national family the DAR helps to name and shape.

Certainly the DAR is not the only women's patriotic organization to devote itself, at least in part, to policing the boundaries of the white family and the white nation. The Mount Vernon's Ladies Association, for example, famously resisted any mention of slavery or slave life for generations. Women's organizations in the South, such as the United Daughters of the Confederacy, celebrated the memory of the confederacy (and the memory of white power and the white family) with a frenzy of memorial building around the turn of the century. In that same period, patriotic organizations like the DAR took up projects of Americanization and memorialization that also sought to define the nation and the family as white.[20]

One hundred years later, not all members of the DAR were equally committed to policing the boundaries of the white family. At least two other DAR members joined Margaret Johnston in resisting the exclusion of Santos Ferguson. On April 4, 1984, following the story in the *Post*, two members from Massachusetts held a press conference decrying the treatment of Santos Ferguson. Joyce Finley told reporters that King's contention that the Ferguson problem did not involve race was simply not true. "There appears to be," she told reporters, "substantial evidence that runs contrary to Mrs. King's public statement on the Lena Ferguson/race discrimination case and other disputes that could seriously threaten the continued existence of the DAR."[21] Finley and Faith K. Tiberio called for King's impeachment. Finley promised to produce evidence at the upcoming annual DAR Congress. Instead, Finley and Tiberio were reprimanded by the national board and threatened with expulsion from the organization. In October 1985, the two were found guilty on three counts: "Conduct calculated to disturb the harmony, conduct injurious to the good name [of the DAR], and conduct tending to hamper the work of the organization."[22] Tiberio had been a member of the DAR since 1945 and a member of the Children of the Revolution for nine years before that. Her ancestors were Quakers who chose to fight in the Revolution, and she told the *Post*, "I would not have been true to my ancestors ... if I had not spoken out."[23] The board immediately voted to suspend the disciplinary action, but it had made its point. Dissent on the question of race was not taken lightly in the DAR.[24]

Outside the DAR, however, King's blithe assertion that being black wasn't the only reason some women were kept out of the DAR did not go unnoticed. In 1984, when she was saying this, federal law prohibited discrimination in organizations that benefited from a tax-exempt status, as the DAR did. In the District of Columbia, an underresourced, nearly 70 percent African American city, the DAR's tax-exempt status saved them $534,497 a year in property taxes on their building.[25] Following the earlier story in the *Post*, D.C. city council chairman David A. Clarke introduced a bill to revoke the DAR's tax-exempt status.[26] In response, King invited Santos Ferguson, still not a member of a local chapter, to be her guest at the annual congress, and she invited Alex Haley, the author of *Roots*, to speak to DAR members. For Santos Ferguson, this was still not enough.

Lena Santos Ferguson certainly had grounds for a lawsuit against the DAR, but she resisted this option, insisting that she wanted to join rather than damage the organization.[27] Instead, when the D.C. law firm Hogan and Hartson volunteered to get involved, Santos Ferguson and the firm began to negotiate with the DAR. Hogan and Hartson would represent Ferguson in her struggles with the DAR for over seventeen years. In 1984, the combination of the tax threat, the legal threat, and the wave of press interest pushed the DAR to offer Santos Ferguson full membership. She accepted and joined the Elizabeth Jackson chapter, which folded—as predicted—a few years later. Santos Ferguson remained committed to preventing other black women from suffering her fate. She continued working with Hogan and Hartson, who negotiated a multipart agreement that required the DAR to amend its bylaws to stipulate that the DAR would "keep track of, and help, minority descendants become members; advise women that they could be eligible regardless of their race or the race of their ancestor; offer scholarships to graduating seniors in D.C. schools; conduct a seminar on blacks in the Revolutionary War; and identify *everyone* of African descent who served."[28] The DAR also promised to undertake an affirmative action program that included "promoting the goals of H.J. Res 454 honoring black patriots who served in the Revolution."[29]

The DAR vowed to ban further discrimination. They promised to research and identify all black soldiers who served or had been involved in the Revolutionary War and to honor the memory of these soldiers. King wrote to Santos Ferguson's attorney, "If, at any time, there is doubt in your mind or in that of Mrs. Ferguson regarding our integrity or commitment, we want you to let us know. . . . [W]e feel very good about all of this and feel that many good things have come to our Society and we have achieved a great deal in the past two weeks."[30] But the DAR's promises turned out to be complicated to keep.[31]

The response to the Santos Ferguson case in the *New York Times*, the *Washington Post*, and the *Wall Street Journal* reveals both indignation about the prejudice Santos Ferguson faced and avoidance of the obvious lurking question of miscegenation. Only one opinion piece in the *Post* directly addressed this question. Historian Adele Logan Alexander writes, "What is ignored (by the DAR and in *Washington Post* articles as well) and seems almost impossible for white Americans to accept, discuss, or articulate, is miscegenation."[32] She continues, "No, formal marriages between slaves were not permitted prior to the Civil War, but more important, marriage and even cohabitation between the races was forbidden by law in most states from the colonial times. . . . [I]n many jurisdictions these bans remained in force until 1967." For Alexander, what needs to be said is that "no other people on earth display greater variation in skin color, facial structure, or hair texture than we do, yet white America hesitates to admit why this is so. . . . [C]ertainly in our country's early history some few black men sired children by white women, but more commonly we twentieth century black Americans are descended, somewhere along the line, from black women who were sexually coerced by white men." Alexander is interested in this obvious, unspoken truth in the context of the DAR: "The tough question then is not so much whether the DAR members accept the handful of black members who will join the organization and who, for the most part (other than skin color) will greatly resemble the present members in education and background . . . but rather how they will deal with these women whose presence must continually remind them of the illicit, coercive and often violent acts of their mutual forefathers to whose valiant patriotic deeds their organization is dedicated?" And, one might add in the context of Barboza's project, whose presence must remind them of the importance of African Americans to national life from the start.

As Barboza puts it, "Those ladies understood what they were doing. . . . They knew that their families were related to black families. . . . They wanted a sanitized, controlled history."[33] This desire shaped the research they had promised, which was very slow in coming, only appearing in print in 2001.[34] They hired the much celebrated African American genealogist James Dent Walker as a consultant. However, it took them seventeen years to identify 2,400 slaves and free blacks who had fought in the war.[35]

Progress in the research was slow, in part because the DAR's investment in legitimation had a complicated impact on the research itself. Their definitions of whiteness and blackness troubled the research; the unspoken question of miscegenation shaped and slowed the DAR research even more than the sloppy recordkeeping of the Revolutionary War–era military. According to Barboza and historian Gary Nash, the DAR did not use census records, which had valuable information about race, and their use of other historical documents was compromised by the DAR's insistence on counting only soldiers listed as "black, "Negro," or "mulatto." In a 2004 *New York Times* opinion piece, Barboza and Nash argued that many other racial designations were used in these records, including "colored," "yellow," "brown," and "light." In failing to recognize these terms, the DAR research was missing soldiers and underreporting the service of African Americans.[36]

Describing the way this played out, Barboza and Nash wrote, "This may give you a clue to the DAR's resistance: when confronted with sixty-four 'brown' soldiers who could have sired members, the organization conceded that as many as fifty-seven may be listed in its index of proven Revolutionary War soldiers (patriots whose descendants became DAR members). Yet, for generations, descendants of 'brown' patriots married 'light' or 'white' mates, thus increasing the chances that white society, including organizations like the DAR, would be a safe harbor for their offspring."[37] As late as 2004, the DAR remained, as Barboza saw it, committed to "writing out anyone with 'unacceptable' bloodlines."[38] There is also the possibility, of course, that "brown" could have included American Indians. Barboza occasionally included language about remembering Indians in his descriptions of the memorial, but this wasn't systematic or sustained or, really, what he was interested in. And he does not press for more exploration of this in the research, thus reifying a black/white dichotomy for thinking about race and the nation and belonging. It leaves untouched other possibilities for understanding not only the Revolutionary War but also crucial details of African American history.

In fulfillment of another promise to Santos Ferguson, in 2003 the DAR convened an academic conference, the Forgotten Patriots Symposium, at DAR headquarters. Participants in the symposium included some of the most respected historians of the Revolutionary War era, Sylvia Frey, Greg Dowd, Gary Nash, Greg O'Brien, Andrew Cayton, Julie Winch, Woody Holton, Ira Berlin, Warren Hofstra, Colin Calloway, Debra Newman Ham, John Garrigus, and Gwendolyn Midlo Hall. This event signaled the DAR's commitment to the highest quality research.

By 2008, the DAR research seemed to have moved beyond some of its earlier limitations. That year, the DAR published a much more ambitious and significantly retitled 854-page book, *Forgotten Patriots: African American and American Indian Patriots in the Revolutionary War*. It includes the names of 6,600 African American and American Indian "patriots."[39] *Forgotten Patriots* also includes a smart, careful appendix, "Documenting the Color of Participants in the Revolution," which takes up this question with seriousness and precision. Twenty-four years later, two of the initial DAR promises seemed to have been fulfilled. The other promises that Santos Ferguson and Hogan and Hartson negotiated with the DAR in 1984 were less tightly defined. They generally concerned encouraging "minority" membership—and therefore were more complicated in what were, Santos Ferguson aside, heady days for the DAR.

In 1985, when this research was begun, the change-resistant DAR was, in fact, flourishing despite the controversy. It was a moment of ascension for the DAR, and the membership seemed to be forging ahead in their work to maintain the boundaries Adele Logan Alexander described. On April 19, 1985, the *Washington Post* ran a story with the headline "DAR, in Step with the Times." Describing the ceremonial opening of the Ninety-Fourth Continental Congress of the National Society, Daughters of the American Revolution, reporter Jane Leavy writes, "In an instant the air is filled with a profusion of red, white, and blue, held aloft as if by sheer emotion. . . . [T]he Daughters of the American Revolution stand, united and secure, knowing they have done their part to ensure that the Stars and Stripes are indeed forever."[40] Leavy continues, "They have been called racist, sexist, elitist. They have seen the flag they love patching the bottom of tattered blue jeans. They have seen the presidency assailed during Watergate and their country humiliated in Iran. They never wavered. They knew America would come to its senses." Jubilant members asked Leavy, "How can anyone think we are wrong?" "How can any one think we're doing evil?" "How could you not love your country, this country?" and "How could you not love people who love their country?"[41] These questions reveal both a love of the social power their organization gave them and a willful blindness to the costs and consequences of that power. Citing the Tall Ships, the election of Ronald Reagan, and the 1984 Olympics, Leavy concludes, "It is a good time to be a Daughter of the American Revolution." Indeed, the so-called Reagan Revolution and its rhetoric of family values spoke to some of the DAR's core principles.[42] There was much for them to celebrate in this moment.

At this meeting, the DAR fulfilled part of its promise to Santos Ferguson. It also made a bold statement of white supremacy. Members voted, as King had agreed that they would, to amend the bylaws to prohibit chapters from discriminating on the basis of race or creed, but the same document included a resolution in support of apartheid in South Africa. Dismissing "the disinformation and protest movement against South Africa now prevalent in the United States," members voted to support the government of South Africa.[43] The DAR is perhaps best known in the twentieth century for refusing to let Marion Anderson sing in Constitution Hall in 1939, a refusal that led Eleanor Roosevelt to publicly denounce the organization and withdraw her membership. The faith that most members had in 1939 and 1984 that "things would come back around" was profound—and is expressed in this bold support for apartheid in South Africa. In the context of Santos Ferguson's struggle to join the DAR, this resolution—when the brutalities of apartheid were being decried around the world—is hard to see as anything but an aggressive assertion of the racial boundaries they hoped to maintain.

Nonetheless, Santos Ferguson and Barboza persevered in their efforts to force the DAR to make a place for Santos Ferguson and women like her. In the years after the settlement, they continued to work with Hogan and Hartson to monitor the research produced by the DAR and to urge the DAR to move more quickly. Twenty years after the settlement, the DAR was confronted with a vivid personification of the women Alexander described in 1984, whose presence must remind them of the illicit acts of their ancestors. Inspired by Santos Ferguson and Barboza, Essie Mae Washington-Williams, the African American daughter of the late Senator Strom Thurmond, sought membership in the DAR in 2004. Washington-Williams is the child of Thurmond and Carrie Butler, who was a fifteen-year-old household servant working for Thurmond's family when Washington-Williams was conceived. Thurmond never publicly acknowledged Washington-Williams, and she did not speak out about her father until after his death.[44] She sought to join the DAR to support efforts to build the Black Revolutionary War Patriots Memorial and to carve out a place for women like her in the history of the United States.

Washington-Williams also sought membership in the United Daughters of the Confederacy and told Tavis Smiley on his PBS talk show in 2005 that she wanted to join "because I have relatives who died in the wars, and I do know that with the Daughters of the Confederacy, there were many black soldiers who were killed in the Civil War. . . . And then in the Revolutionary War, we know how many there were killed, something like maybe five thousand or more, and these people were never recognized, and we feel that they should be recognized."[45] Her lawyer told the *New York Times,* "She hopes to encourage other blacks in a similar position to do the same."[46] In a statement, she explained, "It is important for all Americans to have the opportunity to know and understand their bloodline. Through my father's line, I am fortunate to trace my heritage back to the birth of our nation and beyond. On my mother's side, like most African-Americans, my history is broken by the course of human events."[47] Barboza sought from the start to address this break. It became apparent after a few years that changing the DAR would not be enough. Barboza needed a broader, more public platform. He turned to the idea of a memorial on the Mall.

THE UNBUILT MEMORIAL

Between 1980, when Santos Ferguson first tried to join, and 1984, when the *Post* published the first story on her battle with the DAR, she and Barboza tried unsuccessfully to generate interest in her story. Frustrated particularly by the DAR's determination to deny Santos Ferguson's legitimate connection to an American past, Barboza—a congressional lobbyist by trade—first tried to claim a place in history for black Revolutionary War veterans through a gesture from Congress. In September 1983, he approached Representative Nancy L. Johnson of Connecticut. She agreed to introduce a bill to honor black Revolutionary War soldiers and "liberty seekers." For Barboza, it was initially "a way of prodding the DAR."[48] Johnson was successful, and Ronald Reagan signed Public Law 98–245 in an Oval Office ceremony on March 27, 1984, coincidentally just a few days after the *Post* ran the first story on Ferguson and the DAR.[49] But the law, "honoring the contribution of blacks to American independence," generated little interest. It was not reported in the *Washington Post,* the *New York Times,* the *Wall Street Journal,* or any other major news service. Barboza was gratified but not satisfied; the law had not claimed space in the popular imagination.[50]

A few months later, with the DAR still pushing back despite the bad press, Barboza began thinking about how else he could stake a claim for African Americans in national life. In November 1984, he began to think about building a memorial. It occurred to him that a memorial might do something that neither Public Law 98–245 nor the fight with the DAR had been able to do. He wanted to "show a common heritage," to fulfill "the promises of liberty that black soldiers fought and died for," to make the point that those "black patriots are the clear and unadulterated roots of what we enjoy today."[51] He wanted to claim a place in the national story, articulating not just a common heritage but a common lineage for black and white Americans. And he wanted to do it indelibly.

A memorial seemed like a good way to do this, and a war memorial seemed like the most likely kind of memorial to get built. Barboza casually links his desire to build a memorial in 1984 to the Vietnam Veterans Memorial; the two-year-old memorial was bringing a new relevance and vitality to the Mall, and the attention paid to sacrificing soldiers on the Mall did not escape his notice.[52] So Barboza went back to Representative Nancy Johnson with the idea for the memorial; she was willing to introduce a bill to get it built. He now needed a senator to introduce it in the Senate. He also needed to form a foundation to see the memorial through the design and building process and to raise money. He went to DAR president King and Margaret Johnston and asked them to serve on the board. They both agreed.[53] So did Lena Santos Ferguson and D.C. city council chair David A. Clarke. A few weeks later, on a plane home to Tennessee, King ran into an acquaintance, then senator Al Gore.[54] She asked him to sponsor the bill in the senate. Gore agreed.

The Black Revolutionary War Patriots Memorial Foundation held their first press conference on Memorial Day, 1985. King, Clarke, Ferguson, and Barboza sat at a conference table and called for "a lasting honor to the more than five thousand black patriots of the American Revolution."[55] Barboza argued that a memorial was needed because "there are no statues in Washington, no motion pictures, and no Fourth of July speeches extolling their bravery."[56] David Clarke added, "I firmly believe that the memorial to black freedom fighters will provide a long overdue symbol of the valuable contribution which black Americans have made to the establishment and maintenance of American Freedom."[57] Patriots were to be honored, black Americans were to be reframed as granters of freedom with a stake in the nation from its earliest moments, and a memorial process was underway.

Clarke's use of the word *freedom* and Barboza's use of *liberty,* here and throughout his long fight for the memorial, are important. Liberty is associated with the Revolutionary War for obvious reasons, but for Barboza it has a particularly important resonance. Freedom was emerging as the central trope for the new memorials on the Mall during the fight with the DAR, but freedom is complicated when linked to pre-emancipation African Americans. A memorial for African American freedom fighters in the era of the Revolution would add one more layer of complication to the already seriously knotty project of making visible a common lineage. So while Clarke evokes freedom here and it comes up in some conversations about the memorial, the central trope for Barboza throughout the memorial struggle is liberty.

In 1985 the bills were introduced, and they passed with little debate in 1986. The bills' supporters made bold assertions about the importance of honoring the service of African Americans who fought in the Revolutionary War. King, Barboza, and others testified. Ronald Reagan signed Public Law 99–558 on October 27, 1986, authorizing "the Black Revolutionary War Patriots Foundation to establish a memorial on Federal land in the District of Columbia and its environs to honor the courageous slaves and free black persons who served as soldiers and sailors or provided civilian assistance during the American Revolutionary War and to honor the countless black men, women and children who ran away from slavery or filed petitions with courts and legislators seeking their freedom."[58] Section 2 of the bill stipulated that the memorial would be built with "non-Federal funds."

The details of the language of the bill, which remained unchanged throughout its many return trips through Congress between 1985 and 2005, are worth noticing. Barboza leads with the soldiers and sailors, but then adds runaway slaves and those who petitioned for their freedom in this period. The emphasis in the testimony to Congress and in the foundation's public statements, however, was always on the patriots—the soldiers. Barboza says he did not start with idea of honoring runaway slaves; he started with the idea of honoring soldiers.[59] But, as he thought about what those soldiers fought for and the conditions under which enslaved people fought, he wanted to expand the notion of who should be honored. He wanted to build a memorial on the Mall to runaway slaves. This seemed like a pretty radical notion, but he describes the inclusion of the runaway slaves and those who petitioned for their freedom in terms of the pursuit of liberty. He wanted to honor all those who were pursuing liberty in the Revolutionary War era. He says he "didn't want the memorial to be too exclusive; he didn't want to create a black DAR."[60] Congress and the press have taken up the question of the soldiers—extolling the virtues of the war patriots and the long-overdue debt the nation owes them—but I have found no mention anywhere of the runaway slaves.[61]

Barboza is right to claim that "black patriots are the clear and unadulterated roots of what we enjoy today." African Americans have been always

inseparable from nation formation in the United States, but neither "unadulterated roots" nor "what we enjoy today" is a simple proposition. Black military service, for instance, was a complicated and serious issue in the Revolutionary War.[62] Four hundred thousand of the two million people in the
colonies were black. The British offered freedom to slaves who would fight for
them, and tens of thousands joined them for this reason. When the Continental Army was initially formed, blacks were barred from service and those
serving in state militias were removed. But recruiting troubles led to a loosen-
ing of this ban, and eventually the army recruited free blacks. Congress even
tried to buy male slaves from individual slave owners, offering the slaves fifty
dollars and their freedom at the end of the war if they served well, but this
plan was so unpopular with slaveholders that it was never realized. Barboza's
loose framing of black soldiers simply as patriots erases much of their experience and the complications of the freedom for which they fought.[63] Some of
those who fought on the American side volunteered, some were slaves sent
to fight by their masters, but they all fought for "liberty" in a slave society.
Historian Sylvia Frey has argued that the Revolutionary War involved white
Americans, British, and African Americans in "a complex triangular process"
in which the British promise of freedom for slaves enraged white southern
loyalists and made American patriots of them.[64] In this formulation, many
whites were fighting partly in defense of slavery, and many of the runaway
slaves Barboza wanted to memorialize ran to the British to fight for their
freedom. But this would muddy the waters for Barboza; he was working to
make a white story into a black *and* white story.

Congresswoman Nancy Johnson, at the first press conference, made
the most compelling statement of the ideas the foundation wanted to see
expressed in the memorial. She identified the logic for building the memorial quite explicitly when she said that she hoped that the memorial would
turn heads and help people to realize "their own ignorance and the profound
implications of that ignorance.... [I]f you really don't know that the nation
was founded by both blacks and whites, it is easier to be racist."[65] The memorial was supposed to rewrite national "legitimation" narratives to legitimate
the miscegenation on which the nation had been built. It was to disrupt the
past protected by the DAR and replace it with a past in which race and nation
were synonymous in a new sense. And the builders of the memorial turned to
the figure of the soldier, the idea of the soldier at the end of the twentieth century, to do this, without worrying too much about the historical specificity
of the experience of real soldiers and the material circumstances of the war.

The first negotiation for Barboza and the foundation was to secure the location they wanted for the memorial. Barboza's ambition for the memorial and what it could do for black Americans was reflected in his ambition for the site. He wanted the memorial to be built on the Mall, in Constitution Gardens, adjacent to the Vietnam Veterans Memorial. Perhaps a less auspicious site would have led to a less fraught memorial process with less anxiety on the part of the reviewing agencies. But Barboza was set on this site because it would place the memorial roughly equidistant from the Lincoln Memorial, the Washington Monument, and the DAR's Constitution Hall. This triangulation was important in his thinking, as it claimed Washington, Lincoln, and the DAR in his refiguring of the black soldier and the nation.

Despite its humble origins and the modesty of its design, Constitution Gardens would become a crucial part of the memorial process. Constitution Gardens had been occupied by temporary military buildings for forty years before the Nixon presidency. These buildings infuriated Nixon, who wanted them removed and replaced with something like the Tivoli Gardens, Copenhagen's startlingly pristine Hans Christian Anderson–themed amusement park and gardens. Skidmore, Owings, and Merrill, the firm that had been working sporadically since 1965 to build on the McMillan Plan for the Mall, designed an elaborate park for Nixon, but he was soon distracted from this project, and the Commission of Fine Arts "rejected the scheme as being far too busy and functionally inappropriate."[66] As CFA chair J. Carter Brown writes, "We believed that the structure of the Mall was now so established that something of a much more relaxed nature was warranted for this space."[67] The CFA-supported plan was realized in the mid-1970s. It includes a naturalized lake, open meadow, wooded pathways, and one memorial—the Signers Memorial. The Signers Memorial is a low stone memorial to the fifty-six signers of the Declaration of Independence. Built in 1982, it was a gift from the American Revolution Bicentennial Administration. It is the embodiment of understatement, reflecting the modest, even occasionally humbled patriotism of the bicentennial. This modesty would have serious implications for Barboza's project.

The bureaucratic mechanisms in place to oversee the building of a memorial on the Mall are an enormous challenge for any memorial project. Congressional approval was required for getting a site. The design then needed approval from the Commission of Fine Arts, the National Capital Planning

Commission, and the National Park Service, which would assume responsibility for the completed memorial. When a memorial to commemorate the service of African Americans in the Union Army during the Civil War was proposed to Congress in 1991, it passed H.J. Resolution 320 without much debate. A site was selected well off the Mall at Vermont Avenue and U Street, and the memorial—with four armed and uniformed black soldiers—was dedicated eight years later. This Civil War project was not entirely without struggle, but it had to contend with a dramatically different level of oversight, far fewer restrictions on the design, and much less anxiety about what it might say because it stands, with its armed black soldiers, off the Mall in a traditionally African American neighborhood.

The bill authorizing the Black Revolutionary War memorial had guaranteed a site "on federal land in the District of Columbia and its environs." To be built on the Mall, the subject of the memorial had to be designated "of preeminent historical and lasting significance to the nation," according to the 1986 Commemorative Works Act.[68] This act, a response to the rush to build memorials on the Mall in this period, sought to slow the pace of memorial building on the Mall by limiting the kinds of memorials that could be built. It emphasized war memorials but discouraged memorials to "lesser conflicts" or aspects of a particular war. Barboza needed an exemption to get space on the Mall, and he got it with the help of secretary of the interior Donald Paul Hodel, who described the memorial as a "significant part of the fundamental *military* struggle that gave birth to the United States as a separate and free Nation."[69] Hodel does not mention runaway slaves, rather emphasizing the importance of the memorial in a military context. Public Law 100–265, passed in March 1988, guaranteed the Black Revolutionary War Patriots Memorial a site in Area 1—on the Mall. [70]

But both the Commission of Fine Arts (CFA) and the National Capital Memorial Advisory Commission worried from the beginning about the relationship of the memorial to the Signers Memorial and Constitution Gardens. J. Carter Brown wrote in his report to the Parks Service, "The Commission notes, however, the concern expressed by the National Capital Memorial Advisory Commission regarding the potential scale of the project and counsels the designers to provide a discreet scheme in scale with the Signers Memorial and in harmony with Constitution Gardens as a whole."[71] Brown's conception of a "discreet scheme" and the knee-high dimensions of the Signers Memorial would have profound, ultimately debilitating, consequences for the design and the memorial.

The Black Revolutionary War Patriots Foundation was charged with getting the memorial built. They needed to raise money, find a design, and meet the five-year, 1991 deadline written into the legislation approving the memorial. And though they did develop a design, the foundation raised little money beyond what they spent, and they did not meet the deadline. The problems at the foundation led to problems with the deadline and, eventually, to extensions from Congress in 1991, 1993, 1996, 1998, and 2000. The authorization for the memorial finally expired on October 27, 2005.

The Black Revolutionary War Patriots Foundation (BRWPF) was a complicated organization from the outset. Barboza, Santos Ferguson, Clarke, Johnston, and King were at once adversaries and founding members of the foundation. Margaret Johnston, Santos Ferguson's first supporter and sponsor at the DAR, soon became a central figure in the foundation. Johnston was married to an executive at General Motors, which had indicated interest in giving money to the foundation. She quickly became cochair of the foundation. Together, she and Barboza assembled an impressive advisory board that included Colin Powell, Andrew Brimmer, and the president of General Motors. Early on, they held a dinner at the Sheraton in Washington to kick off their fundraising campaign. Brimmer and the others attended. Powell spoke. GM gave generously, and the event brought in $250,000. The night was likely the high point for the memorial and the foundation. But financial disorganization and stalled fundraising bled the coffers and scared away some board members—perhaps eventually derailing the project.[72]

Barboza's account of the problems at the foundation has everything to do with Johnston. In his words, she went from being their only ally at the DAR to being their "worst nightmare."[73] He claims that Johnston wanted control, that she did not have the experience required to run an organization, and that she did not try to fundraise. He suggests that her principal interest seemed to be in undermining the organization.[74] Barboza does not directly claim that Johnston intentionally tried to sabotage the memorial, but he does suggest that the DAR used the foundation to cut off the memorial at its knees, exacting revenge on Santos Ferguson and himself. What he says most directly is, "I had no power: I only had the power of the story and my knowledge of Congress" and that Johnston "poisoned the well."[75]

From 1988 to 1992, Santos Ferguson and Barboza argued with Johnston and struggled to raise money. In 1992, Johnston ousted Barboza from the foundation, effectively removing him from the project. Santos Ferguson resigned in protest. She told the *Washington Afro-American*, "The greatest wounds Maurice and I suffered, and the worst thing we could have done to the memorial's cause, was to allow my white DAR sponsor, Margaret M. Johnston, to chair the Board of Directors of The Patriots Foundation.... [T]his person, whom we considered a lifelong friend, betrayed us."[76] She went on, "In 1992, she used her familial connections to a major donor, General Motors Corporation, to manipulate the Foundation and removed us from the project like what America did to the history of African Americans; she has denied my family the opportunity to pass on the pride of this potential achievement to future generations." Santos Ferguson's description is interesting. She speaks in quite literal terms of her desire to see her grandson standing before the memorial, but she also makes a larger point: Johnston did to her just what she and Barboza had hoped the memorial would undo on a national scale. She sees it as a generational interruption: they were denied the opportunity to pass on pride.

These claims would have little credibility if, with Santos Ferguson and Barboza removed from the foundation, Johnston had managed to get the memorial built. She did not. Joanne Jones stepped in as her cochair after Barboza was ousted, and together, with significant help from GM, they were able to get the authorization for the memorial extended. Between 1991 and 2005, Johnston and her successor kept the memorial alive. This must have taken considerable effort and dedication; the project did not immediately die on the vine when Barboza and Santos Ferguson were removed. And it is hard to imagine that her motives were "to poison the well." She supported Santos Ferguson when it could not have been easy, and she put tremendous energy into the foundation. She was not, however, able to raise the money required. Before 1992, the foundation raised $250,000 from GM. According to Barboza, it was thwarted in its efforts to raise more by tensions at the foundation and problems with the design.[77]

According to Barboza, from 1986 to 2005 over $4 million was raised for the project.[78] Between 1992 and 2005, when the authorization expired, the foundation raised $1 million though the Black Revolutionary War Patriots Commemorative Coin Act, $1.5 million from corporate sponsors including GM and Phillip Morris, $1 million in a fundraising pledge from San Francisco Mayor Willie Brown, $50,000 from Ghana, and the rest from a few private donors.[79] In 2000, Reed Abelson reported for the *New York Times* that the foundation had lost the support of early corporate donors and "has had little luck replacing them."[80] Board chair Wayne Smith described the fundraising process as "kind of a lonely business."[81] Barboza says that nearly all the money raised was spent on salaries and overhead, with less than $1 million going to memorial development.[82] When the foundation finally dissolved with the 2005 expiration, there was no memorial and no money left.

It is important to note that other memorials built on the Mall in this period had living veterans who were anxious, or whose children were anxious, to see a memorial built. The Korean War Veterans Memorial and the National Japanese American Memorial to Patriotism during World War II, for instance, were built largely with money raised by veterans—even though the veterans raising the money did not necessarily embrace the memorial designs. Not only did the Black Revolutionary War Patriots Memorial have no living veterans to support it, but the point of the memorial was to make visible the service of African Americans whose descendants are frequently unaware of their families' contribution to the founding of the United States. In other words, they had no living veterans, and the families of the veterans often don't know that their forefathers fought and thus are a hard crowd to fundraise from.

Despite the trouble at the foundation—and perhaps compounding it— the memorial design development went forward. Before Santos Ferguson and Barboza were removed from the board, they did get a design approved. To date, there have been three designs. If Congress ever reauthorizes the project as proposed in 2005, 2009, 2010, and 2011, there will likely be a fourth.[83]

THE FIRST DESIGN

The bronze figures . . . gave the memorial a feeling of monumentality it should not have.

NEIL PORTERFIELD, COMMISSION OF FINE ARTS

In 1990, Maurice Barboza and architect Marshall Purnell presented a preliminary design to the Commission of Fine Arts. Purnell described the design: "The lawn area rising from the lake to an elliptical plane, paved in granite, on which were placed thirteen seven-foot-high bronze figures—the number coming from the thirteen colonies—each holding a scroll that gave information on events and people."[84] Purnell also described a "teaching function" for the memorial, a separate adjoining area with low formal seating.

The CFA members were unanimously opposed to the design concept.

J. Carter Brown commented, "The placement of any figures would have to be looked at very critically."[85] Vice-Chairman Porterfield reminded Barboza and Purnell that, when the site was approved, "the Signers' Memorial was in everyone's mind" and told them that "a landscape solution was expected."[86] The members thought "the bronze figures and the hard edge, especially the stone enclosure walls, gave the memorial a feeling of monumentality it should not have." They felt that this monumentality "defeated the feeling of discovery and spirit of the place [Constitution Gardens]."[87] The members didn't like the wall that the figures and scrolls would form. They thought there was too much going on, that "it would not be an intimate, poetic experience" and that the "point of the memorial was being lost." This language of "discovery" in the context of Constitution Gardens was important to the CFA and ultimately crushing for the memorial.

Purnell responded that the Signers Memorial had its own well-defined space and would not be altered by his design. He also was very clear that a landscape solution would be problematic because "he thought visitors needed to see black people depicted, they needed to have heroes, and it was necessary to portray those who had fought for freedom."[88] Brown responded that, when the site was approved, the commission "had in mind a poetic, landscape solution, not one involving free-standing sculpture, which he did not consider appropriate to the site." Brown went on to say that "he hoped that [the designers] would see this." He added that "whatever elements were involved, they should not pierce the green ridge behind the memorial area."[89] This proved to be determinative. The CFA wanted not only a landscape solution, which precluded figures, but a landscape solution that was not visible from more than a short distance. The commission concluded by rejecting the design, asking Barboza and Purnell to develop a new design and to get a sculptor involved.

The CFA response expressed clear expectations of the memorial: they wanted landscaping instead of figures; they did not want monumentality; they wanted it to be an "intimate" experience upon which one might stumble; they didn't want it to be vertical; they didn't want it to be disruptive; and they wanted it to be "poetic" rather than "attention-getting." The figures and their size were, in the minds of the CFA members, undermining the point of the memorial. But, for Barboza, the figures *were the point* of the memorial. Purnell was very direct: showing black people was the reason to build the memorial. But the commission was not deterred. Their insistence that Barboza should have understood from the approval process that the site was fit only for landscaping is not supported by the minutes. The CFA "cautioned" about the size of the memorial in relation to the Signers Memorial but was not explicit about landscape, figures, or scale.[90] Brown assumed that considering the memorial in relation to the Signers Memorial would lead Barboza to imagine a smaller, more modest, less conspicuous, and figure-free memorial for black Revolutionary War soldiers and runaway slaves. To paraphrase Brown, he had in mind a memorial that wouldn't wave its hand. But this was very much at odds with what Barboza wanted the memorial to do.

In his April 5, 1990, letter to the Park Service reporting on the meeting, Brown wrote that he was troubled by the design. "The figures themselves," he explained, "present an aspect that appears at variance with the larger context of the Constitution Gardens."[91] (Given that many of the signers of the Declaration of Independence named on the Signers Memorial were slaveholders, this statement from Brown, which is most obviously about aesthetics, seems to entirely miss the point of a memorial for free blacks whose experience was indeed at variance with the larger context.) Brown continued, "The thirteen larger-than-life statues, in conjunction with extensive grading of the site, will have a presence that exceeds the quiet and low profile of the Signers Memorial."[92] "If," he wrote, "the Memorial Foundation believes free standing figurative sculpture is necessary, then the scale of the program should be reduced." The scale of the Signers Memorial is knee high. It is hard to imagine a design solution with knee-high figures. Though this may seem too literal an interpretation of the CFA's requirements for the memorial, it was taken seriously; the CFA told Barboza that any sculpture would have to be "very small not to be visible over the ridge," and Brown suggested a low wall with bas-reliefs. The March 1990 meeting clearly established very modest, contained, limited, knee-high parameters for the memorial design.

THE SECOND DESIGN

They wanted it to be abstract. In this city, our nation's capital,
there was an issue with putting black faces on the National Mall.

ED DWIGHT

In 1991, Barboza and Purnell went back to the Commission of Fine Arts with a new design and sculptor Ed Dwight.[93] They had held an unusual design competition. Barboza and Purnell invited a series of sculptors and designers to come to Washington. They brought them into a conference room with thirty designs and asked them about the designs: "What do you like?" "What would you change?" Dwight describes it as "the stupidest god-damned thing."[94] They were, according to Dwight, pushing an 8' × 8' × 8' granite block "with text that said something like blacks were here and they fought."[95] Dwight told them what he thought and asked for some paper. He started to make drawings. As he tells it, Marshall Purnell turned to Barboza and said, "I think we have found our man."[96]

The design Dwight eventually developed looked like figures emerging from a swirling rock in the eye of a hurricane. The idea was that the figures were "escaping, had been buried and the wall was chipped away, ripped open to reveal their history and to release their energy."[97] This design started with small figures, but it ended with full-size, standing, armed figures who have emerged triumphant from the rock. Dwight had pieces of rock thrown off the wall and strewn through the plaza. The design was dynamic, explosive, and not deferential to the Signers Memorial or the CFA's desire for a modest surprise. It aspired to express release. It aspired to reveal African Americans in the bedrock of national life. And it aspired to make this seismic claim on the Mall. To do this, it included multiple armed black figures. From his first meeting with Purnell and Barboza, Dwight was adamant about the need for black figures. For him, too, the point of the memorial was black figures. He wanted them to come screaming out of the wall because they had been held there in bondage. "Black kids," he argues, "need to see black faces. A two-year-old needs to see these figures."[98] His figures would convey something that no landscape solution could.

Presenting this design to the CFA in 1991, Barboza began by describing his vision for the memorial. He made an emotional plea, telling the members that "this should not be considered a war memorial; it was intended to honor the vision, effort, and extraordinary courage of the black people who served during the birth of our country."[99] Having secured his site with the secretary of the interior based on the *military* significance of the memorial, he shifted here, playing to a different audience; he still wanted figures of soldiers but was pitching them to the CFA as representing not war but a more abstract service to the nation in the name of liberty. He was trying to get the figures he wanted by emphasizing honor and service rather than war. He didn't need a war memorial; he needed a soldiers' memorial. This logic is not unlike the logic that shaped the Korean War Veterans Memorial, which was well under-way in 1991. The point of both was not so much the wars themselves as the uses to which the soldiers who had served in them might be put. Barboza's problem was that his soldiers could not be "traced with race"; they needed to be black. Their blackness was intended to make a point beyond military service, to make blackness visible in the national story, and to legitimate the not-white political and reproductive roots of the nation. But this is not the language Barboza used; he simply reminded the commission that the dream of the soldiers to be honored had not been realized for two hundred years, and he called on the CFA to help realize this dream.

Marshall Purnell tried to convey the sincerity of the foundation's efforts to address the CFA's concerns. He told the commission that, after their last meeting, the BRWPMF had reduced the memorial to three elements: sculpture, structure, and text. He described the new design as something closer to a landscape solution, as "three curved walls and a paved plaza: a bronze sculpture wall, nearest the lake; the plaza, a low seating wall, and farthest to the south, a granite wall for inscriptions."[100] Echoing Brown, Purnell made a point of saying that the memorial "should not have to shout across the lake." He went on to say, "Nor should it be a destination in itself; the intent was to pull in the visitor as he walked along the path on his way to other destinations."[101] This certainly spoke to the CFA's requirements for the memorial, but it did not really correspond to Dwight's design. And it is a little baffling.

Landscape architect Roger Courtenay then described some details of the design, emphasizing its relationship to the "spirit" of Constitution Gardens. He described a "plaza area, about 30 by 50 feet, that would be paved in light-colored granite, the stones radiating out from the free-standing sculptural figures in a vortex-like pattern."[102] He took care to call attention to their responsiveness to the CFA's push for a low, unassuming memorial. He emphasized that "the memorial would have a horizontal emphasis, with its highest point at elevation 19, the top of the flood levee."[103] This last point would take on significance with the National Park Service, which was both enthusiastic in its support for the design and adamant that the memorial not penetrate the berms they had planned to surround the memorial.

Courtney was followed by Dwight, who spoke in dramatic terms. He said his "task had been to memorialize a group of people having a common experience during the period from 1775 to 1783, and in portraying them, to release the energy buried inside." His work, as he described it, would start at the low end of the low wall in bas-relief. The relief would become higher "with the portrayal of blacks' petitions for freedom and their questioning of their roles in the war and the new nation." "Finally," he continued, "the wall would disintegrate and full figures would emerge in a call to arms, battle, and lastly a

FIGURE 7. Black Revolutionary War Patriots Memorial design with Ed Dwight. (Courtesy of Ed Dwight Studios, Inc.)

post-war scene with a family looking towards the future."[104] Dwight would use the low wall that the CFA had requested to stand for the bondage from which his figures were struggling to emerge. And his figures would emerge— first as armed combatants and then as a freestanding family unit.

The CFA's response was more positive this time. They expressed a general sense that there was too much going on in the memorial. They were also concerned that the walls were too dark and the freestanding sculpture might be too much, that they might become "clumpy." Brown also pressed Dwight to keep the relief "a little longer before changing to full figures," to minimize the number of full-sized figures.[105] However, in his report to Robert Stanton, the regional director of the National Parks Service, he cheerfully described a "spirit of cooperation" and remarked that they were witnessing "the design review process at their best."[106] For Brown, the sculpture wall was

FIGURE 8. Black Revolutionary War Patriots Memorial figures. (Courtesy of Ed Dwight Studios, Inc.)

the perfect solution to the problem of the tension between figures and the Signers Memorial. Small figures emerging from the wall worked for him. He expressed a desire to see the other elements diminished and for some emphasis to shift from the figures back to the bas-relief, but the design was approved and there was relief in the tone of his report. Brown wasn't trying to kill the memorial; he believed it needed to be deferential to the Signers Memorial and saw progress in this direction. For him, the less figural the memorial was, the more deferential.

The design did not change much between 1991 and 1996, when the new BRWPMF appeared before the CFA to receive final approval of the design. Purnell, presenting the design with the ousted Barboza, repeated their desire to avoid disrupting Constitution Gardens and the Signers Memorial, and to avoid calling attention to the memorial they were building. In the end, the design that was approved was a mix of the BRWPMF's ambitions, the CFA's constraints, and Dwight's powerfully rendered compromise—a few figures emerging from a low wall teaming with figures in relief. Figures emerging from the wall seemed not only a good solution to the CFA's concerns, but also a compelling way to represent people pulling themselves out of human bondage. In the models, there is some awkwardness around the scale of the figures. In the wall, the figures seem lilliputian. As they start to get bigger but before they emerge from the wall, they seem especially and strangely child-sized and miniaturized. The last figure in the wall is a crouched soldier who appears to be in a low run into battle, his rifle barely raised. Just behind him, a figure who does not seem to be wearing a uniform and whose weapon is not drawn, is oddly small in comparison to the runner. He seems diminished, maybe even caricatured. But these are details likely to have been worked out in the development of the memorial.

The key points about Dwight's design are that he was able to get figures approved and that he shifted emphasis from arms and declarations of rights to the family. By reducing the armed black soldiers from thirteen in the original design to four or five, he softened the design considerably. The soldiers in the wall are in uniform and armed. And his design culminates not with a single victorious soldier but with a well turned-out family gazing gratefully, if anachronistically, at Lincoln. The first figure to emerge fully from the wall holds a rifle tightly with both hands, horizontally across his hips. His head is tilted back slightly, and his shoulders are thrown back. He appears to look far into the distance. A few paces in front of him stand the family. The woman holds a child in her arms. Between her and the first figure stands an older man. The child stands straight at his mother's shoulder and gazes into the distance. The soldier/father is set just slightly apart. He wears a military uniform and his tricorne is held low at his side. He is carrying a rifle, its barrel pointed toward the ground. His right foot is set a few inches in front of his left and his right knee is slightly bent, as if he is leaning into the future. It is a potent, complicated design, expressing and containing the power of the black soldier and linking liberty with the legitimate black family.

The CFA approval did not end the design process. The struggle continued with the Park Service over the landscaping and the containment of the memorial. Ed Dwight, who considers the design his best work, would become quite disenchanted with the process, telling the *Washington Post* in 2005, fifteen years after his initial involvement with the project, that the memorial was stalled by concerns about black figures on the Mall. When asked about the fate of the memorial, he replied, "They wanted it to be abstract. . . . [I]n this city, our nation's capital, there was an issue with putting black faces on the National Mall."[107] The Park Service wanted to build large berms to "shelter" the site or intensify the surprise felt in stumbling upon it. Dwight describes an obsession with making sure that the rifles or the heads of the figures did not penetrate the berm: "They kept telling us that this was sacred ground and that we couldn't penetrate the berm." Of course, for Dwight, the whole point was that it was sacred ground and the berm needed to be penetrated; the black figures needed to be seen.[108]

Dwight contends that concerns about armed black men on the Mall—the pressure to hide and minimize the memorial—did not come from a single source or from any federal policy: "This was about individual anxieties, but a lot of individuals who were in positions to shape the memorial."[109] Although he seems to want to avoid accusing Dwight of dishonesty, Maurice Barboza, who is still trying to work with some of these individuals and agencies to get his memorial built, resists this summation. He is adamant that he never heard anything about black faces on the Mall. When asked about Dwight's remark, Barboza said, "No one ever said that to me."[110] But Dwight's point, which is compelling, is that they didn't have to say it—they didn't even have to fully articulate it to themselves—in order to shape the memorial. For Dwight, the fact that the CFA and NPS repeatedly insisted that the memorial be essentially hidden behind berms and that, even then, the figures needed to be shoved as far back into the rock as possible, be contained in the knee-high wall, made little sense outside of an anxiety about the black figures. He describes the embarrassing problem of trying to sell the minimized memorial to potential donors—of walking into a room full of receptive folks and having to struggle to explain why the figures had to be so small and why the memorial needed to be a surprise in the landscape.[111]

Barboza, whether or not he thought the design issues were linked to anxiety about race, not only never gave up on the figures, but he never gave up on *armed* figures. The issue of weapons was nearly as important to him as the figures. Barboza did not want just any black figures; he wanted to represent particular kinds of armed black figures. In the Revolutionary War period, laws prohibited black men from owning weapons, so to portray the black patriot with a weapon gives him "back the manhood that this law took away and at the same time serves as a reminder that he didn't turn that rifle on his master—he was loyal both to the master and the pursuit of liberty."[112] The family depicted in the memorial is evidence of this manhood.

For Barboza, the weapons in the hands of these figures are emblems of the soldiers' masculinity and loyalty—loyalty to the nation and to the masters for whom they fought. But, of course, this formulation is complicated and raises other questions. How could these men have been loyal to their masters in the pursuit of liberty? Doesn't loyalty to a master fundamentally deny liberty? (Doesn't serving on behalf of a master legitimate the state rather than the individual? Does it legitimate bondage in the name of liberty?) Barboza here applies to eighteenth-century soldiers a trumped-up twentieth-century notion of military service as an enactment of the virile citizenship that is the ultimate expression of freedom. This is tricky for twentieth-century soldiers, and perhaps impossible for eighteenth-century soldiers. The struggle over the soldiers at the Korean War Veterans Memorial is relevant here. The tension between the desire to figure the soldiers as powerfully masculine (no limp wrists) and as unswervingly loyal (blindly devoted) is similar to the tension Barboza, perhaps inadvertently, describes above. These representations of soldiering try to conflate masculinity and obedience. The great distinction between the two projects is, of course, that the purpose of the Black Revolutionary War Patriots Memorial is to pull the requirement of whiteness out of the equation. At the Korean War Veterans Memorial, which did get built, soldiering is represented as an expression of masculinity, obedience, and a kind of whiteness. The Black Revolutionary War Patriots Memorial sought to shift the racial logic in this figuring of the soldier. Certainly, this posed a great design challenge.

In the end, Barboza was not happy with Dwight's design. He said it was "too tragic." This is in keeping with the desire of other memorial builders of the period to avoid grief at all costs.[113] Barboza describes himself as wanting more of the triumph of the family. He said Dwight gave him "old men with haggard faces" and suffering.[114] Barboza's final analysis of the design was that "nobody gave me money for that design."[115] Barboza complained that the "soldiers were old men, crouching small looking, powerless." The figures were not heroic enough, not powerful enough somehow. He talked about how so many African Americans think that their ancestors "didn't do anything." This is what he wants to change, and the Dwight design would not do enough to change it. In the bas-relief in the wall, Dwight's design portrayed a lot of grief and anguish; it represented suffering where Barboza wanted to represent patriotic heroism in the pursuit of liberty. He didn't think the design addressed the problem of African Americans "not seeing themselves as worthy." Barboza was sure that "the design brought us down."[116]

This memorial was not built. The relationship between the CFA and NPS requirements, the design, the tensions at the foundation, and the stalled fundraising is not entirely clear. Nor is the larger role of the DAR in the memorial process. The project faced so many challenges and involved so many complicated personalities that there does not seem to be a simple answer to the question of why it was not built, but there are some indicators of the central problems. The fraught terms of the relationship of the DAR to Barboza, Santos Ferguson, and the memorial were a problem from the start. The limitations imposed on the design by the approving agencies likely made fundraising difficult; it is hard to generate interest in a memorial that is not supposed to be monumental or call attention to itself. In either case, Dwight's design died with the Black Revolutionary War Patriots Memorial when congressional authorization lapsed after nearly twenty years, in the fall of 2005. For the ever-persistent Barboza, this end enabled a beginning. With the memorial went the foundation that he had founded and that had prohibited his involvement with the project. When the fate of the memorial seemed sealed in the spring of 2005, Barboza founded the National Mall Liberty Fund and began his efforts anew.

STARTING AGAIN:

THE NATIONAL LIBERTY MEMORIAL

Like the Black Revolutionary War Patriots Memorial, the National Liberty Memorial (NLM) promises to honor "over 5,000 enslaved Americans and free persons of African descent, who volunteered to serve as soldiers and sailors during the American Revolution; tens of thousands of slaves and free persons who rendered civilian assistance that helped win the nation's Independence; slaves who ran away to freedom; and thousands of men, women, and children who petitioned state courts and legislatures for liberty during that era."[117] And the NLM aspires to expand this project: "Through the memorial to black patriots, National Mall Liberty Fund D.C. will educate Americans about these patriots' contributions to the founding of the nation and fill large gaps in our children's textbooks. . . . [A]n understanding of our common heritage will eliminate stereotypes, heal racial wounds passed on for generations and foster a sense of 'One Nation' among Americans."[118] The fund promises further, "Near these and other symbols of liberty, the memorial will illuminate lost history and tell us that blacks: served honorably under General George Washington, and beside their white compatriots, in military and civilian roles; struggled to win freedom and equality decades before Lincoln's birth and the emancipation proclamation; aspired to make the ideals of the Declaration of Independence a part of the Constitution and a reality for all citizens; and fought and died in all wars, from the Revolution to Vietnam (including the Civil War)."[119] This links the memorial not only to the Signers Memorial but to all American wars through Vietnam. Interestingly, in 2005, it does not include either war with Iraq or the war in Afghanistan.

As Barboza describes it, this memorial is pointedly for young African Americans: "This project seeks to revitalize the spirit of the nation's African American youth and to inspire them to achievement and exemplary citizenship.... [T]he memorial will demonstrate historic African American values at work in the founding of the nation and in the achievement of universal liberty."[120] At the same time, the new name for the project drops *Black* and *Revolutionary War* and replaces them with the more generic, apparently unraced terms *Liberty* and *National*.

The NLM Fund has made some progress. In April 2006, Senator Christopher Dodd of Connecticut introduced S. 2495. The bill, cosponsored by Senators Grassley, Byrd, Allen, Obama, Dole, and Chafee, would pass the BRWPM rights and authorization to the National Liberty Memorial Fund and would enable the fund to "renew the cause and design, construct and dedicate the memorial."[121] The bill, which has not been passed, reads: "To authorize the National Liberty Fund D.C. to establish a memorial on Federal land in the District of Columbia to honor slaves and other persons that fought for independence, liberty, and justice for all during the American Revolution."[122] Like the organization's new name, this new bill deemphasizes race. It does not refer to black soldiers or black patriots or American Indians, only to slaves and "others" who fought. The new bill also drops runaway slaves. Barboza wanted to add whites who had helped blacks, but the committee asked that this language be removed.[123] Barboza defends the changes in language by arguing that his vision has always been broad and that he has always been interested in honoring the pursuit of liberty in the broadest terms. But there is a distinct tension between eliminating race and the war from the name of the memorial, the name of the organization, and the wording of the bill and creating a mission statement that promises to speak directly to African American youth. Though Barboza rejects Dwight's contention that black faces on the Mall were a problem, he dramatically changed the language of the pitch when proposing a new memorial.

In June 2006, the National Capital Memorial Advisory Commission met to hear the fund's appeal for transfer of the preexisting site approval. This was crucial because the Commemorative Works Clarification and Revision Act of 2003 banned building memorials in Area 1, the Mall, without preexisting site approval. Barboza brought to this meeting his well-rehearsed arguments about the need to honor Revolutionary War heroes. He also brought two African American teenagers with black ancestors who fought in the war. Yolanda Wade and Daysha Christian were told just a few weeks before the meeting that their ancestors had served, and the girls agreed to join Barboza in testifying before the commission. Wade told the *Richmond Times-Dispatch,* "They didn't get recognized, and I wanted to take a stand for them since they're not here to do it." Thirteen-year-old Christian added, "The monument can show that somebody actually cares."[124] Senator Dodd sent a statement to the hearing affirming, "I continue to believe that this memorial highlighting the heroic efforts and the diversity of the men who fought in the Revolutionary War deserves a place within Constitution Gardens on the Mall."[125] The memorial required approval from the commission to stay alive, and it got it.

In a letter to Senate president pro tempore Ted Stevens, written in support of S. 2495, historians Henry Louis Gates and Gary Nash express loftier ambitions than highlighting diversity or showing that somebody actually cares. They argue that the Mall will not be a complete work of art until the memorial takes its place there, where it will "redefine how Americans perceive the nation's birth, 'all men are created equal,' and our future as one nation based upon enduring principles, instead of color and race." They also lend compelling language to the ambitions of Barboza and Santos Ferguson, writing that they "realized America could become a more inviting home for descendants of slaves if the tarnish of slavery and second-class citizenship were removed from their ancestors with a permanent statement on the nation's most visible landscape."[126] This clearly articulates Barboza's determination to use the memory of black Revolutionary War soldiers to redraw primary boundaries of national inclusion. It contends that representing these men as soldiers rather than slaves, on the National Mall, will change how people understand their place in the nation.

Barboza continues to fight for this rewriting of the Mall. However, his link to the Mall was seriously threatened in 2007, when secretary of the interior Dirk Kempthorne rejected the fund's bid to hold onto the Constitution Gardens site. Bills introduced in 2009, 2010, and 2011 challenge this decision and keep hopes for the memorial alive.

THE THIRD DESIGN

A classical and timeless design . . .
NATIONAL MALL LIBERTY FUND

The National Liberty Memorial Foundation will not have rights to and does not seem interested in Ed Dwight's design for the memorial. They have commissioned classically trained sculptor David Newton to mock up a new direction for the memorial. His design expresses Barboza's interest in emphasizing the family's role in the struggle for liberty; it drops the struggle and the soldiers and simply puts the black family on a pedestal.

Newton's design consists of three figures—a man, a woman, and a child—raised on a pedestal. The pedestal is set in the center of a plaza defined by a low, white neoclassical wall. The entry to the plaza is flanked by two very tall flagpoles with American flags. The figures are arranged in a circle with a bronze American flag connecting them. At the center, the man holds a rifle diagonally across his chest. His sleeves are rolled up, revealing strong, muscular arms. One knee is raised and he appears to lean slightly backward to look in the direction of the Lincoln Memorial. He is not wearing a tricorne hat and does not appear to be wearing a uniform; his status as a soldier is ambiguous. The woman points at Lincoln. Her back heel is lifted as if she is poised to take a step forward. The child, to the left of the man, is wearing a tricorne hat and carrying a drum, with drumstick poised to strike. They are a clean, contained, well-ordered, family, surrounded by the flag and focused on Lincoln.[127] For Barboza, the design's focus on the family is crucial. The idea for the memorial came out of his own genealogical quest; he wanted to stake his claim to be part of the national family and undo the painful exclusion of Lena Santos Ferguson's rejection by the DAR.

STILL UNBUILT

Twenty years after Congress approved it, and fifteen years after Dwight's design was granted CFA approval, the Black Revolutionary War Patriots Memorial has not been built. Why? The financial problems of the foundation are difficult to unscramble, but there is not much evidence to support outright thievery. It costs money to raise money, and the foundation's ambitions never seemed to match the money they were able to bring in. They did not have a long list of corporate supporters; Johnston's connection to GM was their best source of support. The Black Revolutionary War Patriots Memorial did not have a constituency of living veterans to contribute to or lobby for it. The military muscle in Washington—the ABMC in particular—had no stake in the memorial. The DAR's interests were conflicted at best. And, as powerful and moving as Dwight's design concept was, it was diminished, contained, hidden by Commission of Fine Arts and National Park Service anxieties about the memorial disrupting the Mall. It is not hard to imag-

FIGURE 9. National Liberty Memorial rendering. (Courtesy of C. J. Howard/Franck & Lohsen Architects.)

ine the difficulties of generating support for a memorial that involved confrontation with the DAR, a design process that resulted in a nearly hidden memorial, and most powerfully, the enormous challenge of making legitimate the place of African Americans in the national family. The fighting over the scraps that came in became increasingly bitter. As a result, there is no memorial on the Mall for blacks who served in the Revolutionary War.

However, another memorial was erected on public grounds in recent years, and it does some of what Barboza hoped to do, although not on the Mall or on Barboza's terms. The state of South Carolina built a memorial to Strom Thurmond on the State House grounds after his death in 2003. It is a full-size figure of Thurmond in midstride. The base is carved with inscriptions and a list of the names of his children: Nancy Moore, James Strom Jr., Juliana Gertrude, and Paul Reynolds. After Essie Mae Washington-Williams came forward as Thurmond's daughter, legislation was passed to add her name to this list and change the number of children from four to five. This change is jarringly scratched into the stone, smudging and blackening the memo-

FIGURE 10. Strom Thurmond Memorial. (Photo by Ranee Saunders.)

rial. Her name is carved in nearly but not quite the elegant, formal font used for the other names. It is rough and striking, and in the context of the hard, painful history it represents it could hardly better evoke the sensation of clawing to get in. It stakes the claim Barboza wants to stake in powerful, visceral, and monumental terms.[128]

But this startling, heartbreaking, thrilling revision of the Strom Thurmond Memorial is not on the Mall, not at the monumental core, and not in the shadow of either Constitution Hall or the Lincoln Memorial. What the Black Revolutionary War Patriots Memorial has been able to accomplish on the Mall is nothing, yet. The soldier and the nation that soldier might define are not reimagined on the Mall, not written in stone as not-always white. The effort to use the figure of the soldier in this legitimation project failed. The sacrifices of black Revolutionary War soldiers—even in a moment of great interest in celebrating the sacrificing soldier—were not enough, it would seem, to overcome the long history of efforts to make them illegitimate. The ascension of the soldier was complicated, and not necessarily the ascension of the soldier who was not white. The anxiety about noses that were too broad and lips that were too thick at the Korean War Veterans Memorial clearly reflected anxiety about representing race and soldiering, and the story of the Black Revolutionary War Patriots Memorial demonstrates, in part, the limits of the ascension of the soldier and the terms in which he or she might be celebrated. Barboza tried and failed to take advantage of the revived status of soldiers and war memorials to revive the status of American Americans.

Ultimately the failure of the memorial is complicated, with no single glaring source of blame, but it is also abundantly clear that the effort was held in check by anxiety about figures of black soldiers. The struggle to get the memorial built reveals much about what was speakable about soldiers at the monumental core in this moment. Maybe if the memorial's proponents had given up on the figures, had been satisfied with landscaping and a plaque, there would be a memorial there today, but that memorial would not have rewritten the place of African Americans in national life and would not have transformed centuries of illegitimacy.

THREE

The Nearly Invisible Women in Military Service for America Memorial

Make their contributions a visible part of our history.

MARY ROSE OAKAR

THE STORY OF THE WOMEN in Military Service for America Memorial is about the fight to recognize the service of women in the U.S. military. It is also the maddening saga of the practically invisible rendered nearly invisible; it tells of an effort to carve out a place in the public imagination, and on the National Mall, to acknowledge and celebrate the contributions that women have made to the U.S. military. It recounts the successes and failures of an attempt to move women, to paraphrase Anne McClintock, beyond the role of "symbolic bearers of the national," and to represent them as active national agents.[1]

The story begins in the fall of 1985, when the Senate Committee on Energy and Natural Resources' Subcommittee on Public Lands, Reserved Water, and Resource Conservation held a hearing on five bills, each proposing the construction of a memorial in the District of Columbia. The proposed memorials included a Third Infantry Division Memorial, a Korean War Veterans Memorial, a monument celebrating U.S.-Moroccan relations, a Black Revolutionary War Veterans Memorial, and a memorial to American Women in Military Service. In the documents for the hearing, all but one of the bills had usefully specific, descriptive titles. S.1107 was to "authorize the Society of the Third Infantry Division to erect a memorial in the District of Columbia or its environs."[2] S. 1379 was to "authorize the erection of a monument given to the American people as a gift of the Kingdom of Morocco, on public grounds in the District of Columbia."[3] One bill, however, read only "S.J. 156 Authorizing a memorial to be erected in the District of Columbia." This is puzzling in light of the number of memorial propositions before the Ninety-Ninth Congress and may well be the result of an administrative oversight, but the resulting invisibility of the object to be remembered—women who have served and are serving in the U.S. military—captures a great deal about the fate of the memorial and the visibility it has been able to achieve for women who have served.

In 1985, veterans who took up the fight for a women's memorial wanted their memorial to challenge the figuring of the soldier in the United States as necessarily *male*. This, it seems, required a seismic shift in the figuring of the nation. And it turned out to be nearly but not quite impossible. The idea for the memorial was met, at turns, with studied indifference and determined resistance.[4] Military agencies, in the midst of negotiating thorny public and internal debates about women in the post-Vietnam military, as well as most veterans' groups, refused to actively support it. Corporate sponsors did not rally around the project. And the commissions overseeing the memorial design process vigilantly contained its visibility. In the end, the memorial was built because interests outside the United States supported it. It was enabled by the service of American women in one of these new American wars—the Gulf War. Without money from those with whom and for whom the United States fought, it is quite likely that the women's memorial would never have been built. The crucial money came from outside the boundaries of the nation, from parties invested in the bodies of U.S. soldiers not as emblems of white male heroism around which the nation might be constructed, but as spendable forces in wars defending their interests.

In 1985, the Third Infantry Memorial was dismissed as redundant; it was reduced in scale and eventually built as a modest cenotaph in Arlington National Cemetery. The Moroccan Monument was not approved by any of the federal bodies that the law required. It was determined to be of less than paramount national significance. The women's memorial was also denied approval, initially.

After a long struggle, however, it was dedicated in July 1997. Its story is a fascinating example of the process through which the dominance of the symbolic reign of the heroic white male soldier is maintained without specific policies or mandates. The women who testified before Congress in 1985, and the hundreds who would join them in the fight to get the memorial built, saw a conversation developing on the Mall about the figure of the soldier, and they wanted to get in on it. They wanted to use this moment of interest in celebrating the soldier to refigure the soldier as potentially female. (Which, of course, she was in increasing numbers on the ground). They wanted to challenge the idea of the heroic male soldier as the only soldier imaginable.

In this moment, however, this was fundamentally at odds with the celebration of sacrificing soldiers emerging on the Mall. If the agencies building the Korean War Veterans Memorial were concerned that limp wrists and pregnant-looking ponchos might work against their aspirations to inspire future blind sacrifice, it is not hard to imagine that feminizing the soldier in more dramatic terms might meet serious resistance.

Just as remembering black Revolutionary War veterans would shift the nation imagined on the Mall, refiguring the soldier as female—even as more women are serving in all capacities in the military—would also shift the nation imagined on the Mall and therefore the terms of U.S. nationalism as it was imagined in the capital, in ways that were apparently nearly untenable in 1985 and beyond. Such a refiguring might, in fact, threaten the very idea of the nation at its root—as a cognitive terrain constructed by male subjects that drew from its inception on gendered notions of family and the public.

Nonetheless, the women working for a memorial to women in the military fought hard—and they did get a memorial. They also got a museum, a theater, and a registry for women who have served. It is important to stress that they achieved something extraordinary. But it is all literally buried and nearly invisible, hidden in plain sight, built underground with the stipulation that it could not be visible from the exterior. The only visible exterior aspect of the memorial is one very modest, temporary, brown and white Park Service sign that reads, "Women's Memorial." This remarkable state of affairs evokes two powerful questions: Why did the women's memorial, which so explicitly sought to bring visibility, need to be invisible? How did the process work? Answering the first question requires answering the second question. Answering this second question requires working through the details of the memorial process.

THE QUEST FOR VISIBILITY

"It was all driven by the Vietnam Veterans Memorial," says the president of the Women in Military Service for America Memorial Foundation, Brigadier General Wilma Vaught."[5] The origins story of the Korean War Veterans Memorial is about veterans responding to the Vietnam Veterans Memorial with the question "Where is my memorial?" The origins story of the National World War II Memorial is about an Ohio World War II veteran taking this same question to his congresswoman. The origins story for the Women in Military Service for America Memorial is also about World War II veterans from Ohio taking nearly this same question to their congresswoman. These women veterans—proud former WACs—were responding to the Vietnam Women's Memorial just southeast of the Wall, which was approved by Congress in 1984 and dedicated in 1993.[6] Word of the proposed memorial inspired a group of female World War II veterans to go to Washington to meet with Congresswoman Mary Rose Oakar. They asked her why there was no memorial for women who had served in World War II. Her reply was that all memorials are for all veterans. The veterans claimed that this was not true, that the service of women had not been memorialized and that the time had come. Oakar promised to do some research and get back to them.

Mary Rose Oakar, a Cleveland Democrat and one of a very few Arab Americans in the House, came fairly quickly to understand the veterans' frustrating sense of invisibility. She turned to the American Veterans Committee (AVC), a liberal veterans' organization formed after World War II as an alternative to the American Legion and the Veterans of Foreign Wars. The AVC had begun a modest campaign to build a memorial for women in 1982, just as the Vietnam Veterans Memorial was dedicated. In 1985, Oakar and the AVC joined forces to establish the Women in Military Service for America Memorial Foundation.

The Vietnam Veterans Memorial and the Vietnam Women's Memorial provide useful contexts for understanding the push to build a comprehensive women's memorial, as do the broader, more abstract issues of constructing nationalism with the memories of soldiers. The specific history of this particular moment in women's service in the military is also vital. When the draft ended, one unexpected change brought by the all-volunteer military was a dramatic increase in the participation of women. This fueled heated debates about women in the military through the 1970s and 1980s.

Of course, women have participated in, provided support for, and served in all American wars. More than 2.5 million women have served or are now serving.[7] Until the twentieth century, they had to pass as men to join the military, and today they still have to contend with restrictions on the kinds of service they can give. Famously, Deborah Sampson served, under the name Robert Shurtleff, for three years in the Fourth Massachusetts Regiment in the Revolutionary War and was discovered to be female only when she was treated for a fever.[8] Lucy Brewer served, as George Baker, on the USS Constitution in the War of 1812 and has since been hailed as the "first girl marine."[9] These women who fought are, however, exceptions that highlight profoundly different expectations for men and women not only in the military but as citizens and national agents. Their service is hardly representative of what women have contributed to the military.

Women served on both sides of the Civil War, and their participation as women—rather than women passing for men—expanded dramatically; they worked in every kind of support service, but as civilians rather than enlisted people.[10] When the army needed over a thousand nurses to deal with a typhoid epidemic during the Spanish-American War, the female nurses were hired as civilians.[11] Some women were granted limited access to the military when, in 1901, the Army Nurse Corps was established, with the Navy Nurse Corps following in 1908, but nurses serving in these corps did not yet get "full military status, equal pay, or equal benefits," and these organizations were stopgap measures.[12]

It wasn't until May 14, 1942, with the formation of the Women's Army Auxiliary Corps, which would later become the Women's Army Corps (WAC), that women achieved something closer to regular military status. The WACs were segregated and were not trained for combat; instead, they were "intended to free men for combat."[13] The WACs were also segregated along racial lines; African American WACs had different assignments and status and did not serve with white WACs. The same was true for the Navy equivalents—the WAVES.[14] In all, nearly 350,000 American women served in World War II. Most of this service was in health care and administration, but "women demonstrated their competence in virtually every occupation outside of direct combat—they were employed as airplane mechanics, parachute riggers, gunnery instructors, air traffic controllers, naval air navigators, and the like."[15] The 1948 Women's Armed Services Integration Act "provided regular status" for women in the military but capped enlistment of women at 2 percent of total enlistment, required written consent from the parents of all women under twenty-one, and excluded women from Navy vessels and Air Force aircraft that might engage in combat. Perhaps because of the limited service women could offer, or perhaps because in 1949 pregnant women and women with children were summarily removed from the military, the cap was never reached in this period. From 1948 to 1969 "the percentage varied between 1.0 and 1.5 percent."[16] In 1967, the Department of Defense lifted this cap and expanded benefits for women, but it still kept women out of combat and combat zones.[17]

The 1970s were marked by fiery public debates about the role of women in the all-volunteer military. The end of the draft, the struggle to pass the ERA in this period with its implications for the military, and the activism of feminists all stirred changes in women's access to service. Following the removal of the 2 percent cap and, a few years later, the ban on women with children, the number of women the military rose steadily. By 1976 women made up 5 percent of the services. Women were permitted to command men and were admitted to military academies. Slowly, women were granted access to a wider range of service. However, resistance was, and continues to be, quite intense.[18]

It was not until the 1989 invasion of Panama that Captain Linda Bray became the first woman to command soldiers in battle. Her service was so controversial that she left the military as a result.[19] In 1991, forty thousand American women served in the Gulf War in situations increasingly close to combat. The 1992–93 National Defense Authorization Act officially rescinded some female combat exemption laws.[20] Women serving in Iraq and Afghanistan are still restricted from combat battalions. The debates about these restrictions have turned on three key issues: upper body strength, pregnancy, and morale within the units. These restrictions do not, however, keep women from combat situations, and many women serving now find President Bush's January 2005 declaration—"No women in combat!"—to be out of touch.[21] The circumstances of these new wars don't allow for service to be easily distinguished from combat.

The story of Jessica Lynch is particularly telling regarding the contortions of logic required by these restrictions and the confusion in the military about how to deal with women.[22] Army Private First Class Lynch was caught in an ambush, captured, and then rescued as Pentagon-placed cameras recorded the drama. Lynch was represented as a heroic soldier fighting as she went down—she says she did not actually fire her weapon because, like so many supplied to U.S. soldiers in Iraq, it was faulty and jammed immediately—and also as a blonde victim of cruel Iraqi soldiers. Much was made of reports that she was raped in captivity, which she denies. Bush's declaration did not keep her out of combat, but once she was there, the army tried to frame her as heroic *and* as a female victim. Lynch rejected this framing and insisted that the most important part of her story was not about her but about her best friend, Lori Piestewa, who was killed in the ambush.[23] Piestewa was the first American woman killed in the Iraq War and the first American Indian woman killed in combat while serving in the U.S. military, but there was very little interest in her story.[24] That Piestewa was a woman killed in combat despite the army's restrictions and that she was Hopi and Mexican American made her death a challenge to the insistent figuring of U.S. soldiers as white and male. It made her story less compelling for many compared to the tale of Lynch's heroic rescue.

Lynch and Piestewa's commanding officer, Brigadier General Heidi V. Brown, has said that at the war's start "there was a lot of debate over where women should be," but as the war wore on, "you don't hear about it. You shouldn't hear about it."[25] This rough naturalization of women in the military, however, was still a long way off as the effort to build a women's memorial got underway.

In the 1980s and the 1990s—before Lynch and Piestewa, as the question of women in the military continued to be a source of friction though women were joining the military in increasing numbers—when the Vietnam Veterans Memorial inspired a wave of interest in war memorials, women who had served in World War II, Korea, and Vietnam came to Washington and asked to be recognized as military actors. Over and over, they insisted that their contributions be seen. In 1985, Congresswoman Oakar introduced legislation for a women's memorial. H.J. Res. 36 read simply, "to authorize the Women in Military Service for America Memorial Foundation to establish a memorial on Federal lands in D.C. to honor women who have served in the armed forces."[26] In her testimony in support of the memorial, Oakar spoke of the contributions women have made in all American wars from the Revolutionary War forward. She pointed to the sacrifices of these women, reminding her colleagues that, "contrary to popular belief, in all wars, women have been killed, maimed, disabled, and injured psychologically."[27] Arguing that these contributions have been "overlooked," that women's roles in the military were still too limited, and that women had a particular interest in peace, Oakar established a broad definition of women's contributions. She told the committee, "We know that the issue of peace in the world is of particular importance to women as mothers, wives, sisters, and daughters.... [T]hey have sacrificed their lives, the lives of their sons, husbands, brothers, and loved ones." She concluded, "We are about two hundred years late in memorializing the participation of women in the military.... [T]heir efforts have too long gone unnoticed."

At this relatively early stage of advocacy for the memorial, Oakar articulates three logics: Women have sacrificed their bodies, they have sacrificed the bodies of their families, and these sacrifices have been overlooked. She is the only person on record to try the argument about sacrificing sons and husbands and fathers. Throughout the process, the memorial's supporters focused their arguments on the sacrifices of women who have served and outrage that their sacrifice has gone unnoticed. Overlooked. Unnoticed. Not visible. The redundancy in the language used in these arguments and my emphasis on it here underscore the connection between being remembered and being made visible. It is important to draw out this emphasis because of the contradictions and contortions the memorial process would require of this powerful desire to be seen.

In 1985 as the approval process proceeded, however, none of these arguments won over the National Park Service (NPS) or the secretary of the interior, Donald P. Hodel, whose support the memorial would need.[28] Speaking for Hodel and the NPS, Dennis P. Gavin, deputy director of the National Park Service, referred to National Capital Memorial Advisory Commission guidelines for public memorials in the District of Columbia stipulating that "for military memorials, the committee's policy is that only memorials commemorating *all* members of the Armed Forces identified with a war or other significant event, or branches of service of the Armed Forces should be authorized."[29] Citing language of the legislation for the Vietnam Women's Memorial and the U.S. Navy Memorial referring to "men and women," Gavin argued, "To the extent that S.J. 156 purports to confer additional recognition upon women who served in the Navy or who are Vietnam veterans it is in duplication of memorials already authorized."[30] He concluded, "Because this resolution is not consistent with the policy of the military memorials adopted by the Secretary's advisory committee and because the memorial would duplicate the commemorative effect of two memorials already authorized, we recommend against its enactment." Too many war memorials for women hardly seems like a convincingly pressing problem, but this is what Gavin offered.

In the rest of his testimony, Gavin suggested that the question of the Black Revolutionary War Patriots Memorial should be deferred "until the Secretary has the opportunity to consult with and obtain the advice of the Secretary's National Capital Memorial Advisory Committee. . . . [W]hile the committee has established a policy on military memorials which we have referred to in our testimony . . . the committee has not yet set forth a policy on historical figures such as would be commemorated under this proposed legislation."[31] He did not know what to do about the black Revolutionary War veterans; it was much easier for him to dismiss the Women in Military Service for America Memorial (WIMSAM). Perhaps even more revealing of the status of the WIMSAM is Gavin's response to the Moroccan memorial; he also proposed deferring action until the secretary could consult with the National Capital Memorial Advisory Commission, revealing that the memorial celebrating the history of U.S.-Moroccan relations was a more complicated proposition for him than the memorial for women.

A lobbying campaign by the American Veterans Committee, however, led to approval by the National Capital Memorial Advisory Commission. The AVC was able to get the Veterans of Foreign Wars, the American Legion, and the Department of Defense to state that they "had no objections" to the building of a women's memorial.[32] This was not much, but it did grant tacit permission without lending support, and it was enough to sway the commission, which brought along Secretary Hodel. In 1986, legislation was passed, and on November 6, 1986, President Reagan signed Public Law 99–610, which stated, "The Women in Military Service for America Memorial Foundation is authorized to establish a memorial on Federal lands in the District of Columbia and environs to honor women who have served in the Armed Forces of the United States, using non-Federal monies."[33]

Oakar's framing of the memorial in terms of a belated recognition of women in the military eventually won the day. Speaking to a *Los Angeles Times* reporter, the WIMSAM Foundation's executive director, June Willenz, said, "When you talk about veterans, most people think of men. They don't think about the women."[34] She continued, quoting from a letter written in support of the memorial: "Before I die, I want to take my daughter to Washington to see the statue dedicated to American women veterans." "The Memorial," she concluded, "is really something that is long overdue."[35]

After approval had been won, General Wilma Vaught became the memorial's principal champion. Brought in by Oakar and the AVC to get the memorial built, Vaught has a lifetime of experience as a woman in the military, and she is something of a powerhouse. She has been the "first woman" throughout her career. A brief selection from her biography in the National Women's Hall of Fame reads:

> In 1966, she became the first woman to deploy with a Strategic Air Command bombardment wing on an operational deployment. In 1972, she was the first female Air Force officer to attend the Industrial College of the Armed Forces. In 1980, she became the first woman promoted to Brigadier General in the comptroller career field. In 1982, she was appointed Commander, U.S. Military Entrance Processing Command, North Chicago, Illinois, the largest command, geographically, in the military. In addition, she served as

Chairperson of the NATO Women in the Allied Forces Committee and was the senior woman military representative to the prestigious Secretary of Defense's Advisory Committee on Women in the Service. When she retired in 1985, she was one of only seven women generals in the Armed Forces, and only one of three in the Air Force. She has received numerous military decorations and other honors, including the Defense and Air Force Distinguished Service Medals, the Air Force Legion of Merit, the Bronze Star, and the Vietnam Service Award with four stars.[36]

Vaught is no shrinking violet; members of her staff proudly describe her as a force of nature.

She argued from the beginning that the memorial should make women's service visible, inspire other women to serve, tell the stories of servicewomen's heroism, and make "their sheer hard, unglamorous, but necessary work in the military" seen.[37] She summarized her vision for the memorial: "What was needed was a memorial that would make the contributions of American servicewomen, and other women who had worked closely with the military, a visible part of our nation's heritage."[38] This was more easily said than done, and Vaught made tactical decisions early in the process that would get the memorial built but seriously limit the visibility it could achieve.

THE SITE

When the memorial was authorized and a site selected, Vaught's vision would encounter a rough irony. The site for a memorial is always essential, but, in the case of the WIMSAM, it proved to be particularly defining. In his brief book celebrating the memorial, Brent Ashabranner writes, "General Vaught believed that a site on the National Mall was out of the question. No space was available for the kind of memorial building needed; even if a place could be found, approval for a Mall location could take years."[39] Vaught's practical thinking and her keen eye for bureaucratic hazards got her memorial built. But the initial decision to forgo a site on the Mall is puzzling. Why assume that the women's memorial was not of sufficient national significance? Why let this go without a fight? For Vaught, it was a matter of picking her battles. She had five years to raise the money and see the memorial built, and she anticipated that the fight to get on the Mall would "slow us way down" and therefore endanger the memorial.[40] She was undoubtedly right.

The search for a site off the Mall was, however, frustrating; according to

Vaught, "every available location was remote and too far from Washington's major attractions."[41] She was looking for something off the Mall but still on the tourist path. As Ashabranner tells the story, "On returning to National Park headquarters at the end of a day of fruitless site searching, the committee drove past the entrance to Arlington National Cemetery."[42] The grand neoclassical Hemicycle, 270 feet of semicircular stone and concrete wall at the entrance to the cemetery, caught Vaught's eye. She asked David Sherman, her Park Service guide, what it was and what it meant. The Hemicycle, designed by architects McKim, Mead, and White, was part of the design of Memorial Drive and Memorial Bridge, the tail end of the McMillan Plan for the National Mall. Memorial Drive and Memorial Bridge literally and symbolically connect the Mall to Arlington National Cemetery. The Hemicycle was intended to signal the ceremonial entrance to the cemetery, but the construction begun in 1934 was never completed, and the Hemicycle had fallen into disrepair.

Despite its state in 1986, the Hemicycle had seriously ambitious origins. McKim, Mead, and White, building on the McMillan Plan, wanted to extend L'Enfant's original vision of the Mall. When L'Enfant was designing the capital, the fallen soldier was not yet sacralized in the United States; this did not happen until the Civil War, when the need arose for a national military cemetery. As fate would have it, Robert E. Lee's ancestral home, which was also in George Washington's lineage, was available and close enough to both Bull Run and Washington, D.C., to be a logical site for just such a cemetery.

The history of Arlington National Cemetery starts in 1802, when the adopted grandson of George Washington, George Washington Parke Custis, designed and put his slaves to work building an estate on the site.[43] Custis, descended from Martha Washington's son from her first marriage, had one child—a girl named Mary Anna Randolph Custis—who married her distant cousin Robert E. Lee. Lee and Mary Anna lived in the house until 1861, when it was seized by federal troops. The estate was legally confiscated in 1864 for unpaid taxes. That same year, Arlington National Cemetery was established. The first burials were the casualties of Bull Run, more than 1,800 of them, buried together in a twenty-foot-wide, ten-foot-deep vault. Although Custis had intended estate to be a "living memorial" to Washington, Arlington House (often referred to as the Lee House) is, in fact, a Lee museum that tells the story of his life there and the lives of his slaves.

The revisions of the Mall inspired by the post–Civil War memory boom

FIGURE 11. Women in Military Service for America Memorial, before restoration. (Courtesy of Orion/ Women in Military Service for America Memorial, Inc.)

expanded the cemetery and its place in the symbolic life of the nation. The McMillan Plan linked the proposed Lincoln Memorial to the bodies of the sacrificing soldiers he had celebrated with a proposed Memorial Bridge across the Potomac to Arlington. The Memorial Bridge was to empty onto Memorial Drive, which would end at the gates of Arlington, at the foot of the bodies of the soldiers, quite literally. But economic depression and war left little money and less appetite for completing the McKim, Mead, and White scheme. So the Hemicycle languished untended for more than fifty years.

Ashabranner writes, "Charles Follen McKim had a deep love of neoclassical Greek architecture, and the Hemicycle was undoubtedly his idea."[44] He continues, "The wall had no symbolic meaning appropriate to the cemetery, and in time it became nothing more than a retaining wall holding back the soil of the cemetery, which inclined steeply toward Arlington House behind it."[45] Both of these comments deserve a little attention. The neoclassical architecture was not an arbitrary matter of the architect's taste but part of the style of the McMillan Plan; it was meant to convey both democratic ideas and the power of the state, just as it had at Chicago's 1893 World's Columbian Exposition, which inspired the rethinking of the Mall. The Hemicycle wall was embedded with plenty of symbolic values; its public just had not needed its symbolism for the previous fifty years. This would change dramatically when it was slated to be restored as a women's memorial.

Sherman and Vaught soon determined that the Hemicycle was administratively not part of Arlington National Cemetery but, in fact, part of the National Mall. It had been intended to mark the official end of the Mall, but this idea was not taken up in practice. The Mall seems to end quite emphatically with the Lincoln Memorial, while Memorial Bridge and Memorial Drive seem to serve more as infrastructure than as symbolic gesture. They function as conduits, carrying people into and out off the city rather than delivering them to the gates of Arlington National Cemetery. This helps explain the run-down condition of the Hemicycle in 1986. Prerestoration photographs of the site reveal overgrown landscaping, crumbling blocks, moss creeping across laurel and oak leaf wreaths carved in the stone, and damaged ceremonial urns. Once she found it, General Vaught was determined to have the site, whatever its condition. She was, according to the Commission of Fine Arts minutes, "elated by the possibility of having the site at Arlington because of its prominence, accessibility, and its strong military link."[46] She was happy to bind her project to Arlington.

Testifying before the CFA in an effort to get approval for the site, the National Park Service's David Sherman argued that restoration of the site would enhance the entire Arlington Cemetery gateway. He was followed by Major Jeanne Holm, who stated that "fighting of a war was a team effort, that everyone who participated, in whatever category, contributed to the defense of the country, and that each person should be made to feel that he or she was essential to the whole endeavor."[47] Vaught claimed that this idea had been neglected and "the purpose of the memorial was to correct that."[48] She went on to assure the commission that the memorial would restore the Hemicycle while building a visitors' center, theater, and computer room that would not detract from the dignity of the Hemicycle or the surrounding area.

CFA chairman J. Carter Brown's response was both determinative and telling. According to the CFA minutes, he "thought the site highly appropriate and was enthusiastic about the historic preservation possibilities, but was somewhat nervous about a large-scale open competition for the design, since people tend to get carried away with grandiose schemes; he was also concerned about the possibility of disturbing the area in front of the Hemicycle. . . . [E]ven an underground scheme would necessitate getting access to it." He concluded, "The design would have to be a subtle one."[49] This turned out to be one of Brown's trademark deep understatements. Brown was concerned about protecting the integrity of the Hemicycle—despite the fact that it had been abandoned and neglected for fifty years. It had an architectural pedigree to be sure, but this pedigree—the site of the gate to Arlington—and the vision for the gate had held precious little value until Vaught took an interest.

Vaught told Brown that she was well aware of these concerns, "particularly the fact that the site was still the Great Entrance to Arlington Cemetery, where both men and women were honored." She continued, "Although the memorial would be dedicated to women, their partnership with men in a joint endeavor should be brought in."[50] She made a concession Brown did not appear to ask for, without directly addressing the chairman's insistence that the Hemicycle remain unchanged. In his postmeeting letter to Jack Fish of the National Park Service, Brown's interest is clearly in preserving the Hemicycle. He comments that "the historic preservation dimension of the idea is particularly welcome," adding, "Our only caution was that the selection of this site, an integral part of the Memorial Bridge–Entrance to Arlington composition, requires that great care be taken so that the broad effect of the Hemicycle, as it now stands, will not be altered."[51] Though Brown wrote "the broad effect of the Hemicycle," what he and the other agencies meant was closer to "even the smallest detail of the Hemicycle." This emphasis on preserving the Hemicycle was never explicitly linked to a desire to diminish the memorial for women. The meetings did not include conversations denigrating the service of women or expressing a desire to suppress the memory of their service, but they did produce a diminished memorial.

"The Women in Military Service for America Memorial Foundation's mission became," as its website explains, "one of restoring and transforming this imposing four-acre site, preserving the existing structure while simultaneously creating an inspirational and dynamic memorial that educates as well as honors."[52] The latter part of this mission proved to be much more difficult and met with far greater resistance than the former.

THE DESIGN

Vaught says she was never interested in figural representations for the memorial. The memorial was to be for all women in all wars, and she thought it would be impossible to find a figure or group of figures to represent all women in all wars.[53] In this sense, it was not problematic for the Hemicycle to become the memorial. But the Hemicycle would need extensive, expensive renovation and would need, somehow, to memorialize women in service without being altered. Certainly, this was a daunting design proposition.

Despite J. Carter Brown's caution about the "grandiose schemes" that a large, open design competition might generate, a national design competition was held in 1989. The competition required a design at the site of the Hemicycle that restored it without altering it, that included a theater and an exhibition space, and that incorporated a space for veterans to generate an online archive. This left designers few options as they imagined the memorial. It had to be both behind the existing Hemicycle and underground. The competition guidelines did not require it to be invisible, but such a requirement would have simplified the rest of the design process.

One hundred and thirty designs were submitted. Because none of the designs "solved this difficult three-part challenge completely,"[54] three finalists were selected and asked to rework their designs in response to the jurors' concerns. The three designs were known as the Grove, the Spiral, and the Pylons. The *Washington Post* described the Grove as " a rectilinear arrangement of forty-nine bronze trees in the center of the courtyard created by the memorial gate" and quotes jurors describing it as "a powerful image that creates a very special sense of place."[55] The Spiral was a seven-foot-deep bowl in the center of the Hemicycle, with spiraling paths symbolizing "the continuous service of women as having no beginning and no end." The Pylons were "ten 18-foot high prism-like forms built of glass and arranged in an arch atop the Memorial Gate." The jury praised this design as "the most visible of all of the entries, especially at night when the internally illuminated pylons would glow." It was this entry, designed by Marion Weiss and Michael Manfredi of the New York firm Weiss/Manfredi, that was ultimately selected.

Before the foundation could present the design to the Commission of Fine Arts, Brown saw the design in the *Post* and was outraged. He called the National Capital Memorial Advisory Commission immediately to say that the design had to be stopped.[56] It did not take long for the message to get to Vaught that the CFA, the NCPC, and the Park Service were dead set against the design. "It can never go forward," she was told.[57] So, for the next few years, Vaught focused on fundraising and trying to convince the architects that the pylons had to go.

By October 1992, when the WIMSAM Foundation took the design to the CFA for approval, the pylons—the ten glass prisms on top of the Hemicycle—had disappeared, and the design was focused on the interior space and not disrupting the exterior of the Hemicycle in any way. The pylons had been replaced by 108 flat glass panels that would not be visible from below, inscribed with quotes by and about women serving in the U.S. military. The concern about the pylons had been that they were too visible, too likely to compete visually, especially at night, with other sites at Arlington, particularly the Custis-Lee Mansion and the Kennedy gravesite. The glass panels—thick glass tablets—were designed to sit along the balustraded top of the Hemicycle and to act as skylights, letting light into the underground building below. They would make the presence of women who have served visible on the exterior of the building by emitting light at night.

Over the next few years, the four Commission of Fine Arts discussions about the memorial paid little attention to the interior of the building; rather, they focused on protecting the integrity of the Hemicycle. In 1992, the design was approved, but there was concern about the stairs and the lighting, which both necessitated changing the existing Hemicycle. In the Weiss/Manfredi design, stairs to an open area on top of the Hemicycle were visible coming in through the niches. The CFA required the stairs to be further recessed. The CFA was also concerned about lighting: "How visible would any proposed night lighting, as well as light escaping through the sky lights, be from the Mall and how would it affect the views of the Kennedy grave and the Custis-Lee Mansion?"[58] The implied answer: too visible.

A 1994 meeting with the CFA began with an assurance that the WIMSAM Foundation had made the 1992 modifications. The stairs had been recessed. Marion Weiss addressed the lighting: "It was very important to the spirit of the memorial and had been carefully considered as it would be visible from the Lincoln Memorial and from up close, as one entered the Court of Honor, and as it would affect the other Arlington memorials."[59] Brown was not appeased. After much discussion, he said his "principal concern was the night lighting; he was afraid the skylights would upstage the Hemicycle, the Custis-Lee Mansion, and the Kennedy Grave."[60] Anticipating this concern, Weiss introduced lighting designer Howard Brandston, who assured the commission that he was sensitive to their anxieties about the lighting and promised that "no more than a soft glow from the skylights would be seen through the balustrade." He further promised that there would be no lights in the skylights, which "would not be visible above the structure of the Hemicycle."[61] This seemed to satisfy the commission; the memorial would not be visible, and no light would escape.

CFA board member Robert Peck asked about the entrance to the memorial. Weiss explained that there would be two entrances, at the north and south walls, and a "revision to the concept design showed the doors recessed, to avoid the jarring effect of modern glass doors at the face of the wall and also to provide protection from the weather."[62] At the CFA's request, the doors were further recessed to be entirely out of sight.

More concerns were expressed about the exterior site plan. Again, these concerns were not about the meanings that the women's memorial might generate, but about how much the Hemicycle or the surrounding landscaping might be altered and how visible the memorial would be. The Weiss/Manfredi plan called for rows of pleached lindens (trees planted close together with their branches woven together to form a screen). They would be set back from Memorial Drive to protect the view of the Hemicycle.[63] Weiss and Manfredi also proposed a water feature in the center of the courtyard formed by the Hemicycle: a small rill emptying into a simple circular reflecting pool. The commission found the plan too stark and too distinct from the existing landscaping, and wanted the "hard-edged" quality reduced. Mr. Peck took the position that "the less done to the McKim, Mead and White design the better." Ms. Chatfield-Taylor thought the rill was "too middle-eastern" and "thought it might be better just to keep the beautiful classical basin and put a fountain in it." Vice-Chairman Hartman expressed similar concerns about the rill, the formal pleached trees, and the attention these elements might call to themselves. The courtyard area, in his assessment, "needed to be regularized and not transformed." General Vaught argued that the formality of the pleached trees was not out of place in a military cemetery. Commissioner Abrahamson disagreed, commenting that "once you entered the cemetery you were in a different world, a sacred precinct, and the landscape should be different; the women's memorial should invite the visitor into that world."[64] In other words, not only should the memorial not disrupt the existing landscape but it should draw visitors into the cemetery. In the context of commission concerns, this seems to require that the women's memorial draw as little attention to itself as possible. Weiss and Manfredi hoped that the landscaping would "beckon" and act as a "passage"; the commission seemed to agree that it would do this, and they didn't like it.

Though Brown's comments indicated general agreement with his fellow commissioners, his assessment was slightly more generous. He did not mind the "Alhambra-like" quality of the rill. In fact, he thought it "had a memorial function, gave the new reflecting pool some meaning, and showed that this was not just a restoration of the exedra."[65] This comment stands out in the CFA minutes as the only reference to the meaning of the women's memorial.

In the end, having successfully redesigned every element of the memorial's exterior to minimize visibility, the WIMSAM Foundation won final approval for the memorial design. They were not, however, given approval for the site plan. Brown wrote, "In spite of the softening effect that had resulted from changes to the 1992 concept, there were misgivings about the stark effect of the paved area and the formality of the pleached trees, which provides a sharp contrast to the informality that characterizes the landscaping at Arlington."[66] He concluded, "On the whole the Commission is pleased with the design of the memorial and the way in which it will be incorporated into the Hemicycle, and with the plans for the restoration of this historic landmark. . . . [W]e look forward to reviewing final plans for the plaza area."[67]

The final CFA discussion of the memorial took place in March 1995. Weiss pointed to three themes of the memorial beyond the restoration of the Hemicycle: "Water, passage, and light." She told the commission, "The stairs in the niches, in breaking through the wall, symbolized the barriers and the passage through those barriers experienced by women in the service; the jets of the water in the Hemicycle niche represented women's voices, which would be brought together in the channel and flow into the pool."[68] Weiss and Manfredi responded to the commission's concerns about the landscaping by giving up on the pleached trees, reducing the number of trees by half, and pushing them off to the periphery. They responded to concerns about the rill by revising the water feature to include a fountain in the Hemicycle niche, "which consisted of a circle of water jets, about four feet high."[69] They essentially promised to fill the space that had been originally designed for a fountain with a fountain.

Vice Chair Harry Robison and the other members of the commission were satisfied with the dramatic and complete concessions. In a letter to Roger Stanton of the Park Service, he wrote, "The members agreed that the reduction in the number of trees, the less formal pruning, and the increase in the size of the planting beds will provide a better transition to the informality seen elsewhere in Arlington. . . . [T]he revisions to the water feature will also bring a more harmonious relationship with the existing Hemicycle architecture." Robinson approved the final plans with one caveat: "With the understanding that concerns have been raised over not planting trees flanking the north and south gates of the cemetery." Robinson suggested another round with the architects and a mock-up, but no formal meeting was ever held. After the 1995 meeting, the trees that Weiss and Manfredi had hoped would mark the space as somehow distinct or as a place one might enter were quietly dropped from the design.[70] Their last attempt at exterior visibility quietly died.

FUNDRAISING

Kuwait saved me.

GENERAL WILMA VAUGHT

Raising money for this memorial was not easy. As was typical of the memorials built on the Mall in this period, the legislation stipulated that federal funds not be used. The renovation of the Hemicycle made the memorial significantly more expensive than building a new structure. The foundation's goal was to raise "$18 million for restoration and preservation of existing structures and new construction of interior space of the Education Center" and to "raise an additional $13 million for equipment, furnishing, exhibits, and establishment of an on-line registry."[71] Money came in very slowly. Vaught went to the Park Service for money for the restoration of the Hemicycle, and they eventually gave $9.5 million toward the restoration, half of what it would cost, but this left $22 million to be raised. AT&T gave $1 million, but this was spent on overhead. Ross Perot, whose generosity had been important to the Vietnam Veterans Memorial Fund, offered $250,000. But when he saw the design, saw that the women would be honored underground behind an existing structure that would not be altered to make the memorial visible, he withdrew his offer. Vaught says he is the only donor to explicitly make this complaint, but it is not difficult to imagine other potential donors having the same response.[72] A local builder donated a house, which was raffled as a fundraiser; that they would have to hold a raffle for the memorial indicates the difficulties they had raising money. Adding injury to insult, the raffle actually lost money.[73] The memorial was essentially dead in the water until they were "saved by Kuwait."

In desperation, Vaught went to some Saudis with whom she had contacts. They gave her $850,000. They arrived at this figure by putting a value of a little more than twenty dollars for each woman who had served in the Gulf War. (Roughly $21 a head times 40,000 women who served.) The Kuwaiti government matched this donation. This gave Vaught enough money to convince other donors that the memorial was a viable proposition. Money started to trickle in. General Motors gave $500,000, Merck Pharmaceuticals gave $500,000, Kodak gave $500,000, and the memorial was on its way. It took Vaught until some time after the memorial was completed to raise all the money she needed, but she did. And she is adamant that she couldn't have done it without the Kuwaitis and the Saudis.[74]

It is hard to know what to make of this, except that the Saudis and Kuwaitis were not deterred by either a memorial for women in the U.S. military or an invisible memorial. Certainly, there is something very strange about countries in which women were unable to vote—and, in the case of Saudi Arabia, drive or travel unattended by a male guardian—supporting a memorial intended to celebrate the service of women in all aspects of military life. A memorial of this kind would be unthinkable in Saudi Arabia, and yet the Saudis were happy to express their gratitude to the American women who fought on their behalf. Clearly, the kinds of wars waged at the end of the twentieth century involved interests well beyond the national boundaries of the United States—interests willing to invest in the celebration of the service of American women in their national space, and willing to donate a price per head.[75]

THE UNSEEN MEMORIAL

As visitors approach the completed memorial, no exterior architecture indicates that the structure is a memorial. No permanent signage on or near the Hemicycle indicates the presence of a memorial—or anything else, other than a blank ceremonial gate. Even the landscaping is blank, remaining unchanged for the length of Memorial Drive as it enters Arlington and deadends at the Hemicycle. Visitors have to know that the memorial is there, and then peek around the Hemicycle to find the recessed entrances.

Asked if the lack of signage was a source of frustration for the Memorial Foundation, Marilla Cushman, head of public relations for the memorial, paused and replied, "I don't think frustration is the right word." A seasoned military professional, Cushman couldn't have made her point more effectively. "Of course," she said, "We'd like to have a big neon sign if we could."[76] Set a few feet in front of the entrance on a slender wooden stand, the small, temporary Park Service sign reading "Women's Memorial" is itself not easy to find.[77] Every year, 4.5 million people visit Arlington National Cemetery.

FIGURE 12. Women in Military Service for America Memorial. (Courtesy of Carol Highsmith/Women in Military Service for America Memorial, Inc.)

Two hundred and fifty thousand stop at the Women's Memorial.[78] Imagine how many more might visit if there was a permanent sign out front.

Though the memorial did get built, it has not yet achieved physical visibility for women in military service. Why did it need to be so invisible? Because the Mall was not ready for a gendered refiguring of the soldier at the end of the twentieth century? Because this moment of interest in nationalism and militarism at the monumental core did not extend to women in the military? This seems too easy, yet impossible to ignore. The protection of the McKim, Mead, and White Hemicycle did not, for instance, have to be absolute. In this moment, interest in the figure of the soldier was driven by a desire to hold on to a particular past, to shore up the nation of a "simpler time," and to ensure future sacrifice. Making visible the contributions of women was not necessarily broadly shared as part of that drive.

THE RESPONSE

The women who have visited the memorial in the ten years since it was dedicated have responded with gratitude and enthusiasm. They travel great dis-

FIGURE 13. Women in Military Service for America Memorial with sign. (Photo by Hank Savage.)

tances to see the memorial. They donate their papers to its archives. They bring their uniforms and their mothers' medals. They tell their stories on the online registry. They study the exhibits.[79] They bring their daughters and sons. They complain that they can't find it, but, once they do, they are happy with it and make good use of what they are able to get.[80]

Some with a less emotional investment responded with muted praise. The day before the dedication, the *Washington Post* ran a review titled "A Memorial Passes Muster." Ben Forgey offers this restrained description: "One good test of a new work of architecture is the degree to which it improves its surroundings. By this measure the Women in Military Service for America Memorial is a resounding success."[81] He goes on to add, "Even though it is a bit reticent, the memorial enhances an already splendid setting in a number of ways." Forgey continues, "From a distance you would hardly know it is there, for the memorial has been subtly built in front of, on top of and behind an existing structure—the elegant semicircular stone retaining wall that for more than six decades has marked the ceremonial entrance to the cemetery."[82] He makes this observation in neutral language, but for a memorial that explicitly sought visibility for women, to hardly know it is there is troubling. Forgey assures his readers that "up close you notice the transformation right away.... [I]n front of the wall is a handsome stone-paved plaza with a dark circular pool in the center." He continues, "Four of its eleven blind niches have been opened up for stairwells leading to the roof.... [T]here, you'll find a newly paved walkway and angled glass 'tablets,' many engraved with sayings about women's experiences in the military." From the rooftop and the interior, the changes are dramatic—he is right about this. The problem is that you have to somehow know to go into a building that doesn't appear to have an entrance.

Forgey praises Weiss and Manfredi: "The memorial is insistently respectful of its honorary place, and therein lies its greatest strength.... [W]e are correct to worry about building too many memorials in Washington, but this one looks right and feels right in this particular spot because it is part of a larger whole." This doesn't read like a description of a memorial that claims a place in the public imagination for women in the military; it reads like subordination.

BARRIERS AND PASSAGE

Despite the insistence on exterior invisibility, if you can find it, you will discover that Vaught and Weiss/Manfredi built a remarkable building behind the Hemicycle. Describing the design that was built, Weiss and Manfredi write, "Our design for the memorial, winner of a national design competition, cuts openings in the formerly blank niches of the hemicycle's granite retaining wall, a barrier between the cemetery and the city. These openings lead to glass-enclosed stairways that ascend to the cemetery. Passage through the historic retaining wall mediates the change in grade along one of Washington's important monumental axes while serving as a metaphor for women's passage through the barriers that they have faced to serve their country."[83] Passage is an interesting metaphor here, but it is not an accurate description of the experience of the exterior of the memorial. The barriers, from the exterior, are irrefutably present.

Inside the building, however, the memorial is startling. It is a light and expansive place. Weiss and Manfredi write, "An excavated arc of space between the Hemicycle and the cemetery forms a commemorative gallery, the central spine of the project. This space is defined by the Hemicycle's buttress like concrete counterforts and a new marble wall concentric with the original structure. Openings cut into this marble wall lead to exhibition spaces,

FIGURE 14. Women in Military Service for America Memorial, entrance. (Photo by Hank Savage.)

a theater, the hall of honor, and a computer register of the women who have served and their stories."[84] Literally squeezed between the faded pomp of the nineteenth-century vision of imperial, monumental nationalism and the bodies of the dead soldiers celebrated in that same moment, the architects created an opening that feels like a fissure in the earth, like a small, abrupt seismic opening—the monumental core torn open just a little bit.

Weiss and Manfredi describe their subterranean meddling with the Hemicycle: "The four glass-enclosed staircases pierce the historic granite structure and ascend through the interior space of the memorial gallery to an upper terrace. The curved terrace affords views to the cemetery above, the gallery below and the City of Washington beyond."[85] Given the limitations they faced, the pressure for visual containment they encountered, this description opens up a modest possibility for seeing the capital in a new way. Standing on the women's memorial, on the sacrifices of these women, might afford a new way of seeing the city.

Perhaps most wrenchingly, Weiss and Manfredi offer this description: "A 240-foot arc of glass tablets, held in place by a stainless steel armature, is suspended over the gallery. Like the pages of a diary fanned across the cemetery, these tablets are carved with text by and about women who have served. Sunlight passing over the inscriptions creates legible shadows on the marble wall of the gallery; ephemeral memories and histories are thus told by shadow and light."[86] What do they make legible? Ephemeral memories and histories told not with imperial bombast or heroic striding figures, but by shadow and light. This is the refiguring of the masculine soldier that the memorial has been able to achieve, to date.

When Anne McClintock writes about the role that women have played in national spaces as "the symbolic bearers of the national" who are denied "any direct relation to national agency," she could be writing about this memorial process. She continues, "The representation of male national power depends on the prior construction of gender difference," suggesting something useful about the apparent need to keep women's service invisible.[87] Acknowledging women soldiers—or women warriors—might not only challenge soldiering as exclusively male but also threaten to expose and unsettle the way constructions of the national depend on constructions of gender.

It seems likely that Vaught was taking the long view when she chose this site and met the demands of the CFA. Her memorial does not achieve a dramatic refiguring of the sacrificing soldier; it reveals, in fact, the unspoken investment in figuring that soldier as male. Nowhere in any of these conversations was the service of women in the military directly belittled; nowhere in any of these conversations was the need to figure the soldier as male directly expressed; but the result of these conversations is a subdued, limited, repressed celebration of the not-male soldier. Maybe Vaught assumed that she could not get more than this when the memorial was built. But she did get her memorial built. It is on the Mall. It claims some national space, however modestly, for women who have served. And it is there to stay. Maybe one day it will get a sign.

Finally, it is crucial to add here that despite the limited visibility achieved by the memorial, Vaught's impulse to get this high-visibility site is already paying off in one significant way. Not long after the dedication of the memorial, the signage was changed on the George Washington Memorial Parkway, which runs parallel to the Potomac past Arlington National Cemetery. The signs alerting drivers to upcoming exits for the cemetery now include "Women in Military Service for America Memorial." Millions of people drive by these signs every year. This may not be the kind of visibility that Vaught and so many others fought for, but it is undeniably a great deal of visibility.

FOUR

Impossible Soldiers and the National Japanese American Memorial to Patriotism during World War II

Here we admit a wrong.

. RONALD REAGAN

THE NATIONAL JAPANESE AMERICAN Memorial to Patriotism during World War II sits on a triangular plot on the Capitol grounds, between the Capitol and Union Station, at the far eastern edge of the axis linking Arlington National Cemetery to the Capitol. It has five principal elements: a bronze sculpture of two cranes wrapped in barbed wire, a plaza lined with panels inscribed with the names of the internment camps and the numbers held there, a pool of water with rock islands, a list of the names of the more than eight hundred Japanese American soldiers killed in the war, and a "traditional Japanese" bell. It is quite remarkable. Its startling inscription, "Here We Admit a Wrong," its graceful bronze birds struggling to free themselves from biting wire, its stark granite panels carved with the names of camps where U.S. citizens were detained, and its list of soldiers who gave their lives while their families were in these camps are powerful. These elements of the memorial work together to create a sense of gravity ("Tule Lake, 18,789. Manzanar, 10,046. Heart Mountain, 10,767. Poston, 17,814. Amache, 7,318.") and a visceral sense of loss ("Harold Arakawa. Kaoru Fukuyama. Kiyoshi Hasegawa. Arthur Morihara."). They also offer the promise of redemption through the recognition of a wrong.

The memorial is moving, even arresting. And it is complicated by this idea of redemption. Images and inscriptions crowd the memorial and set the terms in which redemption is offered: "Here"—because the soldiers sacrificed—"we admit a wrong." Its statements about "the indomitable spirit of our citizenry in World War II," Japanese American pride, "lessons learned," and "fighting prejudice" suggest, without much subtlety, that the loss of both

FIGURE 15. National Japanese American Memorial to Patriotism during World War II. (Photo by Hank Savage.)

life and freedom should be understood in terms of *service* to a nation that would come *through this service* to see its treatment of Japanese Americans as wrong. The nation is redeemed because the service of soldiers enabled an apology, and the memorial celebrates that apology.

The effect is a volatile emotional cocktail capable of inspiring simultaneous surges of shame and pride. The people suffered terribly while the soldiers served selflessly, and this memorial celebrates a loyalty that requires citizens to give of themselves in the name of the nation, despite what the nation is doing to them or, by implication, what it is doing in the world. This is not simply celebrating the blind devotion of soldiers, as the Korean War Veterans Memorial aspired to do. This memorial is celebrating blind devotion in the hot, klieg-lit glare of injustice.

One inscription—"The lessons learned must remain a grave reminder of what we must not allow to happen again to any group"—makes the memorial quite explicitly a cautionary tale. Another inscription, "Our actions are essential for giving credibility to our constitutional system and reinforcing our tradition," uses the cautionary tale to affirm the nation. It makes the

FIGURE 16. National Japanese American Memorial to Patriotism during World War II. (Photo by Hank Savage.)

argument that because we tell the cautionary tale, the nation is redeemed and its promise fulfilled. In this way, the internment is rewritten as an aberration that is healed with the memorial's acknowledgment, rather than the result of at least a century of a racist cultural logic that defined Asians in the United States as "impossible subjects" beyond the reach of true citizenship.[1] The inscription "You fought not only the enemy, but you fought prejudice—and you won" justifies sacrificing the lives of soldiers who died without their freedom as given in a battle to affirm the promise of this not-racist, because-it-apologizes, nation. The inscription that reads, "What motivated these Americans of Japanese descent? We believed a threat to this nation's democracy was a threat to the American dream and to all free people of the world" explains loyalty in the face of bold inequality in terms of the righteousness and the global reach of the not-racist nation. It defends military service to the nation despite the loss of individual freedom in explicitly racialized terms. It suggests that the "sacrificing soldiers" made Japanese Americans less "impossible" as national subjects and fulfilled the promise of the "not-racist nation" without reckoning with how racial thinking and national thinking profoundly shaped the experiences of those recognized by the memorial. Standing before the powerful, suggestive memorial, this is a lot to contend with.

The National Japanese American Memorial to Patriotism during World War II started with the impulse to remember the renowned heroism of the 442nd Infantry Combat Team and the 100th Infantry Battalion and the deaths of more than eight hundred Japanese American soldiers. It started with a push from veterans to remember soldiers who served. What was made of this heroism and these deaths—the celebration of the apology—is an important part of the story of figuring soldiers and nationalism on the Mall; the uses to which these heroes and the war dead are put do not necessarily serve the interests of sacrificing soldiers. The "support our troops" logic, the ascension of the figure of the soldier in this moment, was used in this case to make a claim of national belonging under dramatic circumstances.

LOGICS FOR THE MEMORIAL

Despite the drama it embodies, when the National Japanese American Memorial to Patriotism during World War II was dedicated on November 9, 2000, it was immediately lost in the shuffle. Americans were preoccupied with a still undecided, too-close-to-call presidential election that had taken place a few days before. Most major news outlets simply did not cover the dedication. Architectural critics did not write about it in 2000. Only the *Washington Post* reported briefly on the dedication of the new memorial.[2] This is quite unusual; the *Post* fully covered all the other memorials built and not built in this period. But even when the electoral dust had settled, only a few reporters and critics made their way to the memorial. It was not written about much then and has not been written about much since.[3] This is true of both the popular press and scholars. Even scholars in Asian American studies have paid little attention to it. Elena Tajima Creef, Emily Roxworthy, and Jane Naomi Iwamura have all written recently about nationalism and representations of Japanese Americans and the internment without ever mentioning the memorial.[4]

One of the few stories in the press about the dedication describes Memorial Foundation director Cherry Tsutsumida standing in the rain in front of a crowd of two thousand veterans and supporters, offering an expansive vision of courage: "Courage comes in many forms. Courage isn't just picking up a sword or arrow; it means being able to give of yourself in ways that hold the community and family together."[5] She was talking about the courage of Japanese American veterans, but also about the courage of their wives and mothers in internment camps. Tsutsumida described the courage of women who were evacuated from their homes, who lost their most basic freedoms, and who managed to carry on raising their families and getting through the day. She described, quite movingly, the pain of children listening to their brave mothers weeping in the night. This is an unusual framing not only of courage but also of what might be at stake in a national war memorial. Standing before the memorial, Tsutsumida wanted it to evoke two kinds of courage: the courage to fight and the courage to hold the family together.

For all Asians Americans, ideas about family have long been linked with access to full participation in the nation. In the 1870s, when the first Chinese immigrants in California were vilified by the white working people with whom they competed for jobs, they were often caricatured as overly sexualized opium fiends without families and beyond the reach of any effort to "civilize" them. This framing of Chinese immigrants led to the 1875 Page Law, which prohibited Asian contract laborers and prostitutes from entering the United States. The enforcement of this law limited the immigration of women, making it increasingly difficult to construct families that might have marked Asian immigrants as less difficult to "civilize." The 1882 Chinese Exclusion Act drew on the same logic and effectively ended Chinese immigration. When Japanese immigrants replaced the Chinese as cheap labor, they were similarly racialized and vilified as impossible to domesticate and therefore beyond the reach of civilizing forces. Workingman's Party hero and San Francisco mayor James Phelan summed up these arguments when he told Boston's *Sunday Herald,* "[Japanese immigrants] must be excluded because they are non-assimilable; they are a permanently foreign element; they do not bring up families; they do not support churches, schools, nor theaters; in time of trial they will not fight for Uncle Sam, but betray him to the enemy."[6] This understanding of Japanese immigrants led to the 1907 Gentleman's Agreement that ended the immigration of Japanese laborers. The 1913 Alien Land Law limited the ownership rights of Japanese immigrants already in the United States and made family life increasingly difficult. The final anti-Japanese victory came when Congress passed the 1924 Immigration Act, which effectively ended all immigration from Asia.[7] Asian immigrants were maligned as "impossible subjects." As historian Mae Ngai uses this very helpful term, the impossible subject is a key figure in the history of immigration, labor, and racialization in the United States. The impossible subject is "a person who cannot be and a problem that cannot be solved."[8]

This history of how Japanese immigrants were understood illuminates Tsutsumida's desire to frame Japanese American patriotism in terms of sacrificing soldiers and families kept intact in extraordinary circumstances. Phelan's anti-Japanese screed hit on two key points: Japanese immigrants don't have families, and they won't fight for Uncle Sam. One hundred years later, the memorial sought to address this history of exclusion and its logic, and it used the service of soldiers to do this. For Tsutsumida and the memorial's advocates, the memorial was to demonstrate beyond the shadow of a doubt that Japanese Americans are not only "possible subjects" but exemplary patriots and families at the center of the national family.

Military service has long been a means for the expression of loyalty and for gaining access to citizenship. As Ngai explains, for most of the twentieth century, any alien who served in the military was granted the right to naturalization, "suggesting that loyalty—especially in its ultimate test—qualified one for citizenship."[9] In this moment on the National Mall, the figure of the soldier was being used to refigure boundaries of inclusion. While Maurice Barboza sought to use the service of African Americans in the Revolutionary War to gain access in the public imagination to full citizenship for African Americans, the advocates of this memorial sought to use the military service of Japanese Americans in World War II to call attention to the extraordinary loyalty of Japanese Americans for similar purposes. They sought to rewrite these "impossible soldiers" as exemplary patriots. The story of the National Japanese American Memorial to Patriotism during World War II is the story of a complicated figuring of this loyalty. It was complicated by the problems inherent in linking loyalty to military service and by the ascension of the figure of the soldier as the *not*-not-white, male, heroic emblem of blind devotion on the Mall.

At the dedication, had Tsutsumida's remarks about courage included the courage of those who refused to serve—had her framing of courage for Japanese Americans during World War II been stretched that far—she might have been able to suggest a way to reframe not only courage but also loyalty in the memorial and beyond. But, like the veterans who fought to build the memorial, she did not raise the questions that might have been asked by those who refused to serve about those who did. What the veterans wanted, from the start, seemed simple and reasonable: a war memorial for Japanese American soldiers who fought while their families were interned.[10] As far as the records show, they were not looking to complicate thinking about military service; they intended to *use* thinking about military service in the moment to honor their achievements and to claim national belonging. This effort was complicated by the fact that the ascension of the figure of the soldier in this moment was linked to the maintenance of boundaries of inclusion. The first complication regarded an "ethnic" military memorial.

THE VETERANS MEMORIAL

The origin of the movement to commemorate Japanese American soldiers can be traced to 1987, when the Smithsonian's National Museum of American History mounted a celebration of the bicentennial of the U.S. Constitution. That exhibit, *A More Perfect Union,* represented the internment of Japanese Americans as a grave miscarriage of justice—one of the Constitution's darkest hours—and it depicted Japanese American soldiers as noble and heroic. It inspired a group of veterans to construct a more permanent record on the Mall of the service of Japanese Americans under these strange circumstances. The veterans, led by a veteran of the 442nd and longtime Japanese American activist, Mike Masaoka, formed the Go For Broke National Veterans Association. They set out to build a memorial in Washington to "honor Japanese American veterans."[11] The popularity of the Vietnam Veterans Memorial; the approval of the Korean War Veterans Memorial, the Black Revolutionary War Patriots Memorial, and the Women in Military Service for America Memorial; and the legislation seeking approval for a National World War II Memorial all probably influenced their decision to pursue a memorial rather than, say, a permanent exhibit at the Smithsonian.

In June 1991, with the support of one Japanese American World War II veteran—Senator Daniel Inouye—and one former internee—Congressman Norman Mineta—H.J. Res. 270 was introduced, to authorize the building of a Japanese American *veterans* memorial on federal land in the District of Columbia. It ran into trouble right away. The National Capital Memorial Advisory Commission (NCMAC) immediately discouraged Mineta, who lived in Heart Mountain Relocation Center as a child, from trying to build the memorial in Washington. The NCMAC determined that the Commemorative Works Act "would probably preclude a favorable consideration."[12] They suggested that the memorial "be located on the property of the Arlington National Cemetery or on the grounds of the Pentagon or Fort

McNair where the Commemorative Works Act is not applicable." They went on the say that, in the opinion of the commission, "the proposal could be best presented to the American people as part of a military museum."[13]

The commission described the conflict with the Commemorative Works Act: "The purpose of the act was also to ensure that future commemorative works reflect a consensus of the lasting national significance of the subject involved."[14] The implication was clear: the experience of Japanese American veterans was not of "lasting national significance." This did not go over well with Mineta, Inouye, and their fellow Japanese Americans in Congress. They fired off angry letters to the National Capital Memorial Advisory Commission and the Commission of Fine Arts. These letters made two essential points. First, they expressed concern that the decision was based on a reluctance to define the experience of one "ethnic faction" to be of "lasting national significance." They spoke directly to the "appropriateness of dedicating a memorial to an ethnic faction associated with a great event, such as this group of soldiers who fought during World War II," and reminded the commissions that a proposal to "establish a memorial on Federal land in the District of Columbia or its environs to honor African Americans who died as Union soldiers during the Civil War" had recently been unanimously approved.[15] They suggested that this inconsistency needed to be addressed.

The second point concerned the "lasting national significance" of the service of Japanese Americans. Inouye wrote passionately and at length about the men who had "volunteered from behind barbed wire," looking back with "awe and disbelief that these men who had been denied their civil rights, deprived of their worldly goods and humiliated with unjust incarceration would, nonetheless, stand up and take the oath to defend the country that was mistreating them without due process."[16] He wrote of the losses these men suffered at home and of their triumphs in the war. He reminded his readers that Japanese American soldiers had served in the most decorated units in the history of the U.S. military and suggested that under different circumstances this alone might have merited commemoration.

Inouye ended his letter, "I hope that with this memorial, the lessons learned during the extraordinary and dark chapter in our nation's history will not be forgotten. . . . [R]ather this chapter will remain in our collective conscience as a grave reminder of what we are capable of in a time of crisis, and what we must not allow to happen again to any group, regardless of race, religion, or national origin. . . . [T]he memorial is an indication to those Japanese American war heroes who gave their lives that their sacrifices were not in vain."[17] In this formulation, Inouye shifted the memorial from a purely military celebration of service and honoring of the dead toward a cautionary tale. He moved from the heroic deeds of the soldiers to "a grave reminder of what we are capable of in a time of crisis."

The National Capital Advisory Memorial Commission agreed to reconsider H.R. 271 on April 28, 1992. In his testimony before the commission, Mineta elaborated on the issues he and Senator Inouye had already raised in their letters and emphasized the need to prevent future race-based injustices—the need for the cautionary tale. He spoke of the continued "tendency toward unfounded suspicion" that he found in the experience of Arab Americans: "In 1990, my office began receiving reports of 'interviews' of Arab Americans by agents of the Federal Bureau of Investigation and the Secret Service. Loyal Americans found themselves being asked about terrorist activity in the United States, and about their political views on the war." He went on, "These people had no information about terrorist activity. Their political views on the war were none of anybody else's business, and certainly not the government's.... [O]nce again, a group of Americans experienced having their loyalty thrown into doubt because we found ourselves at war and conveniently forgot the difference between ancestry and citizenship."[18] He suggested that a memorial could help stave off potential mistreatment of Arab Americans.[19] Thus the memorial would do the contradictory work of redeeming the nation as not-racist while acting as a first line of defense against continued racism.[20]

Mineta also argued that the intent of H.R. 271 had been misunderstood. First, it had been described as a "military memorial that should be part of the World War II memorial at Arlington National Cemetery." To this Mineta responded, "It would be ironic if this unique historical American experience were to be devalued simply because it involved the heroic military contributions of Japanese-American veterans and it occurred during World War II."[21] For many Japanese Americans, the rejection of the memorial because it was a military memorial would have had an especially bitter charge. Many of the veterans had served in the hope that their willingness to die for the nation would eventually be recognized as a profound expression of patriotism and would establish Japanese Americans as worthy of respect and full citizenship.[22]

The second misunderstanding, in Mineta's accounting, had to do with the "concern that this memorial could underscore ethnic separatism in our country."[23] The commission, as he understood it, was wary of "ethnic" memorials.

Mineta responded to this concern by arguing that this memorial would be an "American memorial" rather than an "ethnic memorial," because it would "actually emphasize the solidarity of our nation in winning the challenge of World War II." He continued, "The Japanese American veterans displayed such devotion to our democratic principles. This memorial would vindicate their faith and would emphasize the beauty of our system which could right previous wrongs and try its very best to prevent future wrongs."[24] The possibility of ethnic separatism, he implied, could be mollified by the devotion to the nation vindicated by the memorial. In fact, "ethnic" devotion, or loyalty, was, in his arguments, precisely the point. Ethnic devotion during the war offered the possibility of redrawing boundaries of national inclusion, and he wanted a memorial to mark that.

Mineta thought a memorial was capable of doing all this: "The presence of the memorial would speak not to separatism but would actually add to the coherence of the lessons presented by all the memorials in our Nation's capital. This memorial—like the Vietnam Veterans Memorial—would contribute to our Nation's healing of past wounds and development as a truly great democratic system."[25] This argument is important because it frames the Vietnam Veterans Memorial as redemptive and positions the Japanese American veterans memorial as similarly redemptive, suggesting that acknowledgment of wrongs would not only vindicate the Japanese American soldier but fulfill the promise of the nation, helping to develop a "great democratic system." It sets up the memorial as part of the project of "Americans telling themselves that this is who they always were."[26] This framing makes clear that this memorial did not start out as an "anti-Vietnam Veterans Memorial," like the Korean War Veterans Memorial or the National World War II Memorial. Rather, it sought to emulate the Wall, using the moral authority of the sacrificing soldier revived by the Vietnam Memorial to heal the wounds inflicted by internment—and to heal those wounds for both the veterans and the nation at large.

Mineta described the proposed memorial as adding to the "coherence of the lessons presented by all the memorials in our nation's capital." Given that these memorials were built in tension with each other, Mineta's meaning is not entirely clear. Perhaps he meant that this memorial, like the others, would use the service of the soldiers as part of a larger national recovery project. If so, he was right. But the memorial borrows sometimes contradictory elements of each of the new war memorials on the Mall and their various national recovery projects. The memorial for Japanese Americans would draw on the status of the soldier and the nationalist healing of the Vietnam Veterans Memorial, summon the celebration of blind military devotion of the Korean War Veterans Memorial, render women essentially invisible, and would—in anticipation of the World War II Memorial—use the moral authority of that victory to justify all manner of sins. Finally, like the Black Revolutionary War Patriots Memorial, it would seek to use the elevated status of the soldier to remap the racial boundaries of the nation by asserting the contributions of not-white soldiers, that their sacrifices might earn them full membership in the national family.

Mineta ended his testimony with a long quotation from Go For Broke National Veterans Association president William Marutani. Emphasizing the thrust of the Go For Broke argument, Marutani wrote:

> The proposed monument is a tribute to the indomitable spirit of a segment of our citizenry—defined not by themselves but, rather, by the government—who in dire adversities, remained steadfast in their faith in this system of government, who fought for its preservation and in the course of doing so, for their own liberty; and it is a celebration of our system of government that demonstrated the strength and dignity by acknowledging that it had committed a wrong and in doing so, vindicated the faith placed by the Japanese American veterans of World War II. It is, in short, a celebration of America, its system and its peoples. Surely, this unparalleled saga constitutes a "significant element of history" of our Nation—within the very essence of the meaning of Section 2(c) of public law 99–652.[27]

For Marutani and Mineta, the significance of "vindication," "a tribute to the indomitable spirit of a segment of our citizenry—defined not by themselves but, rather, by the government," and, ultimately, a linked "celebration of our system of government" rendered the CFA concerns moot.

Together, Mineta and Inouye made compelling arguments for the historic significance of the experience of Japanese American veterans of World War II, putting forward bold promises about what the memorial might achieve. But this is not exactly what won the day. CFA chair J. Carter Brown wrote to Mineta shortly after the hearing to tell him, "There appears to be a resolution to the opposition that earlier had surfaced."[28] He continues, "As I understand it, the thrust of the memorial would be shifted from a single military focus to one embracing the larger events surrounding the Japanese American people as a whole that occurred in the early years of World War II."[29] The NCMAC and the CFA did not see a place for an ethnic war memorial on the Mall, but they were willing to consider the broader Japanese American experience during the war as worthy of a memorial. Brown uses the language of "larger events" here, but he seems to refer to internment. Why not use the word? The commissions interpreted the Commemorative Works Act to preclude an "ethnic military" memorial but not a memorial to the incarceration of "ethnic soldiers" and their families. The veterans' response to this change was interesting. They chose not to build an internment memorial. The language of the next bill sent to Congress is actually "a memorial in the District of Columbia or its environs to Japanese American patriotism in World War II."[30] That shift did not come from Brown but from the veterans themselves. Memorializing patriotism allowed them to tell the cautionary tale of the internment and the apology *and* to keep the soldiers in the memorial.

The Go For Broke Veterans Association didn't want an internment memorial; they wanted a memorial for soldiers. They returned to Congress with a memorial to patriotism—and this worked. In the end, the Japanese American veterans were able to build a memorial as long as it wasn't a memorial just for Japanese American *soldiers*. They expanded their memorial to include "the Japanese American experience during the early years of the war" as a redemptive story for the nation. They wanted recognition and vindication, and they got it by using patriotism as a stand-in for military service. Despite the Commemorative Works Act, military service is central to the memorial; the nation is redeemed in the memorial through the military service of those who were mistreated. The sacrificing soldier is mistreated, and then used to vindicate his (in this case) mistreatment. And patriotism is equated with military service. It is hard to avoid troubling implications for thinking about war and soldiering in the United States.

THE PATRIOTISM MEMORIAL

The Go For Broke veterans took seriously the shift from a soldier's memorial to a patriotism memorial.[31] They renamed themselves the National Japanese American Memorial Foundation, put together a new board of directors to reflect their expanded mandate, and produced a new mission statement: "The mission of the National Japanese American Memorial Foundation is to create under congressional statute a memorial to the loyalty, courage, sacrifices, and contributions to the greatness of this nation, made by Americans of Japanese ancestry and their immigrant parents during World War II, despite injustices rooted in ethnic prejudices, and as a commitment to an ever greater

America."[32] Soldiers and military service are carefully avoided here, but they do not go away.

George H. W. Bush signed Public Law 102–502 on October 24, 1992, approving the National Japanese American Memorial to Patriotism during World War II. It read, "Authorizing the Go For Broke National Veterans Association to establish a memorial honoring the patriotism of Japanese Americans during World War II." But, as the conversation about the memorial evolved, it was often said to have read, To establish a memorial in the District of Columbia or its environs to honor Japanese Americans interned during World War II. This slippage is everywhere in the documents relating to the memorial—and it is significant. The legislative path of this law is surely confusing, but the distinctions between remembering soldiers, remembering patriotism, and remembering the internment are important; soldiers, patriotism, and internment are not, as this common slippage might imply, synonymous. In the memorial process, however, they were conflated, despite what common sense might dictate.

Even the memorial architect, Davis Buckley—the person one might expect to have the fullest and most precise grasp on the law enabling the memorial—used the language of *both* "patriotism" and "internment" when quoting from the law on consecutive pages of an elaborate report on the memorial process. The report then develops this strange conflation and misreading of the simple language of the law, quoting it as follows:

> The law authorizes a memorial to: Honor American citizens of Japanese ancestry and their permanent alien resident parents who patriotically supported this country despite their unjust internment during WWII; Recognize the sacrifices of the American men, women, and children of Japanese ancestry who were unjustly categorized, evacuated, and interned without reasonable cause; Recognize PL 100–383 in which the U.S. Government acknowledged that a grievous wrong had been committed against Americans of Japanese ancestry; Recognize the strength of the belief in the United States system of government of Americans of Japanese ancestry who volunteered for their country to become the 100th Infantry Battalion and the 442nd Regimental Combat Team; and to Serve as a reminder of the lessons learned and as a constant reminder that those errors will not be repeated to the detriment of any segment of the population regardless of race, religion, or national origin.[33]

This is an awful lot to legislate for a memorial. Erroneously presented in the report as the language of the law, it is not. The law simply says "honoring patriotism." Buckley's report then includes another version of the text of the law in full; in this version, it misrepresents the language ("internment" rather than "patriotism") but accurately includes none of the elements in the long list above. Certainly this represents not only confusion on the part of the designers but also a seemingly unconscious inability to distinguish between patriotism and the internment as the memorial was being designed. As the memorial process moved forward, this problem only got more complicated. In the ensuing conversations about the memorial, patriotism and the internment became mutually dependent. Patriotism and the internment are never, in the memorial or the conversations about it, disaggregated.

THE SITE

Initially, the NJAMF wanted a site at Maryland and Independence Avenues, at the foot of Capitol Hill and just in front of the projected National Museum of the American Indian. A highly visible site, it was also problematic. Concerns arose about its proximity to the museum and about sight lines to the Capitol. The NCMAC was quite concerned and, perhaps because the NJAMF members did not seem to share the commission's concerns, the NCMAC asked the Park Service to produce a list of restrictions that the site would impose on the memorial: "A sculptural element or central focus object will not be included; walls within the garden shall not exceed 18 inches; a water feature may not exceed a height of 3 feet; vista lines will be maintained; no exterior lighting will be added; there will be no enclosed structures above or below grade; the memorial should not rely on audio-visual media; the placement of names of Japanese American patriots or donors will not be part of the memorial design; the memorial must recognize the civilian patriotism and will not be a memorialization of military accomplishments."[34] All except the last restriction make sense in terms of the location and the physical features of the site, but this last restriction was clearly not about sight lines or height requirements. However, it was enough to discourage the foundation from pursuing the site. There was also discussion of a site adjacent to the Supreme Court Building, but despite the appeal of a memorial facing the court that had upheld the legality of the internment, approval for this site seemed unlikely.

In a letter to House Speaker Thomas Foley, Brown complained that "there is an ever-insistent pressure for memorials in this city, and were the Mall and the grounds of the Capitol to be out to such use, it would be no time before they would be covered with a proliferation of monuments."[35] Despite this concern, Brown suggested another site that he hoped would work for the memorial; less centrally located, it was still on the Capitol Grounds, still part of the monumental core. Brown brokered a land deal, trading Park Service land for Capitol Grounds land, to make the site available for the memorial. A wedge of land formed by the intersection of Thirteenth Street, Louisiana Avenue, and New Jersey Avenue, the site was created as part of the McMillan Plan. When the train station was moved northeast of the Capitol, the Capitol Grounds were extended toward the station, and Louisiana Avenue was created to connect the station and the Capitol. Cutting across existing streets, it created the wedge, a small, 0.76-acre lot in a historically significant, low-traffic area. The site was wide open for a memorial. It did not come with an impossible list of restrictions and was happily accepted by all parties.

THE DESIGN

Architect Davis Buckley designed the memorial. There was no design competition.[36] The NJAMF selected him based on his experience with memorials in Washington and his early contacts with Mineta. Buckley got involved with the memorial even before the legislation was approved.[37] In fairly short order, he held three community meetings to generate ideas and support in Washington, D.C., San Francisco, and Honolulu.[38] He described his initial design conception as follows: "The elements of the memorial will focus on the evacuation/internment/denial of civil rights without due process and the steadfast loyalty of all Japanese Americans during World War II as demonstrated by their volunteerism and the heroism of the 100th/442nd and the Military Intelligence Service."[39] Quite explicitly, he envisioned a memorial to patriotism that focused on the denial of rights and used military service in the face of this denial to vindicate patriotism. "To put these events in context," he writes, "they are framed by a preamble and an epilogue. The preamble includes a brief history of Japanese immigration to Hawaii and the mainland. The epilogue reflects on the greatness of our system of government in the rescinding of executive order 9066, the passing of the Civil Rights Act of 1988, 'the apology.' And the reminder that eternal vigilance is needed to protect the rights of all people."[40] He concludes, repeating himself a little, "The forms of the design elements express the concept that through their steadfast loyalty Japanese Americans overcame the unjust denial of civil rights and served their nation with patriotic distinction." This is a lot for any memorial to do. It reads, frankly, like an architectural recipe for disaster. Not only does it raise too many ideas to represent, but some of them are in tension: celebrating loyalty to an entity that mistreated you, for example, is complicated. It requires careful thinking.

The central problem in Buckley's formulation, which he clearly developed with the NJAMF, is that loyalty overcame injustice—"through their steadfast loyalty Japanese Americans overcame the unjust denial of civil rights"— and so it is loyalty that requires emphasis. But, as a framing logic for the memorial, this is problematic because it is historically inaccurate; loyalty, specifically military service as the ultimate expression of loyalty, *did not* earn Japanese Americans an apology. (It did not even earn them a memorial.) This logic erases the generations-long political and legal battles to get the federal government to recognize the wrong. *Loyalty is not what overcame injustice.* Loyalty was the trope that was successfully used to win the legal and political battles, but those battles had to be fought.[41] This failure of Buckley's and the foundation's logic had serious consequences for the memorial.

The memorial was designed to be entered, according to Buckley, "where curbs rise into low walls which guide visitors up a gradually narrowing path, toward a central circular element which represents the evacuation and unjust confinement."[42] He continues, "This element is defined by slightly tapered stone walls which encircle a sculpture at the center. Once within the high encircling walls one feels a sense of confinement." The walls were to be covered with bas-relief and narrative information, and broken in one section to reveal a pool of water with two groups of stones representing "the generations of Japanese Americans interned and future generations, as well as the islands from which they came." The pools were to be followed by panels with the names of the dead, and these would be followed by a bell. He wrote, "From the central space the wall spirals around gradually becoming lower and less confining as it moves along the major pathway toward a 28' tall memorial bell, symbolic of triumph, victory and freedom." He goes on, "As one leaves the central area inscribed on the wall is a short narrative about the volunteerism of the Japanese American Community in industry, the government, and military service."[43] The memorial was to end with "the apology," "a reminder that eternal vigilance is needed to insure that such a denial of justice is never inflicted on any other group of Americans."[44] In this iteration, the design included the walls that create a sense of confinement, the sculpture, the calming pool of remembrance, the release from confinement, the bell, narratives, and "the apology"—all working to celebrate loyalty and convey a challenging series of concepts.[45]

When NJAMF took the design to the Commission of Fine Arts for the first time in September 1997, Cherry Tsutsumida started by describing the purpose of the memorial: "To tell the story of the internment of Japanese Americans during World War II so that such a thing would never happen again to any ethnic group."[46] She and John Parsons, of the Park Service, with whom she and Buckley had been working on the design, stressed that it was neither a memorial for Japanese Americans nor a military memorial, but "would explain the rather complex history of the internment and ultimately the apology from the government in 1976 for the violation of the civil rights of so many Americans during the war."[47] Buckley describes the design concept as representing "the confinement of the Japanese American through a sequence of bas-reliefs and the sculptural elements; a central water element featuring an arrangement of rocks."[48] For Buckley, the rocks in the water held tremendous symbolic value; he "saw the rocks as representative of the generations of Japanese Americans and also as a remembrance of the island homeland, a tension between their ethnic experience, the experience of the internment, and the situation today, when the government has recognized its mistake and made an apology to the people wronged."[49] This is a lot to read into rocks.

Nina Akamu, the sculptor, talked about the memorial having "an integrative social function—it would heal and unify as well as being commemorative."[50] She had designed four sculptural elements in bronze. The largest was the crane memorial, a fourteen-foot-tall composition to stand at the center of the interior circle. "The crane was the symbol of good luck and longevity in Japan," she said, "and was as important to the Japanese people as the eagle was to Americans."[51] The sculpture "consisted of a depiction of two bronze cranes, on a marble base, in identical positions; this represented the duality of the universe. The two free upraised wings were pressed firmly together, representing communal support and interdependency. The lower wings were pressed against the base with strands of barbed wire holding them down." As she describes it, "The birds had turned their heads and were trying to extricate themselves from their painful situation, symbolic of the individual effort to overcome limitations." Her use of a Japanese rather than an American symbol is interesting here. Cranes, not eagles, are wrapped in barbed wire. This represents, perhaps unintentionally, those imprisoned as "other," as still not entirely American, even though most were U.S. citizens. Eagles or eagles and cranes wrapped in barbed wire would have made those interned fully Ameri-

FIGURE 17. National Japanese American Memorial to Patriotism during World War II. (Photo by Hank Savage.)

can and would have suggested a broader condemnation of the nation trapped by its own dangerous racial logic. Wrapping *cranes* in barbed wire avoids this harsher memory of the internment and "orientalizes" Japanese Americans.

Paul Matisse, the stepson of Marcel Duchamp and grandson of Henri Matisse, then talked about his bell, saying he saw it as a chance to "provide a final resolution to the experience of the memorial." Matisse, who had been intrigued by traditional Japanese temple bells when he lived in Japan, explained that, although in Japan they are "generally struck as a spiritual gesture, he thought this kind of expression would be an appropriate addition to the memorial, a way to engage the visitor."[52] He did not mention either victory or triumph, as Buckley had in describing the bell—and this would be tricky, especially considering what interned Japanese Americans faced after the war in terms of prejudice, as well as the economic devastation of internment and the loss of houses, farms, and businesses. Oddly, given Matisse's emphasis, the shape of his bell bore little resemblance to a traditional Japanese temple bell. There is something clearly orientalizing about this broad gesture toward the Japanese "flavor" of a bell. Like the cranes, it "others" Japanese Americans in the memorial, exoticizing them and creating distance between "Japanese Americans" and "Americans."

The CFA was not concerned with these issues. As the September 1997 meeting ended, members of the commission expressed concern about the height of the bell (twenty-eight feet) and the relationship between the bell and the cranes; they didn't want the bell to compete with the cranes. They also had concerns about the walls and cautioned against anything "too slick or shiny." But these concerns were limited, and the concept for the memorial was unanimously approved.

The NJAMF returned to the CFA with revisions just a few months later. Brown started with praise for the "less-is-more" philosophy in revisions suggested by John Parsons—essentially dropping the bas-reliefs, dropping a few sculptures, and adding some inscriptions—but Brown worried that the memorial might not provide enough information. Board member Barbaralee Diamonstein-Spielvogel "thought the memorial was much more powerful with the inscriptions, and thought it was instructive in terms of the World War II Memorial and any others that might come along."[53] The cranes were praised as "almost telling the whole dreadful tale in one image."[54] Finally, they praised the revision for the bell, giving it a horizontal orientation that made it even less like a traditional Japanese bell but eliminated the problem of it competing with the cranes, and the CFA unanimously approved the presented revisions.

After the meeting, in a letter to Terry Carlstrom of the Park Service, Brown wrote, "Our next focus likely should be the quotations, their placement and text as well as the lettering style chosen. The graphics of the lettering will be essential to the success of the design. In this case, the quotes are intended to tell a difficult story and must be selected with care."[55] Brown was an intelligent man with enough experience in building memorials to understand just how understated this observation was. The controversy that arose around this memorial concerned these inscriptions. The white heat of the debates focused squarely on a quotation that celebrated the unquestioning loyalty of some Japanese Americans as a "creed" shared by all Japanese Americans.

Buckley described the arrangement of the inscriptions to the CFA in July 1999: "In the circular plaza area, the location of the crane sculpture . . . the inscriptions there would read as horizontal band, almost as a cap to the 7-foot 3-inch wall. Here would be inscribed the names of the eleven camps." Buckley said he "considered the names to have the strongest visual and emotional impact of anything in that area. Beneath the names would be a short narrative, continuing around the curved area, and below that, quotations from three individuals . . . and beyond that on the main part of the wall, would be the names of the 861 killed in action and more quotations."[56] The CFA liked the changes and made only a few suggestions, one of which was to reduce the number of quotations. Carolyn S. Brody commented that "there were also several quotations mentioned that seemed to be telling the visitors how they should feel; these were thought to be superfluous, and it was suggested that they be omitted."[57] There was little discussion of the content of the inscriptions.

A few months later, in October 1999, the NJAMF presented the memorial inscriptions and locations to the CFA. The historical narrative read:

> After the United States entered World War II, the federal government by Executive Order 9066, forcibly removed more than 115,000 men, women, and children, citizen and non-citizen alike, from Alaska, Arizona, California, Hawaii, Oregon and Washington, to guarded war relocation authority centers on the sole basis of their Japanese ancestry.
>
> Allowed only what they could carry, families were forced into abandoning homes, friends, farms and businesses to live in remote and rudimentary WRA camps. Some were not released until June 1946. In addition, more than 4,000 men and families were detained in ten Justice Department camps, including Sand Island, Hawaii; Kooskia, Idaho; Bismarck, North Dakota; Lordsburg/Santa Fe, New Mexico; Missoula, Montana; and Crystal City, Texas, none of whom were ever indicted or convicted of wrongdoing.
>
> Demonstrating their determined loyalty to America, thousands of Japanese Americans volunteered for military service. The 100thBn/442nd Regimental Combat Team fighting in Europe was the most highly decorated army unit for its size and length of service in the military history of the U.S. Army. The Japanese American Military Intelligence Service, with bi-lingual skills, shortened the war in the Pacific and thus saved countless American lives.[58]

Some minor revisions were made, but this is essentially the language inscribed in the memorial. The other inscriptions presented were:

I am proud that I am an American of Japanese ancestry. I believe in her institutions, ideals and traditions; I glory in her heritage; I boast of her history; I trust in her future. *(Mike M. Masaoka, Japanese American Creed, September 1940)*

In this place we pay tribute to the indomitable spirit of our citizenry in World War II who remained steadfast in their faith in our democratic system. *(Norman Y. Mineta, Interned Heart Mountain Relocation Center, U.S. Congressman)*

Our actions are essential for giving credibility to our constitutional system and reinforcing our tradition of justice. *(Robert T. Matsui, Interned Tule Lake Relocations Center, U.S. Congressman)*

The lessons learned must remain as a grave reminder of what we must not allow to happen again to any group. *(Daniel K. Inouye, Captain, 100thBn/442nd Regimental Combat Team, U.S. Congressman, U.S. Senator)*

Here we admit a wrong. Here we affirm our commitment as a nation to equal justice under the law. *(President Ronald W. Reagan, signing the Civil Liberties Act, August 1988)*

You fought not only the enemy, but you fought prejudice—and you won. Keep up that fight to make this great republic stand for what the constitution stands for. *(President Harry S. Truman, 1946 White House ceremony for the 100thBn/442nd Regimental Combat Team)*

O, America
Imperfect, stumbling, striving
Lessons from the past

Japanese by blood
Hearts and minds American
With honor unbowed
Bore the stings of injustice
For future generations

Both the haiku and the tanka were included without authors' names. (Akemi Dawn Matsumoto Ehrlich wrote the tanka in response to a NJAMF-sponsored competition. Bill Hosokawa, editor of the *Denver Post* and former Heart Mountain Relocation Center internee, wrote the haiku.) The final inscription, to sit under the names of the eight hundred KIAs, read:

What motivated these Americans of Japanese descent? We believed a threat to this nation's democracy was a threat to the American dream and to all free people of the world. *(Spark M. Matsunaga, Captain, 100thBn/442nd Regimental Combat Team, U.S. Congressman, U.S. Senator)*

The CFA's only suggestion about these inscriptions was that the haiku be dropped: "Its meaning would be lost on most visitors to the memorial."[59] About an imperfect, striving America? How would that be hard to understand at this memorial? Brown, however, had praise for the tanka: "It's perfect," he wrote. The only significant concerns were about the Masaoka inscription and the "Japanese American Creed."

The calm tone in Brown's post-meeting letter on concerns he had heard about the inscriptions belied the outrage that would fuel a divisive debate about the inclusion of the "Japanese American Creed." Brown wrote, "One major concern raised by a member of the public had to do with aggrandizing any one individual or organization. The Commission believes this is a reasonable question best taken up by the Foundation. However, retaining the quote in question and eliminating any ambiguous reference to an organization is a possible compromise."[60] Though removing the problematic description of Masaoka's personal statement as a "Japanese American Creed" did seem like a reasonable compromise, Masaoka was an intensely contested figure. Neither his supporters nor his detractors were willing to let the issue go as easily as Brown might have liked.[61] The title "Japanese American Creed" was eventually dropped, after an enormous effort, but this did little to quiet the debate.

MASAOKA

In a March 9, 2000, letter to John Parsons, NJAMF board member Rita Takahashi urged him to delete the quotation from Mike Masaoka. "Masaoka," she wrote, "and the organization he represented, the Japanese American Citizens League (JACL), were highly controversial during World War II and they continue to be controversial today. The memorial should not be the subject of continued turmoil and trouble, even after the memorial is completed. Preventative measures should be taken now (by deleting the quotation), to avoid an on going fiasco."[62] Takahashi and two other NJAMF board members, Francis Sogi and Kelly Kuwayama, formed Japanese American Voice to protest the board's decision to include the Masaoka quote. They urged people to protest to the board, to the National Park Service, and to the CFA. More than seven hundred letters poured in.[63] The fight became acrimonious. Accusations flew of historical inaccuracies—of which there were many in the proposed memorial—and bureaucratic irregularities, which also seem to have been a problem but would have meant nothing in another context. But the heart of the controversy was Masaoka and his "Creed."

The NJAMF board responded with anger to the anger about Masaoka. Melvin H. Chiogioji, board chair in 2000, wrote a letter to the editor of San Francisco's *Nichi Bei Times* on January 8, 2000, defending Masaoka and the board's insistence on including him in the memorial. He described the quotation as "an affirmation of faith in America," arguing that it was clear that it "properly belongs on the memorial."[64] To the charge that Masaoka did not have the authority to speak for Japanese Americans, as the words "Japanese American Creed" would imply, Chiogioji responded, "This causes one to wonder whether the person making the charge would have suggested a nationwide Nikkei election to choose a spokesperson." He goes on to complain that the dissenting voices, "most of whom were not caught up in the evacuation of the West Coast, forget the environment of that period when the attorney general of the U.S. was calling all Americans of Japanese descent 'Japs.' To then assign the shameful results of that official wartime mentality to the actions of Mike Masaoka is absurd at best."

Acknowledging the possibility of removing the quotation as a way to avoid further controversy, Chiogioji writes, "After reviewing the pros and cons, the majority of the board agreed that achievements under Masaoka's leadership deserved recognition on the Memorial. They also cited Masaoka's role in the immigration and naturalization rights for all Asians, citizenship for our own Issei parents, the repeal of anti-alien laws, statehood for Hawaii and the successful fight against real estate escheat cases—all were human rights victories for Japanese Americans which were also significant for the entire nation, and in themselves were reason enough to remember him."[65] The majority of the board was not willing to let Masaoka go.

Much of the evidence for the controversy turns on the Lim Report, a paper commissioned but not well loved by the JACL to investigate its role in the internment. In the report, Deborah Lim, a scholar and lawyer, suggests that Masaoka may have recommended that Japanese Americans be "branded and stamped," that he did not support redress legislation, that he suggested a "suicide battalion," and generally that he was party to JACL "collusion" with the federal government around the internment.[66] In an interview well before the memorial controversy, Masaoka gently cautioned Lim against a too-easy, too-presentist reading of the past: "To try to apply the thinking of today in terms of ethnic diversity to what we had to go through and trying to demonstrate our assimilation is quite difficult, particularly when you consider the circumstances of war and the fact that media and other things have changed so much."[67] He seems to have wanted her to understand the context for his support of assimilation. Lim was apparently unimpressed by this caution and concluded that the JACL and Masaoka had "colluded."

Masaoka represented one side in the struggle to define patriotism and loyalty in the context of the internment. This battle over the place of Masaoka engaged fundamental conceptions of the nation, race, and loyalty as they are linked to military service. Cherry Tsutsumida describes it as a generational problem, telling the *Nichi Bei Times,* "The Nisei love Mike. The Issei love Mike. But the Sansei have a problem with him."[68] In Tsutsumida's framing, for the Nisei (second-generation Japanese Americans) and Issei (first-generation immigrants), Masaoka represents the good fight—the long, slow, patient fight—for equality and full citizenship through unrelenting expression of loyalty. For the Sansei (third-generation Japanese Americans), he represents a polite, obedient assimilationism that they often reject and resent. Supporting this framing of the problem, the *Nichi Bei Times* quoted Stanford student Steve Yoda, who dismissed Masaoka and complained that the "blindly patriotic oath fans the model minority myth."[69] Conflating patriotism and loyalty was a significant problem for the Sansei.[70] However, this conflation was central to the memorial project from the start and accounts for the designers' seeming inability to distinguish between patriotism and the internment.

In one of a very few scholarly responses to the memorial or the controversy, Asian American Studies scholar Larry Hashima argues that "the conflict arising from Masaoka's words and the final impression created by the presence of his quotation provide an opportunity to reconsider another issue hidden within the controversy: the definition of patriotism and its direct association with military service."[71] He points to the origins of the memorial as a veterans' memorial and contends, "Patriotism here is defined explicitly through the conscious act of military service for the nation, a definition that is strengthened given the cloud of suspicion and racism that surrounded Japanese Americans as they entered the Army." And he suggests that military service defines the patriotism of the memorial and the conventional narrative of the internment, and that this enables the traumas of the internment to be given "necessary but tacit recognition as 'patriotic' behavior." The service is used, in this formulation, to justify conflating obedience and patriotism. Hashima concludes, "Masaoka's words on the Japanese American Memorial may easily be interpreted to equate acquiescence and capitulation as the benchmarks for true patriotism."[72] He is right, but this logic did not succeed in removing the "Creed" from the memorial. It is there on the Mall for perpetuity.

In the memorial, obedient military service—the blind sacrifice of the soldier—enables Japanese Americans to be seen as worthy of an apology and therefore vindicated. The soldier is used to obscure the racial logic that made his service so painful and extraordinary. The Japanese American is figured as worthy of an apology, but only in the context of not just military service but blind devotion in military service. Soldiers are celebrated because they put military service above all else. But this is not an accurate reflection of the responses of all Japanese Americans during the war; thinking about those who rejected blind devotion opens up possibilities for rethinking Japanese American patriotism.

SUPPORT

As passionate as Masaoka's detractors were, they did not quell financial support for the memorial. The $11.6 million needed to complete the project was raised in an impressive grassroots campaign that brought in donations of between $1 and $500,000 from twenty thousand individuals and local groups.[73] The memorial foundation formed a capital campaign committee that divided the country into fifteen geographic regions. Each region was assigned a director to develop a regional strategy for reaching individuals in the area. Though veterans' groups, church groups, Buddhist temples, and chapters of the JACL made contributions, the vast majority of the donations came from individuals.[74] The committee does not seem to have sought corporate donations, and though ninety Japanese Canadians contributed a total of $142,568.42, it does not seem to have sought contributions from outside North America.[75]

The Los Angeles region raised $3 million from 6,700 donors. The largest donations came from "George T. Aratani and his wife Sakaye with $500,000, and Dr. Paul Teraski and his wife Hisaka . . . with $250,000."[76] In the Chicago area, 2,300 donors gave more than $2.8 million, and the Pacific Northwest region raised $1.5 million.[77] San Francisco Bay Area contributors gave more than $1 million. Most but not all the donors were Japanese American. According to the foundation, "Jean Lee, a non-Japanese American Florida retiree . . . mailed in $25 every month," and Cal Taggart, who as a teenager had worked as a carpenter building the Heart Mountain camp, sent in $100.[78] They describe the campaign as "an important lesson about making democracy work with patience and commitment."[79] Certainly, given that the lives of virtually all Japanese American families were touched by the internment, there was a deeply invested pool of donors to support the memorial.

RESISTANCE

Takahashi, Hashima, and others have suggested that adding the memory of Japanese American draft resisters to the memorial would have expanded the kind of patriotism celebrated there. U.S. Circuit Court judge and Poston internee A. Wallace Tashima writes of the memorial, "One is at a loss to know why it is called a "Memorial to Patriotism."" He asks, "Is it patriotic to be stripped of all of one's dignity and earthly possessions and forced into exile/imprisonment solely because of one's race or ethnicity? Is it patriotic for a citizen of this country to be regarded as the enemy based on one's race alone? Is it an act of patriotism to bow to the command of the President, literally enforced by the U.S. Army, when there is no apparent alternative?"[80] Those who resisted the draft raised these questions during the war, and remembering them would have kept these questions alive at the memorial. These men who, as Tashima describes them, "out of their understanding of patriotism, defied the draft," offer an alternative to the Masaoka Creed.

At the start of the war, all draft-age Japanese-American men were "reclassified into draft category 4-C, the category reserved for enemy aliens and other undesirables, with the consequence that, despite their citizenship, these men became ineligible to be drafted into the armed forces."[81] The JACL, which supported cooperation with the evacuation and also supported the legal challenges to the internment, lobbied the War Department to allow Japanese Americans "to serve in the military, believing that such service was the best available vehicle for Japanese Americans to regain their rights of citizenship."[82] When the JACL succeeded in its efforts to get the War Department to allow Nisei to serve, the War Department developed a questionnaire for all men of draft age. The infamous "Loyalty Test" included about eighty questions, but two of these questions were more highly charged than the others. Question 27 asked, "Are you willing to serve in the armed forces of the United States on combat duty, wherever ordered?" Question 28 asked, "Will you swear unqualified allegiance to the United States of

America and faithfully defend the United States from any or all attack by foreign or domestic forces, and forswear any form of allegiance or obedience to the Japanese emperor, or any other foreign government, power or organization?" The Loyalty Test stirred deep emotion in the camps. Most but not all men answered yes to both questions, but for many it was one of the most incendiary, wrenching, and damaging experiences of the internment.

Nearly 1,200 Nisei men enlisted, and their success on the battlefield is well known.[83] The story that is not well known is that of the draft resisters, who answered no to the questions and refused to serve.[84] Sixty-three resisters at the Heart Mountain Relocation Center in Wyoming were tried en masse and sentenced to three years in prison for violating the Selective Service Act. Of thirty-three resisters at the Minidoka Idaho Relocation Center, all but one were convicted and sentenced to three years and three months. Only in one case were the resisters not convicted en masse. At Tule Lake California Segregation Center, Judge Louis E. Goodman agreed with the defendants that they were deprived of due process "by virtue of the circumstances" of their internment. Goodman ruled, "It is shocking to the conscience that an American citizen be confined on the ground of disloyalty, and then, while so under duress and restraint, be compelled to serve in the armed forces, or be prosecuted for not yielding to such compulsion."[85] All draft resisters were pardoned by 1947, but theirs has not been the story that gets told about Japanese American patriotism or military service in the war. Tashima writes, "We do not have to label these acts of resistance as 'courageous' to recognize that they were acts of conscience, committed with the knowledge and acceptance of their harsh consequences."[86] But framing them as courageous and patriotic offers an alternative to the Masaoka vision.

The JACL did not support the draft resisters and has struggled to reconcile that position ever since. After a protracted struggle, in 2000 the JACL offered a formal apology to the draft resisters. As Daniel Inouye has written, "I am glad that there were some who had the courage to express some of the feelings that we who volunteered harbored deep in our souls."[87] But this feeling, deep in the souls of the soldiers, is not included in the logic of the memorial. It is not allowed to remake the figure of the blindly obedient soldier.

John Okada begins his novel, *No-No Boy,* about the wrenching struggles of a Japanese American resistor, with a description of his first postwar encounter with an old friend who had served. The friend changes, in the instant when he recognizes the protagonist Ichiro as a No-No boy, from trying to talk him into having a drink to spitting on him in rage. In the novel, Ichiro understands that "the hate-churned eyes with the stamp of unrelenting condemnation were his cross and he had driven the nails with his own hands." Okada describes the soldier passing judgment as "God in a pair of green fatigues, U.S. Army style."[88] Though many Japanese American soldiers may, like Inouye, have softened their judgment in the years since the war, the memorial does not make a place for either the No-No boy or an understanding of the patriotism that drove him to take such a terribly difficult position.

DEDICATION

Speaking at the dedication ceremony, deputy secretary of defense Rudy De Leon asked the veterans of the "greatest generation" to stand and hailed them as "some of the most significant heroes of the twentieth century."[89] He continued, "This memorial will embody not only the pride and triumph of America at its finest hour when America stood courageously against totalitarianism, it will also mark the shame and humility it earned when it fell prey to its prejudice and fears." Celebrating the success of the memorial, he promised, "Visitors will learn a definition of patriotism more personal and powerful than any dictionary could convey. They will learn about people who believed in fidelity to America, even when America was wrong. In the belief that one day it would be right again. They will learn about . . . a loyalty to what America could and would be."

De Leon told two remarkable moving stories of heroism. The first was the story of the 442nd, the Go For Broke team that initiated the memorial: eight hundred soldiers crossing nine brutal miles of enemy territory to save a "lost battalion" of 275 soldiers from Texas. He quoted a veteran as saying, "There was never a thought of turning back, never. No one even mentioned it. We just kept plowing forward to reach the lost battalion, period."[90] The other story was of the 522nd Field Artillery Battalion, "some of whom had family members kept in internment camps back in the United States, who were among the first allied troops to liberate the suffering humanity at the Dachau concentration camp."[91] Imagine.

Listing the honors and medals given to the veterans, De Leon opined, "I believe these honorees would agree, that in comparison to medals of brass, silver, and gold plate, what all the Japanese American veterans and their fam-

ilies earned and kept in the heart of Americans is the greater contribution."
Like the memorial, De Leon conflates being interned and being patriotic;
he figures the interned families as the ultimate war heroes, the real sacrificing soldiers of the Second World War, and he argues that what their loyalty
earned them is greater than any other award. Tightening this conflation,
De Leon concludes, "The founding fathers that signed the Declaration of
Independence dedicated their lives, their fortunes, and their sacred honor.
The generation of Americans that is before us today followed in that same
path. They offered their lives, their fortunes, and their sacred honor. We are
in their debt. We are in your debt. This memorial is dedicated to all of the
men who served, to their families who supported them, and to those loved
ones who endured great hardships. This memorial stands as a monument to
the sacrifice of the greatest generation."[92] The implication here is that what
they earned was membership in the greatest generation. Of course, the distinction that De Leon does not make between the founders and Japanese
Americans is that the founders sacrificed their fortunes and their honors
freely; they were not rounded up and required to do so. Letting this distinction drop—or, in the case of the memorial, letting the tension between
the wrapped cranes and the Masaoka "Creed" be resolved by the service of
the soldiers—erases crucial aspects of the history being remembered. It also
places an enormous burden on the figure of the soldier.

The memorial relies on the *soldier* to establish Japanese Americans as
members of the greatest generation. It does this in a moment of deep nostalgia for the war generation, their triumphs, and the ascension of the United
States as a world power, set against a present characterized by waning global
dominance. In so doing, it risks erasing the history of racial logic—of the
war period and the hundred years before the war, when Asian immigrants
were figured and refigured as "impossible subjects" beyond the reach of true
citizenship—that enabled the internment. Writing about the conventional
understanding of the internment, Mae Ngai argues that it is positioned as
"an anachronism in an era of emerging racial liberalism."[93] The National
Japanese American Memorial to Patriotism makes the same gesture. The
admission of a mistake tells us "who we are and who we have always been" in
no uncertain terms. It posits that unquestioning loyalty in the form of military service can compensate for race. It forges an antiracist nationalism with
the memory of racial exclusion. And it turns on the figuring of the solider.
The soldier is used here three times: stripped of freedom, celebrated for the

sacrifice he was almost barred from making, and made to serve the cause of blind devotion. It seems unlikely that this is what Norman Mineta imagined when, at the beginning of the memorial process, he expressed the hope that the memorial could help protect Arab Americans from the kinds of racism Japanese Americans had suffered. The message, for Arab Americans, seems to be—enlist.

"We Leave You Our Deaths, Give Them Their Meaning"

TRIUMPH AND TRAGEDY
AT THE NATIONAL WORLD WAR II MEMORIAL

GRADUALLY DESCENDING into the National World War II Memorial plaza, the visitor is surrounded by triumphal arches and sharp-taloned eagles bearing ribboned wreaths. Making his or her way around the high-spouting fountains of the reborn Rainbow Pool and past the fifty-six festooned pillars, the visitor comes to a curvilinear wall holding a field of 4,048 gold stars. Facing the wall—a physical dead end—the visitor is turned toward the Lincoln Memorial but unable to see it. Below the wall is a pool of still water with a raised coping inscribed with the words "Here We Mark the Price of Freedom." Almost despite itself, this wall is moving. Despite the kaleidoscopic sensation of multiple architectural forms competing for attention, the wall of stars is arresting to the visitor who knows that a gold star represents a soldier's death during the war. But most visitors do not know this.[1] Though the language of the inscription is evocative, it is also oblique. What does it mean to "mark the price of freedom"? Looking around at the stars and beyond, the memorial seems to be clearly about military triumph on a global scale. It seeks to be epic and heroic, and in this it succeeds. The effervescent fountains, the grand plaza, the towering arches, the soaring eagles, and the scattered edicts issued from generals and presidents all mark victory. They don't mark the price of freedom, and this is a little confusing.

The rhetoric that surrounded the World War II Memorial, as it was debated and built, was nothing if not impassioned. In the 1990s, it suddenly seemed impossible to members of veterans' organizations, children of veterans, movie stars playing veterans, political pundits, talk radio hosts, and members of Congress that the "greatest generation" had not been remembered in symbolic stone in the national capital. Outrage at this perceived oversight ruled the day, and nearly every public conversation about the memorial started with the veterans and the fact that they were owed a memorial—*now*. This broadly shared, nearly untouchable sentiment was a product of its time, as is the memorial. This exploration of the memorial process works to understand the particular terms of the need for the memory of World War II in the 1990s to better understand the confusing way it marks the "price of freedom," and to understand the consequences for how troops are supported and wars are waged.

Unlike the Black Revolutionary War Patriots Memorial, the Women in Military Service for America Memorial, or the National Japanese American Memorial to Patriotism during World War II, the National World War II memorial project is not interested in gender or racial legitimation. It does not seek to redraw boundaries of national inclusion. The figure of the soldier is reduced in this memorial to the small ornamental star, an evocative symbol but one that leaves no room for representing the kinds of soldiers who fought this war or the terms of their service.[2] Instead, the memorial speaks in capacious geographic terms. This is, however, not to say that the memorial avoids figuring U.S. nationalism in gendered and racialized terms—it does. The National World War II Memorial is an emphatic statement of the revived status of war and soldiering in the United States that uses the soldier in a racially and gender-segregated military, a fighting force made homogenous by federal policy, to obscure the problems raised by more recent wars.[3] It is a bold, determined homage to victory in particular terms. This use of soldiers on the National Mall gives "sacrificing soldiers" a painful double meaning.

Throughout the seventeen-year process of getting the memorial built, there was a tension between attention to the veterans and arguments about soldiers and war and the nation that the memorial itself might make. This tension raises a series of questions that will shape this exploration of the memorial: How are the World War II dead and veterans figured in the memorial? What happened in the memorial process to the memory of the bodies those gold stars represent? And most pressingly, what past does this use of the soldiers imagine for the present? These vital questions are not driven by resistance to remembering the incredible sacrifices and service of American soldiers in World War II; rather, they are driven by profound respect for those sacrifices and that service and a deep concern about the uses to which they are put—about how the sacrificing soldier is used. They are driven, to return to Archibald MacLeish, by a deep sense of responsibility to the "young dead soldiers who do not speak" and by the conviction that the meanings made of lives given are vital to national life and seriously consequential.

Stepping back from the field of stars at the memorial and looking at the architecture that surrounds the Rainbow Pool, it is hard not to notice that the principal architectural elements of the memorial are given explicit meaning in global, geographic terms, rather than human terms. The two enormous, forty-three-foot-tall Memorial Pavilions are carved with equally enormous geographic markers: ATLANTIC to the north and PACIFIC to the south. At the foot of each pavilion is a set of pools with cascading water and fountains, their copings carved with names of places and battles: North Africa, Southern Europe, Western Europe, Central Europe, Battle of the Atlantic, Murmansk Run, Tunisia, Sicily, Salerno, Anzio, Rome, Po Valley, Normandy, St. Lo, Air War in Europe, Alsace, Rhineland, Huertgen Forest, Battle of the Bulge, Remagen Bridge, and Germany for the Atlantic Pavilion; China, Burma, India, Southwest Pacific, Central Pacific, North Pacific, Pearl Harbor, Wake Island, Bataan Corregidor, Coral Sea, Midway, Guadalcanal, New Guinea, Buna, Tarawa, Kwajalein, Attu, Saipan, Tinian, Guam, Philippine Sea, Peleliu, Leyte Gulf, Luzon, Manila, Iwo Jima, Okinawa, and Japan for the Pacific Pavilion. The fifty-six seventeen-foot-tall pillars that line the memorial's perimeter are carved with the names of the forty-eight states, the District of Columbia, and the seven territories held by the United States during the war: U.S. Virgin Islands, Philippines, Hawaii, Puerto Rico, Alaska, Guam, and American Samoa. These towering forms define and celebrate the war as an event defined by holding, claiming, and recapturing territory all over the globe. This is the meaning the memorial ultimately produces about the war. This trumps a memory of soldiers in this memory of the war. In its bold first impression, it doesn't seem to have much to do with GIs; rather, it feels like a triumphal monument to military might and imperial swagger.

CONTEXTS FOR THE MEMORIAL

Any consideration of the National World War II Memorial (NWWIIM) must begin by recalling that, in the immediate postwar years, returning veterans did not want memorials. There were battlefield cemeteries, blankets of grass, and great heaving seas of headstones in Europe, which were visited dutifully by dignitaries and grieving gold-star mothers. In the tradition that emerged at Gettysburg, the bodies of the war dead were buried and graves were marked, but at home activist veterans and authors of letters to the editor, as well as city planners and local commissions, turned to living memorials rather than symbolic stone. Living memorials had emerged as a response to loss after the First World War. This modest movement gained popularity after World War II. The idea that memorials should be explicitly about the present and the future appealed to the veterans, who embraced the building of highways, bridges, playgrounds, auditoriums, parks, and swimming pools rather than statuary.[4] I have argued elsewhere that, between the living memorials and the incredible reach of the GI Bill, the nation itself became a memorial to the Second World War in literal and symbolic terms.[5] These living memorials have sewn the war into the fabric of life in the United States. They have made the memory of the war both omnipresent and, with the passage of time, invisible. But they did not make explicit declarations about the war; there was no desire for this in the postwar period.[6] War memorials were out of fashion and did not regain their importance in the United States until after the Vietnam War. (Theorists of nationalism have argued that nations need memory in moments of crisis, not golden moments of global ascension, and the story of the memorials on the National Mall seems to support this.) However, veterans' postwar resistance to war memorials had surprisingly little impact on the growing chorus of voices in the 1990s that claimed World War II veterans had been overlooked. The fact that there was not a national World War II memorial was understood as a slight rather than a conscious decision on the part of those who fought. Honoring veterans with something they had not wanted became an imperative.

Nicolaus Mills, whose *Their Last Battle: The Fight for the National World War II Memorial* is a thoroughly researched, book-length account of the building of the memorial, reflects this double-think:

> The virtues of the living memorial movement that, beginning in the middle 1940s, had such a powerful influence on America over the next decade were also its limitations. In focusing so much attention on the practical issues of community and the future, the living memorial avoided directly dealing with death and sacrifice as well as the task of commemorating the individual lives lost in World War II. With the dedication of the National World War II Memorial on Memorial Day weekend 2004, we have at last begun to make

up for not honoring our World War II veterans with a memorial fifty-nine years ago.[7]

Mills moves from the suggestion that the living memorials allowed Americans to avoid "death and sacrifice" to "we have at last begun honoring these veterans." This is entirely a sleight of hand. He makes this leap without contending with the veterans' desire to think about the future and community as a way to honor "death and sacrifice" and without thinking about the changes in the culture that might have made memorials—once understood as superfluous—seem not just inevitable but vital.

Mills also links honoring the veterans to dealing with death and sacrifice without addressing how the memorial does this; the elision is telling. The links between death, loss, sacrifice, honor, and celebration are complicated in this memorial. They would be complicated under any circumstances. The cost of war in human terms is always enormous. In the United States, especially since Lincoln's speech at Gettysburg, honor and pride have been offered as consolation for the loss of citizen soldiers, and war memorials have increasingly emphasized the sacrifices of the individual soldiers. But too much emphasis on loss, at the Vietnam Veterans Memorial in particular, has provoked anxiety about heroism and the state's ability to recruit bodies for service in future wars, especially in the era of the all-volunteer military. Too much emphasis on the celebration of victory, however, threatens to render loss invisible, to make war glorious, to neglect the sacrifices of those who enabled the military victories, and to speak for the young dead soldier in ways that do not serve young living soldiers or the nation for which they sacrifice.

What changed popular thinking about war memorials between 1947—when vets wanted living memorials—and 1987, when cries for a memorial started to surface? The kind of war the United States was waging had changed, and the ways in which soldiers became soldiers had changed. The Cold War, Cold War proxy wars, the end of the draft, and the troubled status of the soldier in the post–Vietnam War period have challenged ideas about soldiering and war in the United States. As a result, the National Mall has also changed. In 1987, the Vietnam Veterans Memorial was five years old, and the Korean War Veterans Memorial, the Black Revolutionary War Patriots Memorial, and the Women in Military Service for America Memorial had all been approved by Congress. The Mall was being transformed into a site for remembering twentieth-century wars, and the list of twentieth-century wars was certainly incomplete without World War II.

The story of the memorial begins in 1987. Sixty-seven-year-old combat veteran Roger Durbin approached his Ohio congresswoman, Marcy Kaptur,
at a public gathering in prosaically named Jerusalem, Ohio, and asked her
why there was no World War II memorial in Washington.[8] Kaptur, a historian, urban planner, and newly elected legislator, mentioned the Iwo Jima
Memorial. Durbin, a veteran of the Battle of the Bulge, countered that Iwo
Jima was for Marines only. Kaptur was stumped. Had she answered that after
the war most veterans preferred, indeed *insisted* on, infrastructure rather
than statuary, Durbin might have been satisfied—but it seems unlikely.
Given the changing face of the Mall and the rising tide of interest in the war
as the fiftieth anniversary approached, the stubborn Durbin would likely
have continued to insist on a place, next to the Vietnam Veterans Memorial
and the Korean War Veterans Memorial, where he could take his granddaughter when they visited Washington, D.C. At any rate, Kaptur had no
such answer, and the passion to build a memorial was ignited.

This story appears over and over in newspaper and magazine articles about
the memorial; the notion that the idea for the memorial came from a combat
veteran in small town Ohio seems to have been deeply appealing. Nicolaus
Mills starts his "biography" of the memorial with a chapter titled, "Mr.
Durbin Goes to Washington." He is just one of many observers to make the
connection between Roger Durbin and Frank Capra's Jefferson Smith from
the 1939 film, *Mr. Smith Goes to Washington*. In part, this is shorthand for
the story of a patriotic everyman who takes on the Washington powers that
be. But it is worth brief consideration, not only because the classic movie is
a lovingly filmed homage to monumental Washington (pivoting on Smith's
pilgrimages to the Lincoln Memorial), but also because Durbin wants to
refigure the Mall that Capra and Smith so adored—in terms that they might
not have liked. Smith doesn't go to the Lincoln Memorial to revel in the victory of the Union army; as the camera lingering on the end of the Gettysburg
address tells us, he goes to Lincoln to try to understand how to "honor the
dead" with a "government of the people, by the people, for the people" in the
face of good old-fashioned Capra-style greed and corruption. The comparison implies an innocence about the drive to get the memorial built and positions Durbin as taking on the corridors of power. In fact, he became their
agent. This telling misses essential aspects of the story as it evolved and mis-
characterizes the memorial that was produced.

In 1987, Kaptur introduced legislation to "remedy the situation." The legislation called for Congress to authorize the American Battle Monuments Commission (ABMC) to "establish a memorial and museum on Federal land in the District of Columbia or its environs to honor members of the Armed Forces who served in World War II and to commemorate the United States' participation in that conflict."[9] This broad mandate was warmly received, but nothing came of it. In August 1988, Senator Strom Thurmond introduced a companion bill in the Senate, but even this venerable force was unable to move the process forward. Kaptur stood on the floor of Congress with Durbin at her side in 1987, 1989, 1991, and 1993, and decried the absence of a memorial. (It has not escaped notice that it took longer to get the legislation passed than it did to win the war.) Each of these appeals was met with appreciation and inaction. She did not meet any particular opposition but had trouble moving her bill through the required committees and procedures. It was not until continued stalling of the bill began to get embarrassing, and more pointedly, the surge of federal spending, local organizing, and popular interest in fiftieth anniversary commemorative events began to heat up, that Kaptur and Thurmond, eventually joined by ever-longer lists of cosponsors, were able to get the bill passed in 1993.

President Clinton, who praised it with increasingly familiar language about long overdue tributes and "the greatest generation," signed Public Law 103–32 approving the memorial in May 1993. The legislation called for a memorial on federal land and turned the project over to the ABMC.[10] It also required President Clinton to appoint an advisory board to oversee the ABMC's work. Unlike the legislation for the Korean War Veterans Memorial, this law did not require an all-veteran board.[11] The board Clinton selected was different from Reagan's but not a radical departure. On September 28, 1994, Clinton appointed Peter Wheeler, Georgia commissioner of veterans affairs for more than fifty years, as board chair. Three board members did not survive to see the completion of the memorial: William C. Ferguson Sr., a World War II Tuskegee airman; Bill Mauldin, an award-winning political cartoonist best known for "Willie and Joe," about World War II foot soldiers; and Sarah McClendon, a national newspaper reporter and columnist who volunteered for the WACS during World War II and was given an officer's commission. The other members were a diverse group; most were veterans or closely related to veterans.[12] The inclusion of Roger Durbin's granddaughter, who was then studying art history at Bowling Green State University in Ohio, continued the "Mr. Durbin goes to Washington" narrative and put the regular folks who wanted a memorial right in the center of the memorial process, in the midst of the scrapping elites.

THE SITE

The first and greatest controversy for the memorial was about the site. In early 1995, the ABMC looked at six potential sites: immediately west of the Capitol Reflecting Pool and east of Third Street; the northeast side of the Tidal Basin near paddle boats and parking; West Potomac Park between the Lincoln and Roosevelt memorials; the Constitution Gardens platform area between Seventeenth Street, Constitution Avenue, the eastern lakeshore, and the Mall Reflecting Pool; across Fourteenth Street from the National Museum of American History; and Freedom Plaza on Pennsylvania Avenue. The American Battle Monuments Commission and the Memorial Advisory Board unanimously selected the Constitution Gardens site.

But when they took this site to the Commission of Fine Arts (CFA) in July 1995, they were turned away. The meeting opened with the ABMC's ambassador, F. Haydn Williams, who brought a demeanor not usually seen by the commission. Citing what he described as the motto of Daniel Burnham, "Make no little plans; they have no magic to stir men's blood," Williams promised to make this his creed in building the World War II memorial.[13] Leading with Burnham bombast and promising Burnham scale, Williams set the tone for the memorial. He described the war as "the great defining event of the century" and called for a "memorial commensurate with the event." Serious about this extravagant ambition, he laid out criteria for the memorial that the advisory board and the ABMC had developed: "(1) The memorial should be on or in close proximity to the Mall; (2) it should be free-standing, with adequate space around it; (3) it should have relevance to its surrounding, to nearby memorials and structures; (4) it should have great accessibility; (5) it should be evocative of the profound importance of World War II in the twentieth century, as the other memorials on the Mall were evocative of the great events of their time."[14] He argued for the Constitution Gardens site: "It had a commanding location in highly relevant surroundings . . . and would place the Korean and Vietnam memorials in proper perspective; and it was positioned astride the most visited concourse in Washington." He repeatedly stressed the need to be clear about the relative importance of the wars commemorated on the Mall; the World War II memorial would need to be significantly more imposing than the Vietnam and Korean War Memorials.

CFA chair J. Carter Brown, despite his previous reticence about war memorials on the Mall, applauded Williams's approach and met his bombast with bombast. He described his hope for the World War II memorial as a "forecourt to the whole capital memorial experience, with this memorial representing the twentieth century, Lincoln the nineteenth, and Washington the eighteenth."[15] This is a dramatic revision of monumental Washington. He went on to say that "he thought the concept of a horizontal memorial had been pushed to the edge with the Vietnam and Korean memorials," and that "considering the relative importance of World War II, a horizontal memorial would require nearly the entire Mall." (Nearly the entire Mall!) He read a letter from *The Three Soldiers* sculptor and former CFA member Frederick Hart arguing that "he did not think the Constitution Gardens site appropriate for the heroic nature of achievement and loss inherent in the concept of World War II." After a brief discussion, Brown and the CFA rejected the Constitution Gardens site as "not prominent enough" for either aspect of the memorial.[16]

Brown and the CFA proposed the site at the Rainbow Pool—on the central axis of the Mall between the Washington and Lincoln Memorials. The National Capital Planning Commission agreed, and the ABMC was thrilled. At the CFA meeting on September 19, 1995, the site was unanimously approved. In making his argument for the site, Williams dismissed the other sites, including one near Arlington National Cemetery: "The WWII memorial should be a celebratory memorial, symbolizing the triumph of good over evil and would be better situated in a living, vibrant environment than in the shadow of the hallowed ground of Arlington."[17] For Williams, hallowed ground and dead soldiers were not the point; celebrating triumph on an imposing scale was the point, and the Rainbow Pool was the most potent site in the city for this celebration.

Just two months later, on Veterans Day 1995, as the last formal event of the Department of Defense's extravagant fiftieth anniversary commemoration of the war, President Clinton stood at the Rainbow Pool and dedicated it as the site for the National World War II Memorial. Roger Durbin of Jerusalem, Ohio, stood at his side. Together, they buried "sacred soil" from sixteen World War II cemeteries around the world, marking the site as sacred ground.[18] By federal bureaucratic standards, these events unfolded at the speed of light. This would later come to be seen as evidence of a democratic process pushed through by a few elites, but it was hardly the most dramatic assertion of federal authority in the memorial process. As the rhetoric in the CFA meetings indicates, there was enormous confidence in their shared position that the war was *the* event of the century and that it required the most prestigious of sites. Nothing in these conversations indicates an awareness that this position might not be universally shared. They were nearly right about this in terms of their position on the war; it was their position on the Mall that would come under fire.

The absolute confidence these agencies had in their framing of the war as the defining moment of the twentieth century and an unqualified triumph of good over evil that needed to be powerfully present on the Mall was likely reinforced by another controversy on the Mall about the war. In fall 1994 and spring 1995, as the CFA, the ABMC, and the advisory board were selecting the site, a fierce battle flared up at the Smithsonian's National Air and Space Museum over an exhibition featuring the plane that dropped the first atomic bomb on Japan. The furious response to a planned exhibit titled "The Crossroads: The End of World War II, the Atomic Bomb, and the Cold War" revealed a broad investment in maintaining the status of the war as the "good war" in absolute terms. As Tom Engelhardt and Ed Linenthal describe the exhibit, "With the plane as its central icon, that show was to explore the end of a hot war and the beginning of a cold one. As conceived by the Smithsonian's curator and advisers, the exhibit was to examine the bomb's creation, the decision to use it against Japanese cities, the *Enola Gay*'s mission, the ground-level effects of atomic weaponry, the bomb's role in ending the war, and the new era it inaugurated—as well as the ways in which decades of historical research and debate on these topics had altered and deepened our understanding of them."[19]

But this representation of the war was simply untenable to veterans' organizations, ordinary citizens, and members of Congress. Newt Gingrich, then Speaker of a Republican-dominated House, summed up the problem: "The Enola Gay fight was a fight, in effect, over the reassertion by most Americans that they are sick and tired of being told by some cultural elite that they ought to be ashamed of their country."[20]

Gingrich was onto something, but he missed some of the nuance of what was at stake. The controversy was not just about the war but about the status of the soldier derived from the status of the war. In an era in which the Vietnam War had tainted military service and the all-volunteer military required willing bodies, the reemergence of patriotism and the revival of the status of the solider were crucially linked to the status of World War II. An exhibit that questioned, however mildly, the dropping of the bomb was seen as unpatriotic and, crucially, as explicitly disrespectful of veterans. Senator Nancy Kassebaum submitted a remarkable Senate resolution:

> Whereas the role of the Enola Gay during World War II was momentous in helping to bring World War II to a merciful end, which resulted in saving the lives of Americans and Japanese;
>
> Whereas the current script for the National Air and Space Museum's exhibit on the Enola Gay is revisionist and offensive to many World War II veterans;
>
> Whereas the Federal law states that "the Smithsonian Institute shall commemorate and display the contributions made by the military forces of the Nation toward creating, developing, and maintaining a free, peaceful, and independent society and culture in the United States";
>
> Whereas the Federal law also states that "the valor and sacrificial service of the men and women of the Armed Forces shall be portrayed as an inspiration to the present and future generations of America"; and
>
> Whereas, in memorializing the role of the United States in armed conflict, the National Air and Space Museum has an obligation under the Federal law to portray history in the proper context of the times: Now, therefore, be it
>
> Resolved, That it is the sense of the Senate that any exhibit displayed by the National Air and Space Museum with respect to the Enola Gay should reflect appropriate sensitivity toward the men and women who faithfully and selflessly served the United States during World War II and should avoid impugning the memory of those who gave their lives for freedom.[21]

This resolution, which passed unanimously, reflects a climate in which World War II was not only untouchable but untouchable *because* the veterans of that war were beyond reproach. It even legislates, albeit without teeth, that "history be portrayed in the proper context of the times." This invites an obvious question: which times? Certainly plenty of questions about the bomb were raised in 1945, but in 1995, "the times" not only shut down any questions but did so in the name of the sacrificing soldier.

Emphasizing just this theme, on January 19, 1995, William Detweiler, the national commander of the American Legion, wrote to President Clinton and called for cancellation of the exhibit on the grounds that it told the "hundreds of thousands of American boys whose lives ... [were] spared by the dropping of the bomb ... [that] their lives were purchased at the price of treachery and revenge."[22] A few days later, Smithsonian secretary Michael

Heyman cancelled the exhibit, setting a clear precedent for what could be said in the 1990s on the National Mall about the Second World War. Critical thinking about the war was out of the question, and the honor of veterans was at stake; these concepts were linked. In a prescient question raised early in the controversy, curator Tom Crouch asked, "Do you want an exhibition intended to make veterans feel good, or do you want an exhibition that will lead our visitors to think about the consequences of the atomic bombing of Japan?" He continued, "Frankly, I don't think we can do both."[23] The evidence suggests that questions about the war were understood by many as questions about the soldiers, and this was untenable. Questions about the soldiers were unacceptable and would lead to censorship from the highest levels. Any moral ambiguity on the conduct of the war was necessarily an insult to the soldiers who fought it. The implications of this logic for present and future wars are chilling: once our soldiers are engaged, any war is a good war.

This set limited perimeters for how the war might be represented on the Mall. Crucially, it limited what might be said about the war to a statement that it was the good war. Beyond this there did not seem to be much room to maneuver. This was reflected, as the memorial process moved forward, in the remarkable lack of discussion of how the war should be understood. These early conversations about the site are important because they refer, in a limited sense, to the meaning of the war; they establish that the war is important enough to fill the entire Mall, that it was not just the good war but the epic good war.

Just a few months after the climax of this controversy that had preoccupied the Capital, members of the CFA, the ABMC, and the NCPC seemed to be trying to outdo each other in their efforts to align themselves unequivocally with the "make the veterans happy" camp. In Brown's logic, the Constitution Gardens site was unacceptable because it was too far off the central axis of the Mall and smaller than the sites of the Vietnam Veterans Memorial and the Korean War Veterans Memorial. A World War II memorial that was smaller than the memorials for these other wars would represent the war and therefore the soldiers as having less "comparable historical significance," and this would have dramatic long-term consequences for how soldiering was understood in the United States; "our boys" would be the veterans of Vietnam rather than World War II.

The Rainbow Pool was the most prominent site in Washington but also the most riddled with engineering problems. It is a nightmare combination of low-lying reclaimed swampland, a flood plain, and existing structures. All this paled, however, in the face of the opportunity to place the Second World War at the center of the historical narrative of the Mall, linking it, as all parties pushing for the memorial came to insist it should, to the defining moments of the nineteenth century (the Lincoln Memorial) and eighteenth century (the Washington Monument), thus identifying World War II as the defining moment of the twentieth century. This argument—repeated relentlessly as the memorial process progressed—won the day. It would achieve secular canonization of the war, working to make the war forever untouchable in the name of those who served.

Some have argued that the most important element of the memorial is its site—not only on the Mall but in the sacred center of the sacred center, the Rainbow Pool. Though the debates about this memorial revolve around the site, to be sure, it would be a mistake not to carefully consider the design and the fights over it. While the site claims significance in the name of the soldiers, the final design, after years of debate, tries to claim *absolute* significance in particular terms.

THE COMPETITION

Nearly ten years after the proposal for a World War II memorial was first brought before Congress, the American Battle Monuments Commission held a design competition. The call for entries appeared in the April 19, 1996 edition of *Commerce Business Daily*:

> ABMC has been authorized by Congress to establish this Memorial and has secured a preeminent site, commensurate in importance with the war itself. Known as the Rainbow Pool site, it is located on the center axis of the Mall between the Lincoln Memorial and Washington Monument, extending from the east end of the Reflecting Pool to 17th Street. The proposed Memorial offers an opportunity through the civic design arts to honor and express the nation's enduring gratitude to all who served in the U.S. Armed Forces during World War II, as well as to the patriotic and vital support of the American people on the home front. It is an historic opportunity to create a lasting legacy for the nation. The creation of the memorial can be a catalyst to a national reckoning, inviting remembrance of the defining event of the 20th century, the celebration of patriotism and sacrifice, and the bonding of the nation.[24]

Most of this language is familiar, recapitulating the conversation about the memorial: "preeminent site," "commensurate in importance to the war itself," "honor and express the nation's gratitude," "celebration of patriotism and sacrifice." But some language is new: "national reckoning" and "bonding of the nation." "Reckoning" conveys a settling of debts as well as a coming to terms. Its use is striking here because, while it seems to clearly mean the former (thanks owed and finally given), one wonders why the nation might have needed to come to terms with this war fifty years after it ended. The language about "bonding" of the nation might suggest an answer; the requirement that the memorial inspire national bonding expresses a previously implicit link between the memorial and a national recovery project. In the logic of the memorial's advocates, the war was needed *now* to bind the nation.

The call established the competition process. The ABMC brought in the General Services Administration to run a closed competition in which, in the words of Joseph Fishkin, "big firms literally submitted their resumes first and their designs second."[25] It was to be a two-stage process. In the first stage, potential designers would assemble teams capable of getting the memorial built and would provide evidence of their team's experience and capacities. This required a great deal of experience and limited the pool; four hundred designers submitted entries (compared to 1,400 designs submitted for the Vietnam Veterans Memorial and 5,000 for the memorial at Ground Zero in New York). In the second stage, after at least five teams were selected, the teams would develop proposals.

The ABMC did not want an open competition. Feeling that the open competitions for the Vietnam Veterans Memorial and the Korean War Veterans Memorial had been disastrous, they wanted greater control from the beginning. Williams was quite frank about wanting to avoid the battles over the designs that those memorial competitions had engendered. But the closed competition was not well received. It inspired protest from architects and artists across the country, many of whom signed a petition demanding that the ABMC reopen the competition and arguing for the importance of the unexpected in an open competition. (An unveiled reference to the success of Maya Lin's Vietnam Veterans Memorial design.) Paul Spreiregen, a member of the design selection committee that chose Lin's design, wrote in outrage to the *Washington Post* that "such 'invited competitions' are well suited to finding the best designs for buildings, which can have complex requirements. . . . But, open competitions elicit a breadth of designs suitable for memorials. They allow for selection based on performance, not promise. The Vietnam Veterans Memorial is a good example of what can result from open competition."[26]

The ABMC, referencing the unfortunate Korean War Veterans Memorial process, had justified the closed, limited nature of the competition with the argument that it would avoid such controversy. Spreiregen's response was to call on the ABMC to embrace controversy: "Controversy is a proper form of public deliberation, particularly in Washington, and our city benefits from it, tedious as it may sometimes be. Furthermore, the major memorials of our capital city were all controversial in their time—the Washington Monument, the Lincoln Memorial, the Jefferson Memorial, even the Capitol itself."[27] Spreiregen called for a reassertion of the importance of art in the memorial process, arguing that the "design of a World War II memorial will be one of the most challenging projects ever posed in Washington. . . . [T]he memorial must be in harmony with its setting, deferring to the Washington Monument and respecting the distant view of the Lincoln Memorial . . . and yet it must possess its own artistic strength." And then he raised the stakes: "Why, then, limit participation?" Twisting the rhetoric that surrounded the memorial, he wrote, "The heroes of World War II weren't screened for bravery. . . . [N]o one could predict which American would rise to the heights of human courage. . . . [E]qually, no screening of candidates can ensure that a designer will be found who rises to the moment." In response, the General Services Administration did open the competition, but the AMBC held the power to veto the competition jury's selection. The jury ultimately selected a design from the initial pool. The AMBC seemed quite uninterested in either the prospect of controversy or the opening up of possible meanings that Spreiregen hoped to inspire.

The controversy about the terms of the competition flared up briefly and only had staying power with the memorial's more fervent opponents. The guidelines developed by the ABMC, the CFA, and the NCPC in the summer of 1996, however, hinted at the more passionate arguments to come. The two most important elements of these guidelines were: "(1) The vista framed by the row of elms along the Reflecting Pool had to be kept open, with nothing detracting from the view from the Capitol to the Lincoln Memorial; and (2) the design of the memorial had to be respectful of and compatible in configuration and quality with its historic surroundings."[28] Both stipulations were about the Mall rather than the war, and both became complicated, as the various parties clung to them and debated them in the fight over the memorial. The former was open to a wide range of interpretation: how open would an "open vista" have to be? The latter involved the multiple histories of the Mall: that inspired by McMillan and Burnham, the Mall that harked back to the 1960s and 1970s of King and the antiwar movement, and that belonging to 1982 and the Vietnam and Korea memorials. The new militarized Mall of the 1980s and 1990s would eventually rule the day.

The call for the second stage in the revised design process included these stipulations:

> The concept must be aesthetic, functional, operational, comply with the budget, compatible with the site's historic, formal surroundings, fully respectful of the Mall's open east-west vista formed by the rows of elms bordering the Reflecting Pool and the need for central ceremonial space, contextual of memorial structures, have landscaping and the general ambiance and image of the Capital of the United States. The design and scale must take into account the Memorial; stated purposes and philosophy and its national significance as one of the major commemorative places on the Mall. The aboveground design must have a strong identity and the quality of a timeless visible landmark, symbolic of the defining event of the 20th Century. The monument should celebrate patriotism, valor and sacrifice and the bonding of the nation. It must be singularly inspiring and significant without being massive and without exceeding vertical limits. The design, whether abstract or representational in nature, or a combination of both, must represent a true integration and amalgamation of art, landscaping and architecture. The memorial should take full advantage of its preeminent location and consideration should be given to use the entire site. It should represent the best thinking that the various architecture, landscape architecture, related design and engineering professions, and artistic community can bring to bear on its design and realization. The design must fulfill the objectives of the American Battle Monuments Commission as charged by the Congress, to create a special place of great honor on the Mall axis of the Capital to commemorate the lasting significance of World War II on America and the world.[29]

The language here is familiar. This reads, in fact, a little like the results of the survey conducted by advocates for a Korean War memorial at the dedication of the Vietnam Memorial—the memorial needed to be above ground and to celebrate patriotism.

The jury to select the design was chaired by architect David Childs, a man who would shape the next iteration of American memorials through his work on the 9/11 memorial in New York. The other members were architect Hugh Hardy, architect John Chase, former *New York Times* architecture critic Ada Louise Huxtable, Harvard professor and landscape architect Laurie Olin, architect Cathy Simon, National Gallery of Art director Earl Powell, Pepsico CEO and World War II veteran Donald Kendall, World War II veteran and retired admiral Robert Long, and retired general John W.

Vessey, former chairman of the Joint Chiefs of Staff and a World War II veteran. Their task was nothing if not daunting.

THE FIRST DESIGN: BEHEADED COLUMNS

In the end, the jury selected the design most favored by the ABMC from the start—that of Rhode Island architect Friedrich St. Florian. It was a semicircular colonnade of fifty forty-foot-high columns. Twenty-five were to line a large berm to the north of a lowered Rainbow Pool and twenty-five were to line a twinned berm to the south. These columns were, in the initial design, beheaded. Their cut-off tops were intended to symbolize the deaths of soldiers in battle. They were quite dramatic. They would echo the columns of the Lincoln Memorial and mark the cost of the war, with the nation and the soldier still standing but *not* unaltered. They also provided an interesting compromise between a modern and traditional design aesthetic. The classic Doric columns were a staple of the traditional Beaux Arts style of Washington architecture, but the decapitated classic Doric columns and the design's stark, clean lines had a distinctly modern cast. The enormous berms—each 68 feet wide and 360 feet long—would house a museum on one side and a 400-seat auditorium on the other. They were to be densely planted with white roses.[30]

St. Florian's original design worked hard to keep the central axis of the Mall open. The columns wrapped around the Rainbow Pool, and the berms sat to the side of the Lincoln-Washington axis. This was appealing to the jury, as was his negotiation of the problem of abstraction and the capacities of modernism. Jury member Hugh Hardy has written about the problem of an architectural language for memorials, praising the abstraction of Maya Lin's memorial but concluding that it "offered no precedent for presenting the many facets of the Second World War."[31] St. Florian used the most traditional form—the democracy-evoking Greco-resonant column—and manipulated it. But this level of abstraction—this suggestion that abstraction was required in response to the war, this complicated figuring of the soldiers— would not stand.

Truncated and complex though they were, St. Florian's columns were the most traditional forms used by the six finalists. The other designs included glass pillars rising out of the Rainbow Pool, a series of bunkers set around the pool, a garden of great bells strung in the rows of elms that flank the pool, glass spires lining an expanded Rainbow Pool, and an alabaster cube in a

newly black Rainbow Pool.[32] The bell garden was the least visually transformative of the space; St. Florian's design changed the Rainbow Pool the least but could hardly be described as unobtrusive. It is important to remember that, because the designers were judged first by their experience and then by the designs they generated, these designs are more a reflection of the work of successful architects in the 1990s than of a set of ideas brought to the competition about how to memorialize the war. As a result, this limited competition may have yielded more abstraction than an open competition would have. In any case, it left St. Florian as the only option for those not looking for too much modernism or too much abstraction.

His design was first presented to the Commission of Fine Arts at an informal informational meeting in January 1997, just a few days before President Clinton would officially announce the winner. ABMC advisor Bill Lacy introduced the design, describing it as "uncomplicated" and "easy to remember." He stated that "the design symbolized the coming together of the country during the war, with the enclosure by the berms representing the solidity of the nation," and he read from St. Florian's design statement, which spoke of the triumph of democracy over totalitarianism as well as the suffering and sacrifice of war.[33] J. Carter Brown expressed support for the design concept because it did not violate the McMillan Plan.[34] Though there were no urgent objections from the rest of the commission, Vice Chairman Harry G. Robinson, an architect, did tellingly express some concern about the truncation of the columns and suggest further study of the idea.

In July 1997, at the first official design meeting with the CFA, Brown prefaced the discussion of the memorial with a history of the Mall. He was speaking not only to the ABMC and the advisory board but also to a roomful of interested parties who had come to support or attack the memorial. Anticipating trouble, he noted that "the history of the Mall was one of evolutionary change and . . . the Commission of Fine Arts had always adhered to a policy of reason and balance where historic preservation was concerned and could not subscribe to any ideology that viewed the status quo as always incapable of improvement."[35] He reminded those attending that the return to classicism of the McMillan Plan had been terribly unpopular in its time but was much revered now and that now-revered memorials had also been controversial. He defended the site selection, noting two scales on the Mall: "The monumental scale of the Capitol, Washington Monument, and Lincoln Memorial; and the smaller scale traditionally permitted for certain memorials having to do with conflict: the Grant Memorial at the foot of Capitol Hill, the statue of John Paul Jones at 17th Street, the temple form of the District of Columbia World War I Memorial, and the Vietnam and Korean War Memorials." Suggesting that World War II would require something beyond a "simple war memorial," he read from a plaque at the site that promised "a monument to the spirit and sacrifice of the American people and a reminder of the high moral purposes and idealism that motivated the Nation's call to arms as it sought victory in concert with its allies over the forces of totalitarianism."[36] Thus Brown describes the Mall as an evolving landscape, speaks to the modest history of representing war on the Mall, and then calls for a further evolution that would rewrite the history of modest representations of war.

Helen Fagin framed the advisory board's thinking about the memorial: "The Board was acutely conscious of the distinctive place the World War II Memorial would occupy, and of the other memorials among which it would take its place." She reviewed the memories made by the Lincoln Memorial and Washington Monument and argued, "In the 20th century, it was World War II that defined American democracy and American achievement. . . . The memorial would commemorate the more than 400,000 who died, honor the veterans who returned and those on the home front who made victory possible, and celebrate the emergence of the United States as a world leader."[37] She continued, envisioning "the 100th anniversary of the war, and the number of people who would come to the memorial and appreciate and understand the sacrifices that were made so that they could live in freedom and in a democracy emulated all over the world." She concluded, "The nation, the nation's capital, and the Mall deserve the World War II Memorial." As if Fagin had not made this point emphatically enough, Williams added that the memorial would "honor the nation as a whole." Hugh Hardy further upped the rhetorical ante, describing the design as "a temple to the ideas of democracy at one of the nation's most challenging times, a time of unity and extraordinary consensus." This rhetoric was heightened further still by Luther Smith, an architect and World War II veteran, who argued that the columns "symbolized all Americans standing side by side in a common cause, Americans of all races, creeds, and national origins, who protected the country from outside attack, came to the rescue of a world in flames, and raised the nation to its world status." These are arguments for something more than a war memorial. They are arguments for a nation defined by war, and the terms of the definition are crucial. Smith's evocation of the memory of "Americans of all races, creeds, and national origins" who "saved the world in flames" suggest some logical terms for this definition. The global scale of his framing is what emerges triumphant in the memorial process.

In this first CFA meeting, St. Florian began by paying homage to L'Enfant and the McMillan Plan, but added that their work would never be done. He described his design, stressing his respect for the sight lines of the Mall, and described his central concept. In his view, "the column was an archetypical form going back to Greek and Roman antiquity and was meant to be strong and everlasting." In the memorial, he saw them as "anchors." "In their singularity, they stood for the strong, independent, and free American character; in their togetherness they represented the collective will of the American people to uphold their principles and values when challenged; in their purity and solemnity they spoke of other American virtues, modesty and constraint. . . . [B]ecause they were broken, they were a reminder of the lives of so many young Americans cut short by war."[38] He wanted to figure the soldiers as triumphant *and* broken—and, of course, still standing.

St. Florian was followed by senators and congresswomen. Senator Robert Kerrey, reflecting on what he had heard and speaking to what was at stake in the memorial, said he "hoped the discussion did not turn into a test of loyalty to the country—are you for this memorial and for America, or against this memorial and against America?" Given the tenor of the conversation, he could just as well have said, "for the soldier or against the soldier and therefore against America." He expressed doubt that there was any real objection to building a World War II memorial, but maintained that the question of scale was essential. He urged the commission to reject the design and approve something on a more appropriate scale, like the Grant Memorial. Without using Brown's language, he was essentially urging the responsible bodies to stick to the traditions of scale for war memorials on the Mall. Representative Eleanor Holmes Norton echoed this sentiment, describing the design as unnecessarily "invasive."

These elected officials were followed by a series of supporters of the memorial design and the site. Rolland Kidder, a Vietnam veteran and ABMC member, justified the St. Florian design with a comparison to the Vietnam Memorial, arguing that future generations need to understand the difference between the wars: "The ill-defined role and unwinnable mission of Vietnam versus the unity of the nation and the clear mission—to preserve democracy and freedom throughout the world—in World War II." The implication was that a difference between the two memorials would teach the difference between the two wars. This distinction is, in the final design, clear and troublesome. In St. Florian's first design the memorials are more similar in their emphasis on loss.

The last speaker on behalf of the design made a dizzying logical leap. Ken Haapala, representing "families who lost a loved one in the war," repeated the now well-worn refrain about Washington representing the eighteenth century, Lincoln representing the nineteenth century, and World War II representing the twentieth century; he made plain an assumption underlying this logic: "As there is no one leader to memorialize, it was appropriate and fitting to build a memorial to all those who sacrificed, at home as well as on the battlefield."[39] How in this context was Roosevelt different from Washington or Lincoln? In fact, a Franklin Delano Roosevelt memorial—which never mentioned in these lengthy proceedings—had been dedicated just of the Mall on the Tidal Basin, and the Rainbow Pool had never been seriously considered as a possible site.[40] That Haapala could so blithely overlook Roosevelt and assume that his audience would be equally dismissive is a testament both to the rise of the anti-Rooseveltian New Right and the burgeoning status of the military in the period. (The invisibility of Roosevelt as a possibility for representing the twentieth century underscores the double invisibility of someone like Martin Luther King Jr.; an argument might also have been made for the civil rights movement as the defining event of the twentieth century. King has gotten his memorial—near FDR's in the Tidal Basin—but just picture the Mall with King at the Rainbow Pool. What kind of nation would that imagine?)

But this frenzied elevation of the war and, therefore, its memory, was not the only position represented at this meeting, which was ostensibly about St. Florian's design. Paul Spreiregen pushed back against what he saw as a naked celebration of militarism, arguing that Arlington National Cemetery was the place for that, that the capital symbolized "democratic deliberation" and the Mall should reflect this rather than a celebration of militarism. Amazingly, he was the only person to make this crucial point. He went on to say that the design, in his estimation, was a parody of classicism and reflected Fascist architecture. He "thought it would be a travesty to honor America's role in World War II with the architectural symbolism of the oppression we sought to vanquish."[41]

Other architects at the meeting compared St. Florian's design to the work of Albert Speer, Adolf Hitler's friend and architect. Deborah Dietsch commented, "The stripped-down columns were reminiscent of the work of Albert Speer in Germany and could just as easily symbolize a German victory." She also insisted that "an overgrown war memorial had no place on this contemplative site." Robert Miller argued that "the essential symbolic quality of the Mall was its openness, and that the openness was a symbol of freedom, the freedom that was the legacy of World War II; compromising that openness in any way would detract from the symbolism that World War II was all about." He was followed by six more speakers, representing as many organizations, all vehemently opposed to the design and the site, and all concerned about what the memorial would do to the Mall.

In the end, St. Florian's design failed to satisfy even its staunchest supporters. In 1997, the Commission of Fine Arts, the National Capital Planning Commission, and the National Park Service, the three bodies from which the memorial design would ultimately need approval, affirmed their commitment to the site but rejected the original design, describing it as "overbuilt." To some, in the face of St. Florian's rather grand scheme, this sounded like ironic understatement from Brown. Given the scale to which the design would expand, it is seriously ironic. In response, the ABMC withdrew its proposal to add a museum to the site and sent St. Florian back to his drawing board.

As they fought it out in the CFA offices and on editorial pages, the proponents of the initial design misread the scale of its bombast, and its opponents misread the history of the Mall. Neither L'Enfant's plan nor the McMillan Plan was about openness; they were both interested in expressing power in the capital. However, they were not dedicated to a totalitarian expression of power in the way Speer was, and neither was St. Florian. Robert Peck made the best assessment of this comparison: "It was hurtful and untrue to history to compare the architectural style of this memorial or any other in the neoclassical mode to that used by the totalitarian regimes that were defeated in World War II. . . . Just looking around Washington at our public buildings built in the 1930s and 1940s and comparing them to those built in Germany or Italy during the same period would show that there was little, if any, difference in style."[42] Architecture in Washington has always been about expressions of power; this is true even of the monumental core, with the one Mall-altering exception of the Vietnam Veterans Memorial.

THE SECOND DESIGN: ENTER REAL TRIUMPHALISM

In 1998, St. Florian brought a new design to the CFA. It was described as "a smaller, lower, more respectful" version of the original design, but, in fact, it was an entirely new design with an entirely new war to remember. The decision to give up the interior space opened up new possibilities for St. Florian and allowed him to drop the berms. He replaced these with fifty-six "shield-like architectural structures transparent enough to allow for views into and out of the plaza." He specified fifty-six shields to represent the states and territories held by the United States during the war. These shields, twenty-eight on either side of the pool, would be "anchored at the center by monumental granite arches," which would "celebrate the victory won, the triumph of liberty over tyranny." Also new in this iteration was a "ceremonial center of the memorial" in which a "curved granite wall would form an exedra with cascading water falls on either side." As St. Florian described it, "In this place the sacrifice and heroism of the World War II generation would be commemorated, and here would be placed a torch of freedom, passed symbolically from generation to generation."[43]

These changes were enormous and significant. The beheaded columns were replaced by shields representing geographical reach rather than human loss. The western wall, facing Lincoln, was now blocked by contradictory symbols of flowing waters and an eternal flame. Humanity and sacrifice were pulled out from the central features of the memorial and set aside in a special sight for contemplation. The beheaded columns were replaced by soaring triumphal arches, with the bases inscribed with the names of battle sites. The geographic, global nature of the victory—not the sacrifice and loss required by the great victory—was to become the memorial's center.

Herman Herrington, representing the American Legion, was the first to speak. He said that, although he had supported the idea of a memorial, he had not "really had any warm feelings" for the first design. However, he thoroughly embraced the new design; he felt "it had real power." And like virtually everyone supporting the design, he urged quick approval for the sake of the rapidly dying veterans. Also embracing the new design, David Childs observed, "The various elements, classical in feeling and scale, fit the space and defined it without adding architecture to this very sensitive spot on the Mall."

Those opposed to the memorial in this meeting were all actually opposing the site. Nearly all the speakers addressed the problem of the memorial at the Rainbow Pool site. Their concerns about the design related to its impact on the Mall. But, despite these complaints, the CFA thought the design was enough improved that they could approve the concept, and the process moved forward.

RAISING THE MONEY

As the design process moved along, a parallel campaign to raise the $197 million the memorial would cost was also underway.[44] After a slow start, former senator and World War II veteran Bob Dole and Federal Express CEO and Vietnam veteran Fred Smith agreed to take on the campaign. In 1998, when the fundraising seemed stalled, they turned to Tom Hanks, who had just starred in Steven Spielberg's enormously popular *Saving Private Ryan*. Hanks was eager to help. He made a series of TV and print ads in which he declared, "It's time to say thank you."

One of the print ads featured Hanks sitting on the edge of the Rainbow Pool. It read:

It's the right time. It's the right place.

Please help build the National World War II Memorial on the Mall in Washington, D.C.

Because, incredibly, there is still no national memorial to honor the achievements of this great generation.

It's time to say thank you.

Tom Hanks.

The ad made an argument for the memorial as the necessary payment of an obvious debt owed to the whole generation. And it made an argument for the location, not only on the Mall but at the Rainbow Pool. Hanks's face is cleverly aligned on the left of the image with the Lincoln Memorial on the right. His brow is wrinkled in consternation over the lack of a memorial for the greatest generation, and his eyes are searching, imploring Americans to pay this debt and build the memorial.

These ads, produced by the Ad Council, were extraordinarily successful. They generated $90 million in donated advertising and at least $50 million in cash donations the first year. Eventually, the campaign would raise more than the $197 million they needed, from corporations, veterans' groups, and individuals. And the money continues to pour in. Hanks's message struck a chord. Giving thanks resonated with much of the logic that drove the building of the memorial—that national recognition was necessary and long overdue.

At the same time, the use of Hanks made explicit something important about the terms of that recognition: he represented the domestication of the war and the revival of the romance of the common soldier in this moment. He was part of the turn in the 1980s and 1990s toward popular nationalist narratives about war, World War II and the Civil War in particular, that allowed Americans who had been alienated from war and soldiering by the Vietnam War to again embrace war and soldiers. *Saving Private Ryan* is a film about loss in war that begins and ends in an ABMC battlefield cemetery in France. The film focuses on the search for a soldier whose mother has already lost three sons, setting up the ultimate sacrifice: four sons from one family. The struggle to avoid this extreme loss then venerates all loss in deeply domesticated, nationalist terms. Family and nation are profoundly merged in this story. The war itself is domesticated, told as a story about Americans saving Americans for the sake of America. The film's central tension concerns the decision to send seven men to save one. This decision, made by the army chief of staff, is justified by a reading of the Bixby letter, a letter written by Lincoln in 1864:

Executive Mansion,
Washington, Nov. 21, 1864.

Dear Madam,

I have been shown in the files of the War Department a statement of the Adjutant General of Massachusetts that you are the mother of five sons who have died gloriously on the field of battle.

I feel how weak and fruitless must be any word of mine which should attempt to beguile you from the grief of a loss so overwhelming. But I cannot refrain from tendering you the consolation that may be found in the thanks of the Republic they died to save.

I pray that our Heavenly Father may assuage the anguish of your bereavement, and leave you only the cherished memory of the loved and lost, and the solemn pride that must be yours to have laid so costly a sacrifice upon the altar of freedom.

Yours, very sincerely and respectfully,

A. Lincoln[45]

This letter from Lincoln to a mother whom he believed to have lost five sons makes the sacrifice of the soldier tragic but also glorious. In the film, it links the World War II soldiers to the Civil War soldiers, and saving the mother from this outrageous grief becomes something the soldiers need to do for the nation. (It also links film audiences in the 1990s to these soldiers and their sacrifices.) In this way, all the loss and all the risk in the film is American.

This need to save the nation is underscored in the movie by the frame of Private Ryan's memories of the war. In the film, we see his family watching from a respectful distance as Ryan kneels before the grave of Hanks's character. Thus *Saving Private Ryan* is as much about the patriotism of the watching sons and daughters of veterans as it is about the patriotism of the veterans themselves, linking it to the project of saving patriotism in the present. At the end of the film, when Tom Hanks's dying character tells the saved private, "Earn this," Ryan understands he must live up to the legacy of the heroism of the war dead and the epic sacrifices of the soldiers, the families, and the nation. He is expected to make something of this sacrifice. He is asked to speak for the young dead soldiers. This legacy is then passed to his watching son—and to the film's audience. At the center of this legacy is the sacrifice of soldiers and a domesticated framing of this sacrifice. The Tom Hanks character dies and is loved for dying, not for France or Jews in camps or democracy around the world, but for a white American mother from the heartland. (It is an interesting detail of the film that Ryan's father is never mentioned; it is almost as if the inclusion of a father would have disrupted the domestication project enabled by the focus on the mother.) This domestication, this inward turn in thinking about the past recalled by the memorial, removes the war from its context in the world and makes it American.

In historian John Bodnar's reading of the film, one of its central tenants is that "the war was savage; the average American GI who fought it was not."[46] They were good guys, moral guys, diligently trudging through a terrible job. As Bodnar describes it, "The pain of the American combat soldier is revealed, but it is ultimately placed within a larger framework of patriotic valor." For Bodnar, this idea of the soldier—soaked in blood though he may be—as somehow removed from the savagery of war was part of a larger project of reclaiming war in the United States in this period: "Because the Spielberg film attempts to preserve the memory of patriotic sacrifice more than it desires to explore the causes of trauma and violence, however, it is more about restoring a romantic version of common-man heroism in an age of moral ambivalence than about ending the problem of devastating wars."[47] This is a crucial insight about the film and the cultural logic that shaped it and the war and the soldiers it remembers.

It is important to consider this reclamation project in the context of the memorial and the thinking that drove the memorial. The tension between a memorial about loss and sacrifice and a memorial about military triumph is potentially relieved by a new figuring of the soldier as a well-intentioned innocent (who earned all of this for all of us) somehow removed from the brutality of war. As Bodnar describes it, "In *Ryan* patriotic sacrifice as a frame of remembrance stands above both trauma and democracy."[48] Emphasizing patriotism shifts thinking about war away from trauma and allows a more robust celebration of war in the name of the soldier. Money came pouring in to Hanks as a stand-in for the idealized, beloved, moral GI lost to so many Americans after the Vietnam War. As the GI who was distanced from trauma and figured as having earned triumph, Hanks brought in millions of dollars. He offered a frame for thinking about war and soldiering in this moment that likely shaped the terms of remembrance at the memorial.[49]

THE THIRD DESIGN: TALLER, WIDER, AND BOLDER

Negotiating the tension between the figuring of the soldier and the figuring of the war continued to be pivotal in the design process as it moved forward. When St. Florian brought his third design to the CFA in May 1999, F. Haydn Williams described the new design as "stronger and more monumental." More monumental is certainly accurate. He stressed two key changes. First, the arches were "taller, wider, and bolder than before—which symbolized the victory won." Second, the western wall was transformed to become "the sacred precinct," composed of "an eternal light of freedom rising from a jagged, broken plane, symbolic of the depths of destruction of the war; a cenotaph honoring the dead; an enclosed wall at the western end carrying inscriptions; and two bronze wreaths, one honoring our allies and the other symbolizing the tragedy and the sadness of war."[50] All this reintroduced loss to the memorial. Sharply underscoring this, Williams called for inscriptions that would have "the greatest impact," and he closed by reading Archibald MacLeish's "The Young Dead Soldiers Do Not Speak."

The poem, which St. Florian had placed at the center of this new design, brought the war dead into the memorial conversation as they had not been since the initial design was rejected. It brought loss back into a conversation dominated by the specter of epic heroism, evoking something like a beheaded column:

The Young Dead Soldiers Do Not Speak

Nevertheless, they are heard in the still houses: who has not heard them?
They have a silence that speaks for them at night and when the clock
    counts.
They say, We were young. We have died. Remember us.
They say, We have done what we could but until it is finished it is not done.
They say, We have given our lives but until it is finished no one can know
    what our lives gave.
They say, Our deaths are not ours: they are yours: they will mean what you
    make them.
They say, Whether our lives and our deaths were for peace and a new hope
    or for nothing we cannot say: it is you who must say this.
They say, We leave you our deaths: give them their meaning: give them an
    end to the war and a true peace: give them a victory that ends the war
    and a peace afterwards: give them their meaning.
We were young, they say. We have died. Remember us.[51]

The poem makes an argument for a debt owed to the war dead; it moves beyond the recognition of their glorious victory and calls for more peace rather than more war. It introduces a new set of ideas about what it might mean to speak for the dead in the memorial being designed: "an end to the war and a true peace . . . and a peace afterwards."

Though the CFA approved the general direction in which the design was moving—they liked the larger arches and the added eagles—they did not seem moved by this shift toward loss; they had serious concerns about the sacred precinct. St. Florian contrasted the conquest expressed in the arches with the sobriety of a larger-than-life cenotaph, and hoped to bridge these conflicting emotions with a flame "celebrating the triumph of light over darkness that was the essence of the victory of the Allies in World War II." He described a flame set into "a warped, titled plane, laced within the curved center wall. The surface of the plane would be a dark stone, possibly basalt, broken and fissured, with a crater in the center; this would represent the darkness, the earth-shattering events of World War II. Out of the crater would come the flame of freedom."[52] Sculptor Ray Kaskey added that they wanted "this part of the memorial to depart radically from the conventional, classical elements seen elsewhere." The wall above the flame was to be called the "Wall of Freedom," and "would contain the most powerful words they could find that would speak to the essence of Word War II." But the CFA members expressed concern that "the element of death would overwhelm the concept of freedom." St. Florian replied that, although he "felt strongly that the symbol of sacrifice needed to be close to the symbol of freedom, he realized that their relationship needed further refinement." This was something of an understatement and is fascinating in terms of the tension between loss and triumph. For those at the CFA, the soldiers' sacrifices needed to be figured in terms of freedom rather than loss, not both. The final design that was approved a little more than a year later rethought these relationships in dramatic terms, with loss surrendering nearly entirely to military triumphalism, and democracy and freedom present only in a series of oblique inscriptions, leaving the "young dead soldiers who do not speak" still mute.

THE FINAL DESIGN: LOVING THE WAR WITH "A BUREAUCRAT'S IDEA OF CLASSICAL GRANDEUR"

An expanded, much revised design was finally approved in July 2000, and it is very close to the memorial that was dedicated on Memorial Day 2004. St. Florian's fourth design includes, as Michael Kimmelman of the *New York Times* describes it, "a giant sunken stone plaza and reflecting pool, 56 17-foot high pillars, two four-story triumphal arches, 4000 gold stars, monumental bronze eagles, bronze wreaths and fountains."[53] Two semicircles of steles, each representing a state or territory, surround a smaller, lowered Rainbow Pool. Two towering, forty-three-foot triumphal arches on the north-south axis are dedicated to the Atlantic and Pacific theaters of the war. The broad entryway is flanked by bas-reliefs in the style of the Public Works Administration depicting vignettes of home-front efforts, the attack on Pearl Harbor, med-

FIGURE 19. National World War II Memorial. (Photo by Hank Savage.)

ics in the field, women in the military, the Battle of the Bulge, and more. Everywhere there are inscriptions, dedications, and the articulation of surface. These are the elements approved by the CFA and the NCPC in 2000.

The style is essentially neoclassical or, as some have called it, modern classical or simplified classical; it is the familiar architectural currency in Washington, and it is quite different from what St. Florian initially proposed. The modern has vanished. The new style adopted by St. Florian was popular in Washington during the Second World War, for many years after, and in fact, for many years before. The style was frequently used by federal architects in the capital in the various periods of growth in the city. Both the style and the basic design elements (steles, triumphal arches, wreaths, eagles, and fountains) are familiar, and they speak in a clear, emphatic symbolic vocabulary. They look like official Washington, conveying seriousness of purpose and the promise that they are built to last.

But people who think about architectural style and the cultural meanings these styles convey saw more than echoes of Nazi architecture in St. Florian's final design. Albert Speer did, in fact, favor an architectural style that is strikingly similar to St. Florian's design. Though some noise was made about St. Florian's politics and his birthplace—Austria—and some concern was expressed in letters to the editor about the irony of remembering the war with the architectural vocabulary favored by Hitler, these concerns did not capture the public imagination and were secondary to continued concerns about the site. It is, however, worth standing on this comparison for a minute. Speer and Hitler were drawn to the authority expressed in classical and neoclassical forms. But, more than anything else, they embraced scale's potential to express power. For them, this was what architecture could do best—express power—and they went to absurd lengths to heighten these expressions with exaggerated scale. Their most famous collaboration was the Reich Chancellery, which housed Hitler's offices. The scale of the Chancellery was outrageous by any standard; to get to his offices, visitors had to walk the length of a vast hall twice as long as the Hall of Mirrors in the Palace of Versailles. Human scale was mocked for political purposes, and power was indelibly expressed.[54]

The advocates of St. Florian's revisions were not Nazis, however, nor were they advocates of Speer's designs. They did not want to evoke Speer on the Mall, but they did want to make an explicit expression of power. As they saw it, "America saved a world in flames" and earned a position of global dominance through the war—and therefore an outscaled memorial was in order. If the point were not to convey triumph and power, then a different scale might have been called for. The memorial boosters wanted to claim, with all the authority they could muster, the essential significance of the war, its place in U.S. history, and the consequent place of the United States in the world. All this framed U.S. nationalism in terms that militarized the Mall in ways that seemed unproblematic to the memorial's proponents. Opponents were made uneasy by this expression of imperial power in a site they cherished for its openness and its celebration of ideas rooted in law, but those who raised the comparison to Speer did not accurately name the source of their uneasiness. After the first design, the central elements of the memorial were its classical style and its scale. Despite the proposed beheaded columns and the cenotaph, what emerged from the multiple redesigns of the memorial was an expression of American triumph in global terms that draws on the authority of the neoclassical and on dramatic scale to make its points.

This is not to say that there was not, as we have seen, a constant tension in the design process over the problem of representing the war. Sculptor Ray Kaskey's introduction of the eagles in the May 1999 CFA design meeting reveals a little of how this process worked. He described the eagles as "among

FIGURE 20. National World War II Memorial. (Photo by Hank Savage.)

the oldest iconographic symbols": "Their most familiar aspect was that of power, but they also had a more spiritual, transcendental aspect, which was seen here in the position of the wings and in the way the eagles are supporting the laurel wreaths, making them look as though they were suspended and without weight."[55] He could have added, but apparently did not need to, that the eagle as an icon has a strong martial connection. "The eagle grouping," Kaskey continued, "also had an architectural aspect; it resembled a baldachino, with the eagles' wings forming a sort of cross vault resting on the four columns." He wanted the eagles to form a high altar of sorts, but they read more like an expression of power than a symbol of the transcendental. This is also true of another set of eagles in the design: "This time to express power . . . they would be cut out of the end of the stones of the arms, so that they gazed at each other diagonally across the pool and the plaza." In the memorial, this globalizes the reach of power, as the enormous eagles lock eyes over the plaza holding the Atlantic and the Pacific and all else in between in their gaze. This evokes, perhaps, the well-known 1898 political cartoon depicting U.S. expansion as a giant eagle sitting astride a globe with its wings spanning the distance from the Philippines to Puerto Rico and a caption reading, "Ten thousand miles from tip to tip."[56] This is a far cry from the truncated columns with which St. Florian began. In the May 1999 design, in a broad attempt to negotiate between loss and military triumph, the eagles and the arches shared the space with a dark, abstract eternal flame and an oversized cenotaph. In the July 2000 design, the eagles and arches remained, but the cenotaph and flame were gone, replaced by a wall of gold stars.

As St. Florian put it, "A new idea of how to honor the men and women who gave their lives during Word War II had emerged: it was the concept of attaching a field of gold stars to the Freedom Wall at the west end of the memorial plaza, based on the custom during the war of placing a gold star in the window of a home where a family member had lost his life. Each star would represent 100 American war dead."[57] The gold stars may evoke loss, but they are also tricky. In 1917, another industrious Ohioan—Robert Queissner, a U.S. Army captain with two sons serving in World War I—designed a flag to hang in his window. This first service flag had two blue stars to honor his two sons. Before the year was out, Congress recognized the flag, which was used widely to mark service and death; the death of a family member serving in the war was noted by replacing the blue star with a gold star.

By the time World War II began, the flags had been standardized and were ubiquitous.[58] It is easy to imagine the emotional impact for the World War II generation of a wall of stars, but for subsequent generations, especially given that the flags and the stars have mostly disappeared since the Vietnam War era, the effect is quite different. Everyone would understand a cenotaph, but the stars without context are merely gold, vaguely military ornamentation. They allow the relationship between the symbol of sacrifice and the symbol of freedom—which the board asked St. Florian to rethink—to be fudged. For the generation that least needs to be reminded of the sacrifices they made and the losses they suffered, the meaning of the stars is perfectly clear; for subsequent generations, the sacrifice and loss are rendered invisible. Perhaps some indication in the memorial of what the stars meant would have helped, and this was the initial idea. ABMC's Haydn Williams advocated in 2000 that a few lines from the MacLeish poem be carved above the wall of stars:

Our deaths are not ours; they are yours; they will mean what you make them.
We leave you our deaths. Give them their meaning.

This might have given meaning, focus, and real bite to the "sacred precinct."
An indication of the scale of the losses might also have been useful. The

4,048 gold stars are intended to represent 405,399 American military deaths. It is not clear how visitors might know that each star represents one hundred deaths, as it is not indicated anywhere. Indeed, when compared to the names listed on the nearby Vietnam Memorial, the 4,048 stars could have the effect of diminishing the scale of the loss a hundred times.

The eternal flame was still evolving in 2000. It had been intended for the sacred precinct but was moved and radically revised to make room for the gold stars. St. Florian proposed reimagining it as a sculptural element in the center of the Rainbow Pool; he explained to the commission that, although they were asking for final design approval, this element had not yet been designed and would, along with the inscriptions for the memorial, be presented to the CFA at a later date. These undesigned elements allowed the relationship between sacrifice and freedom to be left unresolved when the final design was approved. Both the inscriptions selected and a sculptural element in the Rainbow Pool would have a significant impact on how the memorial would represent the war, determining the relationship between sacrifice and triumph. However, at this stage, the CFA was contending with the growing chorus of protesters who were opposed to the site, and their concern seemed to be moving the process forward.

The July 2000 meeting was moved from the CFA offices to the main auditorium at the Department of the Interior to accommodate the crowd. Advisory board member Helen Fagin told the packed house that what the board most liked about this design, which they had approved unanimously, was its "celebratory aspect." Roughly half the gathered throng agreed with her, while the other half was far more concerned with protecting the Mall from the memorial than with the details of the design. Much of the six hours of testimony presented at this meeting had been heard by the CFA before—and it would be heard again. The National Capital Planning Commission's September 2000 meeting was similar, drawing 106 speakers. In both meetings, proponents thought the site was commensurate to the importance of the war and opponents thought it was disruptive of a sacred civic space. At the NCPC meeting, Representative Eleanor Holmes Norton made a particularly impassioned argument for the Mall as a crucial civic space for African Americans, whose history of using the Mall in the civil rights movement would be erased and threatened in the future by an enormous memorial at the Rainbow Pool.[59]

St. Florian reviewed some new design elements, but his presentation to the CFA had little impact on the conversation. Kent Cooper, architect of record for the Vietnam Veterans Memorial and the Korean War Memorial, was one of very few to speak to the design. He was not impressed. He described it as "totally lacking in conveying any understanding of what this mega-event was all about."[60] He did not "feel that the pylons, arches, and other architectural elements had any meaning, and he found the gold stars a 'pale and impersonal' shadow of the 57,000 names [sic] of the Vietnam Wall or the endless rows of white crosses at Arlington; he saw them as 'inappropriate theatrical glitter.'" He also asked how the commission could possibly approve the plan without seeing the design for such an essential element as the sculpture in the Rainbow Pool.

Brown responded matter-of-factly that "if triumphal arches, victory wreathes, and American eagles did not give a feeling of victory and celebration, he did not know what would,"[61] marking a crucial gap between Cooper's expectation in terms of meaning and Brown's confidence that eagles and arches would clearly express the required meaning. It is perhaps because of this reliance on the most obvious iconography that the memorial, in the end, looks like "a bureaucrat's idea of classical grandeur."[62] This observation, while not particularly complimentary, is also not immediately menacing. But it is worth remembering that bureaucracies are not benign, and that a bureaucrat's war memorial is one that efficiently expresses the position of the state.

THE LAWSUIT

For most of those who opposed the memorial at the CFA and NCPC meetings, details of the design were irrelevant. They did want *any* memorial at the Rainbow Pool. In October 2000, on the heels of CFA and NCPC approval of the design, Judith Feldman and the National Coalition to Save Our Mall, the World War II Veterans to Save the Mall, the Committee of 100 on the Federal City, and the D.C. Preservation League filed suit against the Department of the Interior, the National Park Service, the Commission of Fine Arts, and the National Capital Planning Commission. A last-ditch effort to "save the Mall," the lawsuit charged that the memorial was a violation of the National Environmental Policy Act, the National Historical Preservation Act, the Commemorative Works Act, and the Federal Advisory Committee Act. The National World War II Memorial website provides a useful outline of what was at stake in the lawsuit, including a ten-point response to the memorial's critics:

1. Critics claim that the memorial was approved behind closed doors by a small group of individuals without regard to the law. Not true!

2. Critics claim that the memorial will desecrate grounds made sacred by the civil rights movement and will greatly impede or prevent future public gatherings and marches on the Mall in the vicinity of Washington and Lincoln. Not true!

3. Critics claim the memorial will pave over 7.4 acres, destroying the open vistas and natural beauty that define the National Mall. Not true!

4. Critics claim the memorial will block the Mall's open space between the Washington Monument and Lincoln Memorial, inhibiting pedestrians from walking through this part of the Mall. Not true!

5. Critics claim that the memorial will destroy the historic Rainbow Pool. Not true!

6. Critics claim that the design echoes the Nazi Fascist architectural language of triumph and public spectacle. Not true!

7. Critics claim the WWII Memorial is being built on ground that is part of the Lincoln Memorial. Not true!

8. Critics repeatedly imply that a site in Constitution Gardens was the American Battle Monuments Commission's preferred site for the WWII Memorial. Not true!

9. Critics claim the memorial will create problems of arsenic contamination and flooding, and contaminated ground water will be pumped into the Tidal Basin and Potomac River. Not true!

10. Critics claim that the WWII Memorial will alter the meaning of our National Mall. Not true![63]

These complaints are clearly present in the editorials, articles, and the hundreds of pages of testimony before the commission. Although some of the points argued by the memorial supporters are secondary complaints or smack of legal maneuvering, this list makes clear that the controversy was principally about the site and only nominally about the design and meaning of the memorial.

Regardless of the strength or weakness of the legal claims, it threatened to drag on for years. In spring 2001, the case took several dramatic twists and turns, but they were all rendered irrelevant on Memorial Day. Fearing an untenable delay for the memorial, Alaska senator Tim Hutchison introduced S. 580, which banned "further administrative or judicial review" of the memorial design or the site.[64] Congressman Bob Stump introduced a matching bill. With lightning speed, Congress passed both. President George W.

Bush signed Public Law 107–11 on Memorial Day 2001.[65] This well-crafted law effectively ended all hope for the memorial's opponents and mandated cooperation with the ABMC. Construction soon began in earnest.

The concerns the lawsuit expressed about the Mall, however, are worth thinking about.[66] The memorial does change the landscape of the Mall. It does not, as some had feared, make the north-south axis impassible or prevent future protests on the Mall. But it does change how the Mall might be used; it interrupts the long stretch from Lincoln to Washington, significantly blocking the north-south axis. A large mass of people marching to or from the Lincoln Memorial would be slowed and rerouted into the woods.[67] But this is not the central problem of the memorial as it stands. Though the Mall is changed, it is not rendered impassable or useless as a site of public protest or celebration.

Thinking too literally about the Mall—not engaging it as a symbolic landscape—misses the point. The last counterclaim, that the memorial does not alter the meaning of the National Mall, is hardly tenable. Of course the Mall is altered: that is why the memorial was built. With the Vietnam Veterans Memorial and without the National World War II Memorial, the National Mall imagines a very different nation. The language about Fascist architecture may be seen as a stand-in for the argument about how the meaning has been changed. The commission denies the charge that the "design echoes the Nazi Fascist architectural language of triumph and public spectacle," but it does not (and could not) deny that the memorial is intended to be triumphal and a public spectacle.

The impact of the lawsuit was felt immediately in the decision to begin construction. But the lawsuit's impact on the design is less easy to discern. In May 2001, when Public Law 107–11 was passed, many critical design decisions—the inscriptions, for instance—had not been made. Was debate limited by the mandate to proceed? It is hard to know, but the conversations about these elements were certainly not long, drawn-out debates.

THE INSCRIPTIONS

The CFA discussed the inscriptions in 2002, 2003, and 2004. The two most contested inscriptions were the one for the memorial's entrance, which would explain the project, and the one for the wall of stars, which would speak to loss and sacrifice. The first tried to convey, in the most simple and blunt terms, why the memorial was there. It described the war as the most significant event of the twentieth century, and set the project in the context of memorials to the great events of the eighteenth and nineteenth centuries—as represented by Washington and Lincoln. The asymmetry of this comparison—two men and a war—although never mentioned, created some awkward attempts to properly write the prose. In 2002, hoping to simplify the inscription and perhaps remove the names Washington and Lincoln, or drop the names of the centuries to avoid "an insult to the intelligence of visitors," the CFA turned down the initial language from the ABMC.[68] But, a year later, the ABMC pressed the CFA to reconsider and they acquiesced. The entrance to the memorial thus contains the original ABMC inscription: "Here in the presence of Washington and Lincoln, one the eighteenth century father and the other the nineteenth century preserver of our nation, we honor those twentieth century Americans who took up the struggle during the Second World War and made the sacrifices to perpetuate the gift our forefathers entrusted to us: a nation conceived in liberty."

Thrilled by this language, Nicolaus Mills ends his exhaustive accounting of the memorial process, *Their Last Battle*:

> By its very presence the NWWIIM also changes the way in which America's 20th century wars are viewed on the Mall. In its location on the center of the Mall, rather than off to the side, the NWWIIM upstages both the Vietnam Veterans Memorial and the Korean War Veterans Memorial. The tragedy and hubris that Maya Lin's Vietnam Veterans Memorial speaks to with its somber black granite walls are not nullified by this placement, but what the decision to put the NWWIIM on a direct line between the Lincoln Memorial and Washington Monument does is challenge the idea, which ever since the 1960s has gained wide acceptance in political and academic circles, that the Vietnam War represents the culmination of modern American history. In the Mall's visual continuity it is WWII that is now officially linked to the Revolutionary War and the Civil War, and by extension it is the classicism of the NWWIIM's design, not the stark modernism of Maya Lin's VVM, that is put forward as the architectural language most suited to expressing the values that lie at the root of American life.[69]

Mills accurately describes the intent of the memorial's supporters. He gets it just right, and his articulation of this intent reveals it as a complicated proposition. This inscription revises the past in ways that make General Stilwell look like a stickler for historical detail. It *reorders historical chronology,* putting World War II emphatically after the Vietnam War. How is the Vietnam War, which was fought after World War II, not a culmination of "modern

American history"? It is not politicians or academics, as Mills would have it, who established this chronology, but the march of time. This logic makes the Second World War the culmination of a history lasting fifty years after the war ended. The contortionism required by this thinking is stunning, reflecting the depth of the desire to rewrite the brutal realities and moral ambiguities of the Vietnam War–era United States in terms of the relative moral purity of the Second World War. We cannot will ourselves to be the people who fought World War II rather than the Vietnam War; instead, we are the people who fought World War II, then fought the Korean War, then fought the Vietnam War, and are now fighting wars in Iraq and Afghanistan; no inscriptions in stone on the Mall, no matter how emphatic, can change this.

The CFA followed the ABMC's wishes on the most crucial inscription— the one for the gold stars. From their inception, the stars had been linked to the MacLeish poem. When the November 2002 meeting began, discussion of this quotation was bracketed off, with the promise that the question of how to use the MacLeish poem would be taken up at a later date. At the end of the meeting, there was a short conversation about whether to use a longer or a shorter quotation. General P. X. Kelley, then ABMC chairman, concluded this conversation by saying that something even shorter would be better. He suggested, "Uncommon valor was a common virtue."[70] This is a radical departure from "Our deaths are not ours, they are yours," a quotation that had the potential to transform the memorial.

In April 2003, one month before the start of the Iraq War, when thirty-five of the state pillars were near completion and construction of the arches was well underway, P. X. Kelley and Barry Owenby from the ABMC informed the CFA that a new inscription had been selected for the field of stars. With no mention of MacLeish, Owenby told the commission that the inscription would read, "Here we mark the price of freedom."[71] Several CFA members described the change as "regrettable." To some, this new inscription seemed "too abrupt and literal," though others "thought the Field of Stars was a stark reminder of the sacrifices made during the war, of the price to be paid, and the new inscription expressed that well." A suggestion was made that the poem could be used in Park Service brochures. and the CFA voted to approve the inscription. After more that sixteen years of debate and discussion about the memorial, this dramatic change to a crucial aspect of the design was made remarkably quickly and with little discussion; the whole exchange occupies less that three paragraphs in the CFA minutes. Yet it had profound consequences for the memorial.

It seems unlikely that the significance of this decision would have eluded the CFA, but the usually insistently detail-oriented commission moved very quickly on this vital question. Perhaps the dissenting members of the CFA felt powerless to challenge the ABMC. Perhaps the death of J. Carter Brown in 2002 had diminished the commission's authority. Perhaps the 9/11 attack, the war in Afghanistan, and the weeks-old war in Iraq had brought a new urgency to the project of defining the nation with World War II triumphalism rather than an accounting for loss. Whatever the reason, in one fell swoop, the stars, the sacred precinct, and the memorial as a whole were rewritten. The last trace of the beheaded columns and the acknowledgment of loss for future generations were gone.

"A COMPLETE ARCHITECTURAL RECOGNITION OF THE WAR"

Much of the lawsuit had to do with concerns about disrupting tradition on the Mall. One tradition, however, did not come up. The practice of leaving objects at public memorials began on the Mall at the Vietnam Veterans Memorial, even as it was being constructed in 1982. Before this, Americans did not bring objects to public memorials. The practice has become ubiquitous, defining public grief and the shaping of public memory for the last twenty years. It was born out of a confluence of circumstances: the unsettled social position of the veterans and the war dead after the Vietnam War; the deliberately "unfinished" quality of Maya Lin's memorial design; the impulse to heal, with which the memorial was conceived; and funerary traditions of the communities from which those who died in the war came. The National Parks Service and the American Battle Monuments Commission decided well in advance of the World War II memorial's dedication to actively discourage leaving objects at the memorial and to not collect any objects that were left. Visitors who bring items to leave at the memorial get a polite, well-scripted NPS lecture about the importance of bringing objects to their local historical society or Veterans of Foreign Wars halls.

Bob Carotka, National Park Service superintendent of the Office for the National Mall and Memorial Parks, argues that the memorial is a "complete architectural recognition of the war" and therefore does not need objects to add to, clutter, or complicate its story about the war.[72] This language and its connection to the objects is fascinating, maybe the final words in the loss/

FIGURE 21. National World War II Memorial. (Photo by Hank Savage.)

triumph negotiations. The implication is that personal grief in connection with the memorial is irrelevant. In Carotka's words, "We didn't allow it to take place." According to Carotka, the World War II Memorial is "not a healing memorial."[73] Still, letters, poems, photographs, and medals have been left there.[74] These tokens betray an impulse to make an intimate connection to the memorial or the memory of the war, but the advocates for the memorial didn't want grief or loss.

WHAT HAPPENS TO THE SOLDIERS?

There is an edge to the descriptions of the National World War II Memorial as a "bureaucrat's idea of grandeur" and a "complete architectural recognition of the war." To insist that the memorial, and therefore the nation of heroes it imagines, are complete and unalterable expresses anxiety about possible threats to that memory and a strong will to protect it.

In concluding his book on the memorial, Nicolaus Mills describes it as an "act of self-preservation." This is brilliant but perhaps not as he intended

FIGURE 22. National World War II Memorial. (Photo by Hank Savage.)

it. He writes, "For an America that in the wake of the September 11 attacks has felt threatened to a degree unknown in this country since the bombing of Pearl Harbor, such homage is more than just a final tribute to a parting generation . . . . [I]t is also an act of self-preservation, a way of reminding ourselves of our ability as a nation to come together in a crisis."[75] This conclusion is odd, because the memorial was proposed, funded, planned, designed, and almost entirely redesigned long before the attacks of 9/11. But Mills is right: it is a response to a threat.

Sounding as if he were trying to personify Gary Gerstle's observations about liberals in the 1990s using the citizen soldier of World War II to recover from the problems the Vietnam War presented to their patriotism and their thinking about war, Mills writes:

> As someone who was a teenager in the 1950s, I found the 1960s a period of welcome change. I was part of the civil rights movement in Mississippi one summer. Later I worked in California as an organizer for the United Farm Workers, and like virtually everyone my age I knew, I took part in teach-ins and anti-war marches while the Vietnam War was going on. But then, as now, I viewed the political positions I took in the sixties and seventies as extensions

of an argument that said that from Mississippi to Vietnam we were violating what we stood for as a nation. I was not skeptical about the values I was defending or the history behind them.

In my judgment these same values go to the core of our involvement in World War II. While too young to have a vivid memory of that war, I have a vivid memory of the men who fought it. They included two uncles, one of our next-door neighbors, and the headmaster of my boarding school. There was in my mind nothing inconsistent about opposing the Vietnam War and believing World War II was our "good war." Nowadays, it seems to me a sign of how estranged from ordinary life many who regard themselves as liberals or progressives have become when they cannot imagine a National World War II Memorial that speaks to what is best about us as a nation.[76]

This is a moving and worthy defense of the World War II veterans and the war they fought, but it does not make an argument about how *this* memorial serves them or Mills's aspirations for them. Valuing the service of soldiers does not require rewriting the national monumental core in terms that glorify war.

Being critical of the memorial is not the same as being critical of the GIs or devaluing their service, just as questioning the decision to drop the atomic bomb is not that same as claiming the entire war was a murderous, amoral project. But the difficulties in reconciling these two positions speak to the depth of the problem of the position of the soldier in the United States. In the end, the drive to build the memorial demonstrates a willingness to sacrifice soldiers for the sake of a rebirth of popular militarism—militarism that asks Americans to "support our troops" under any and all circumstances. The memorial is a triumph of this logic, and this is tragic.

Before the memorial was built, architectural critic Herbert Muschamp's assessment of the plans was that they promised to produce a "shrine to sentiment" and a memorial that "does not dare to know." But this isn't quite right. This memorial is a shrine to sentiment, but it *does* dare to know. It dares to rewrite the past in bold terms—as a pure, heroic, simple, righteous past, which justifies the nation in the present and glorifies spending the bodies of soldiers for the state at the turn of the century.

Exhausted by the controversies and design revisions, St. Florian cut to the chase with an interviewer: "The most important obligation of the memorial is to remind future generations of what the World War generation did, namely, to go to war and save the world. So that future generations feel compelled to do likewise. And that is easy to say, but very difficult to do."[77] Future

sacrifice is what the memorial is about. But why assume that future generations would not try to save the world? St. Florian is certainly right about the
difficulty of the task he describes. How do you compel generations that need
prompting to fight? And, further, how do you compel generations to fight to
save the world rather than to fight because war is glorious? How do you compel future generations by refiguring soldiers rather than refiguring war? St.
Florian tried again and again to complicate the soldier and the war, but the
ABMC, and at times the CFA and NCPC, pushed for a blunter instrument,
a blunter representation of the war and its soldiers than St. Florian seemed to
want. The sacrifice of soldiers was to be celebrated, not mourned.

A critical reading of this narrative might sound dismissive of the sacrifices
made in the war or the importance of winning the war. But this is not my
point at all. The sacrificing soldier is used here as a trope in a recovery project, a means of getting at a larger rewriting of the past in the United States
to defend a particular kind of nationalism and encourage future service to
this nation. The problem is not in celebrating sacrifice, but in sacrificing the
sacrificing soldier to build a militarized, post–Vietnam War, all-volunteer-
forces nationalism that enables Americans to embrace war and warriors from
a previous era. St. Florian's broken columns abstracted the figure of the soldier, but this was not the war or the soldier the memorializers wanted to
remember; they wanted unambiguous glory on a global scale in domestic
terms. They got it.

In the end, the Mall is rewritten, and power is expressed in these new
terms. The sacrificing soldier is used to ensure future sacrifice. Ultimately,
the memorial turns triumph to tragedy. Death, even in war, is not necessarily
tragic. Spending bodies manipulated to see war as glorious, however, is tragic
for the cannon fodder and for the nation.

Epilogue

THIS STORY STARTS with Archibald MacLeish's poem "The Young Dead Soldiers Do Not Speak" to evoke the enormous responsibility owed by the living to the war dead. When MacLeish writes, "We give you our deaths, give them their meaning," he calls for a memory of war that not only honors the sacrifices soldiers make for the nation but repays the soldier with a meaning made. The story ends with a rejection of MacLeish's poem by the advocates for the National World War II Memorial because it is at odds with the celebratory spirit of the memorial they wanted to build. They replaced the young dead soldiers with the potentially evocative but certainly oblique phrase, "Here We Mark the Price of Freedom." They chose a platitude that approaches sacrifice without significantly engaging with loss. They chose a memory that makes war deaths palatable rather than palpable. This had become, in fact, the reason to build the memorial: to frame war as heroic, not tragic, for the millions of school groups and families who stand before the memorials year after year after year.

The war memorial boom on the National Mall was largely initiated by veterans of all kinds seeking acknowledgment for their service in a moment of renewed interest in war. In the end, the federal agencies charged with building and overseeing these memorial projects were more interested in selling soldiering and war in new ways than in acknowledging loss. They were interested in recovering the heroic status of the soldier and the linked possibility of wars worth waging, and they have been mostly successful. The triumphal arches and oversized soldiers on the Mall are fully capable of inspiring happy surges of patriotic feeling.

This book emphasizes the process of producing these memorials by following the public debates and controversies that shaped them. This focus allows us to see not only a refiguring of U.S. nationalism in the return of the revered social position of the soldier, but also what is at stake in these representations of soldiers: ideas about what it means to be a soldier, ideas about it means to wage a war, and linked ideas about boundaries of national inclusion.

Witnessing the steady emphasis on the soldier in each of these memorial conversations reveals the ways in which the soldier has become so intensely foregrounded that he (or, with enormous effort, she) often begins to obscure the story of the work that American soldiers have done in the world. What does it mean that the emphasis in these memorials is on the soldiers to such an extent that the soldiers' service comes to trump the wars themselves? This framing enables simultaneous attention to soldiers and avoidance of the details of war.

Witnessing the memorial process also allows us to see other uses to which the soldier, as an abstract figure of remembrance, has been put. The soldier has been inscribed in the national landscape as heroic, but the terms of this heroism are not simple. In response to the revived status of the solider, a multiplicity of actors have tried to put diverse soldiering experiences into memorial form in order to represent the soldier, and therefore the nation, as not always white and male; the soldier has been used in a series of fundamental struggles over national definition. The success of these efforts is mixed at best; other actors have fought with remarkable tenacity to hold onto the figuring of the soldier, and the nation, as white and male.

Further, these memorials all celebrate wars fought *before* the Vietnam War, and yet they are all quite explicitly responses to the Vietnam Veterans Memorial. But mobilizing memories of "good war" nostalgia cannot "unwage" the Vietnam War. Reconstructing support for soldiers in the present with nostalgia about soldiers and wars from previous eras separates the wars from the warriors and avoids difficult questions about soldiering and war *now;* it also allows for a linked return to thinking about the nation in ways that quietly shift attention back onto the white male soldier and away from everyone else.

Finally, the new war memorials were initiated by veterans who wanted to honor sacrificing soldiers, and yet they give the phrase *sacrificing soldiers* a painful double meaning. In one sense, *sacrifice* modifies *soldiers.* These are soldiers who sacrifice—soldiers understood in terms of what they give and, therefore, what they are owed. In another reading, *sacrificing* is a verb and the soldier is the object: (we) sacrifice soldiers. The sacrifice made by the soldier is celebrated, and what the soldier did (or is doing) in the world is obscured by that celebration. This renders invisible the always brutal details of war, allowing a horror-free commemoration of war. In so doing, we enable the sacrifice of future soldiers in wars to come. Thus we allow still more soldiers to be sacrificed, whether they are waging a war worth fighting or not.

NOTES

INTRODUCTION

1. See Nelson, "Martial Lyrics," 2004.

2. A modest memorial to men from the District of Columbia who served in World War I was dedicated on the Mall in 1931.

3. The citizen soldier was not unimportant in the Revolutionary War. Marcus Cunfliffe's still valuable *Soldiers and Citizens* provides a careful narrative of the complicated emergence of both a national military from state militias and the nascent citizen soldier.

4. Faust, *This Republic of Suffering*, p. 101.

5. Soldiers were occasionally buried in marked graves before Gettysburg; what was new there was the practice of burying all the soldiers. See my first book, *Carried to the Wall*.

6. Abraham Lincoln, Gettysburg Address.

7. Laqueur, "Among the Graves," p. 6.

8. Historian Gary Gerstle observes that "most liberals severed their historical connection to war in the 1960s and 1970s when they opposed U.S. involvement in Vietnam." Gerstle sees this position begin to change, however, in the 1990s, when many liberals were drawn to the period's numerous histories and films that encouraged embrace of a soldier-centered, liberal version of war. He contends that audiences embraced the celebration of the individual soldier in World War II and the Civil War as a way to overcome the problems of war and soldiering raised by the Vietnam War. Gerstle, "In the Shadow of Vietnam," p. 128.

9. As Goeff Eley and Ronald Suny write, "Most fundamentally of all, we may mention the attempt to manufacture and manipulate a particular view of the past, invariably as a myth of origins which is meant to establish and legitimate the claim to cultural autonomy." Eley and Suny, "From the Moment of Social History to the Work of Cultural Production," in *Becoming National,* p. 8.

10. Olick, *States of Memory,* p. 3.

11. Ibid., p. 1.

12. Ernest Renan, "What Is a Nation?," in *Becoming National,* ed. Eley and Suny, p. 52.

13. Ibid., p. 45.

14. Anderson, *Imagined Communities,* p. 7.

15. Hobsbawn, *The Invention of Tradition,* p. 1.

16. Anne McClintock, "No Longer a Future Heaven," in *Becoming National,* ed. Eley and Suny, p. 271.

17. Etienne Balibar and Prasenjit Duara are also useful on this point. Balibar is particularly interested in race and nationalism. His essay, "Racism and Nationalism," in *Race, Nation, Class,* ed. Balibar and Wallerstein, begins with a very useful warning against overdetermined models for thinking about either race or nation. In "On Theories of Nationalism for India and China," in *In the Footsteps of Xuanzang,* ed. Tan Chung, Duara pointedly reminds his readers that the value of theories of nationalism is diminished if they are used to obscure prenational pasts: "The scholarly critique can be equally unhelpful when it denies any historical connection between the modern nation and the historical society from whence it emerges."

18. As Lauren Berlant puts it, being national is linked to being "traumatized by some aspect of life in the United States." See *The Queen of America Goes to Washington City,* p. 1.

19. See, for example, Jay Winter's introduction to *Remembering War* and the preface to Jenny Edkins's *Trauma and the Memory of Politics.*

20. Winter, *Remembering War,* p. 1. Winter goes so far as to suggest that memory is eclipsing interest in race, gender, and social class. This seems to me to be an overstatement.

21. See Bal, Spitzer, and Crewe, eds., *Acts of Memory;* and Landsberg, *Prosthetic Memory,* on post- and prosthetic memory, respectively.

22. See Yerushalmi, *Jewish History and Jewish Memory;* Nora, "Between Memory and History"; Halbwach, *On Collective Memory;* and the work of James Young for a start on memory and history. Kerwin Klein, Thomas Lacquer, James Young, Ed Linenthal, Jenny Edkins, Andreas Hussien, and others have written on memory and trauma.

23. Blight, *Beyond the Battlefield,* p. 2.

24. Edkins, *Trauma and the Memory of Politics,* p. xv.

25. Winter, *Remembering War,* p. 3.

26. Savage, *Standing Soldiers, Kneeling Slaves,* p. 162.

27. Linenthal, *The Unfinished Bombing,* p. 4.

28. Ibid.

29. Savage, *Standing Soldiers, Kneeling Slaves,* p. 143.

30. O'Leary, *To Die For,* p. 135.

31. Blight, *Beyond the Battlefield,* p. 125.

32. For a good history of redlining, see Hillier, "Redlining and the Homeowners' Loan Corporation," pp. 394–420. Also see Segrue, *The Origins of the Urban Crisis,* for a broader framing of race and cities in the postwar period.

33. Bailey, "The Army in the Marketplace," p. 3.

34. Ibid, p. 19.

35. Young, "Memory and Counter-Memory," p. 2.

36. Savage, "History, Memory, and Monuments," p. 1.

37. Susan Sontag's rejection of collective memory in favor of "collective instruction," in *Regarding Others in Pain,* is also suggestive here.

38. Joanna Bourke, "Remembering War," p. 484.

39. In the context of thinking about memory and social power, it is worth noting that *witnessing* is a loaded term in a couple of ways. Witnessing the Holocaust has been a key strategy for honoring the memory of the murdered and staving off future horror. And witnessing in African American churches is linked to divine intervention and social affirmation; the phrase "Can I get a witness?" speaks in sacred and secular traditions to a shared sense of the verification of experience that might otherwise go unspoken. Both these uses give the language of "witnessing" a high-stakes charge, as this book turns to the details of the memorial processes to study exactly how the transformation of the Mall, the solider, and the nation happened.

40. Each chapter relies on a variety of primary sources: material from the relevant presidential libraries, the archives of the National Capital Planning Commission, the archives of the National Park Service, the archives of the American Battle Monuments Commission, and the Commission of Fine Arts archives. The CFA archives contain minutes of nearly all the crucial public meetings in which these memorials were discussed and fought over by the parties working to see them built. These minutes are essential to this book and its method; they are an irreplaceable source for witnessing the memorial process.

41. Blight, *Beyond the Battlefield,* p. 3.

42. What follows is, of necessity, a quite brief history of memorial forms on the National Mall. For a book-length account, please see Kirk Savage's *Monument Wars.* Savage focuses on the Mall but argues that the late nineteenth- and twentieth-century proliferation of figural sculpture across the city is an important part of the story of the Mall. Rather than finding cohesion in the meanings made in the memorial landscape of Washington, Savage finds a sprawling, unplanned-despite-the-best-efforts-of-planners, constantly changing array of ideas expressed at the memorial core.

43. Pamela Scott, "'This Vast Empire': The Iconography of the Mall, 1791–1991," in *The Mall in Washington, 1791–1991,* ed. Longstreth, p. 40. L'Enfant was building on Jefferson's "public walks."

44. Ibid., p. 46.

45. Of course, the War of 1812 resulted in extensive damage to both the White House and the Capitol, which required considerable federal and civic resources to repair. Also in 1812 Congress allowed the president to lease parcels on the Mall to individuals who would improve them, but the results were scattershot at best. Ibid.

46. Frederick L. Hary, quoted in Savage, "The Self-Made Monument," p. 233. For details of the fifty-year struggle to get the memorial built, this is an excellent source.

47. Now, too, the size of the monument seems to speak to the task attempted.

Seen as an ineffective attempt to stir nationalist sentiment that might stave off civil war, the monument is perhaps more of a Civil War memorial than the Lincoln Memorial. This can be read in the coloration of the monumental stone. Construction halted in 1854 did not begin again until after the war, and the postwar stone is darker than the original stone. Seen this way, the Washington Monument acts both as a memorial to the desire to stave off war and as a stained, looming reminder of its own failure.

48. The work of the early Smithsonian scientists and scholars was a complicated mix of the promise of developing positivist science and the anthropological project of collecting of artifacts in the wake of the Indian wars. Thus the Mall became a site of pilgrimage for the receipt of particular kinds of knowledge in the service of particular forms of nationalism in particular moments.

49. Thomas Hines and many others have written about the impact of the fair on the City Beautiful Movement—both practically and ideologically. But the Mall as linked to the White City has not had much purchase in American Studies.

50. The American Battle Monuments Commission was also established by the Congress in 1923, as an agency of the executive branch of the federal government to honor the service, achievements and sacrifice of United States Armed Forces. Established in response to the problem of so many bodies lost overseas, its mission involves "designing, constructing, operating and maintaining permanent American cemeteries in foreign countries; establishing and maintaining U.S. military memorials, monuments and markers where American armed forces have served overseas since April 6, 1917 and within the United States when directed by public law; controlling the design and construction of permanent U.S. military monuments and markers by other U.S. citizens and organizations, both public and private, and encouraging their maintenance." "About Us," American Battle Monuments Commission website, www.abmc.gov. The ABMC was not called on often in this latter capacity for fifty years. When it was the language of "controlling the design" and the federalization of the memorial processes, the commission's involvement became vital.

51. The creation of the commission broke a stalemate in the memorial process, and the CFA stood by the McMillan plan, enabling its realization. Thomas, *The Lincoln Memorial and American Life,* p. xxvii.

52. This book focuses on debates and tensions between the CFA and military agencies and veterans groups in the post-1982 period. It is worth noting that these tensions are not new to this period. See Savage, *Monument Wars,* for some of the earlier tensions around the CFA.

53. This is a detail of the history that I love, having argued that after World War II, the nation became a memorial to itself, emphasizing infrastructure rather than symbolic stone. Photographs of the postwar memorial core of the Mall packed with poorly constructed military buildings seemed quite fitting.

54. The Signers Memorial is a small series of knee-high granite blocks with inscriptions. It is consistent with the idea of the federal being remembered in terms of men of ideas about the nation rather than soldiers. Its humility is not consistent with the architecture of the Mall.

55. It is important to note that public protest in the capital city was not new. Continental Army veterans marched on Philadelphia in 1783. Coxey's Army marched on the U.S. Capitol in 1894, and the Woman Suffrage Procession did the same in 1913. In 1932 the Bonus Army camped out on the edges of the Mall and marched on the U.S. Capitol. For more on this, see Lucy Barber's *Marching on Washington*. What began with Marian Anderson was a shift toward Lincoln and the monumental core of the Mall as a site for protest and for evoking the moral authority of Lincoln and his vision of the democratic nation.

56. In a film released a few months later, Frank Capra's *Mr. Smith Goes to Washington,* Jimmy Stewart fairly swoons in the presence of Lincoln at the memorial. Stewart's admiration for Lincoln is explicitly linked to race and the end of slavery when he stares with teary eyes as a young boy reads the Gettysburg Address off the memorial's wall and an African American man steps into the frame bathed in a halo of light as the child reads the word *freedom*.

57. Quoted in Sandage, "A Marble House Divided," p. 136.

58. Ibid.

59. Ibid, p. 138.

60. King's Poor People's March was a more complicated, less shining example of the strategic use of the Mall that has continued into the present. The Million Man March is another important event to include in this trajectory.

61. King, of course, would eventually get his own memorial barely off the Mall in West Potomac Park. Dedicated in fall 2011, the King Memorial is fascinating—not in the least because the enormous figure of King stands with his back to the Lincoln Memorial, staring, with firmly crossed arms, across the Tidal Pool to the lonely Jefferson Monument.

62. Paul Monette, quoted by Charles E. Morris III, "My Old Kentucky Homo: Lincoln and the Politics of Queer Public Memory," in *Framing Public Memory,* ed. Phillips.

63. See Kristin Hass, *Carried to the Wall;* and Marita Sturken, *Tangled Memories,* for detailed discussions of the Wall.

64. There is a local D.C. World War I memorial on the Mall that dates from 1931, but it is now well hidden by overgrown trees. A modest movement is now afoot to restore it and rededicate it as a national World War I memorial. The Navy Memorial was dedicated off the Mall on Pennsylvania Avenue in 1987. Its history goes back to the Kennedy administration, and it celebrates a branch of the Armed Services rather than either a war or the veterans of a war.

65. Interview with Jan Scruggs, May 2007.

66. In architectural historian Dell Upton's chronology of the history of war memorials in the United States, Maya Lin's Wall is the memorial that set off a late-century memorial-building boom after a long period of dormancy. Dell Upton, "Memorials to the Second Civil War: Commemorating the Civil Rights Movement," paper given at the University of Michigan, January 2006.

CHAPTER I

1. Architect Kent Cooper, quoted in James Reston Jr., "The Monument Glut," *New York Times,* Sept. 10, 1995.

2. James Kerin's *The Korean War and American Memory* suggests that the body of Korean War films and literature make the term *forgotten war* paradoxical, but his readings of this film and fiction don't satisfactorily explore the insistence on the war's forgotten status and what it might mean.

3. See Leckie, *Conflict,* for a detailed history of the war.

4. Truman statement dated June 27, 1950, George M. Elsey Papers, Harry S. Truman Library and Museum.

5. Ibid. The precedent of going to war without Congress has turned out to be a dangerous one.

6. Von Eschen, *Satchmo Blows Up the World,* p. 7.

7. This is the number most commonly cited for U.S. deaths in the Korean War, but it includes all Korean War *era* military deaths: 36,576 in Korea and 17,670 in other U.S. military contexts. For a detailed accounting of Korean War deaths, see Tucker and Kim, *Encyclopedia of the Korean War.*

8. Rick Ruffin, "Keep DMZ a Place of Peace," *Korean Times,* Oct. 18, 2007.

9. Schwartz and Bayma, "Commemoration and the Politics of Recognition," p. 947.

10. Christina Klein, *Cold War Orientalism,* p. 9.

11. The number of UN dead—628, 833—is baffling. The number of U.S. deaths (54,246) and the number of South Korean deaths (273,127) combined are just over *half* the figure for the UN carved into the memorial. The significance of these numbers is in their relationship: the U.S. deaths account for 11 percent of the total deaths, but this is not the impression the rest of the memorial conveys. The figure comes from the Washington Headquarters Services of the Department of Defense.

12. *Memorials and Museums Master Plan,* 2001, National Capital Planning Commission files, p. 3.

13. Evans, "The All-Volunteer Army after Twenty Years," p. 40.

14. Quoted in ibid., p. 45.

15. Heidi Golding and Adebayo Adedeji, *The All-Volunteer Military: Issues and Performance* (Washington, DC: Congressional Budget Office, 2007), pp. 6, 15.

16. G. Holcomb, letter to the editor, *Washington Post and Times Herald,* June 15, 1955, p. 14.

17. Barry Schwartz quotes memorial designer Lecky as praising the statue's impressionistic style for leaving traces of race and ethnicity in the figures. I will return to this. Schwartz and Bayma, "Commemoration and the Politics of Recognition," p. 957.

18. Quoted by Albert Parisi, "Korean War Memories, but . . . ," *New York Times,* July 5, 1987, p. NJ1. Notice his language here; he says "freedom in a faraway land" rather than "freedom for a faraway land."

19. Ibid.

20. The source with the most information about Chayon Kim is the Korean War Project website, produced by Hal Baker, an activist Korean War veteran and advocate for the memorial. In fact, he sent the American Battle Monuments Commission the first donation for a Korean War Memorial in December 1984.

21. Testimony of John Kenny, president of the National Korean War Memorial, *Hearing before the Subcommittee on Public Lands, Reserved Water and Resources Conservation, Oct. 29, 1985,* 99th Cong., 1st sess., S.1223, S.J. 184, Washington: GPO, 1986.

22. If Kim's efforts had become the popular origin story of the KWVM, it would be possible to argue that the Mall has been more dramatically reshaped by two Asian American women than by anyone since Senator McMillan. But this is not the story of the KWVM that gets told.

23. Both the *Minneapolis Star Tribune* and the *Miami Herald* investigated the National Committee for the Korean War Memorial and concluded that they spent ninety-seven cents of every dollar raised through direct mail solicitations on administrative costs. Most of this money went into the pockets of committee members, and some of it financed Myron McKee's unsuccessful attempt to run for political office in Minnesota.

24. "Korean War Memorial Sponsors Know What They Don't Want," *Journal of the American Institute of Architects* 72, no. 1 (May 1983): 35.

25. Casey Nelson Blake, "Between Civics and Politics: The Modernist Moment in Federal Public Art," in *The Arts of Democracy,* p. 214.

26. Ibid.

27. E.G. Windchy, letter to the editor, *Washington Post,* Oct. 21, 1982, A18.

28. "Korean Memorial," *New York Times,* Oct. 31, 1985, B12.

29. Editorial, *Los Angeles Times,* Aug. 18, 1985, D2.

30. It is worth noting that there is no record of advocates for a World War II memorial lobbying visitors to the VVM dedication ceremonies. The cry for a World War II memorial would not be heard for a few more years, until after the Korean War Veterans Memorial, the Black Revolutionary War Patriots Memorial, and the Memorial for Women in Military Service for America were all approved by Congress. World War II veterans and their advocates were slower to jump on the memorial bandwagon. This is quite likely linked to the fact that they had not wanted memorials after the war and that they had not needed to negotiate the social position of the soldier or to establish the importance of remembering their war until the memorial frenzy on the Mall was well underway.

31. William Norris, "The Forming of the Korean War Veterans Association," *Graybeards* (March/April 2003): 27, www.kwva.org/graybeards/index.html.

32. Ibid.

33. *Korean War Memorial,* H.R. Res. 523, 97th Cong., 2d sess. (1982).

34. *Korean War Memorial,* H.R. Res. 236, 98th Cong., 1st sess. (1983). J. Carter Brown's response to the addition of "Allied Forces" was that "we see no objection from our standpoint to commemorating the Allied Forces along with our own American forces in this memorial, since it was a unique military action in which the

United Nations as whole was conducting operations." Brown to Augustus Hawkins, July 14, 1983, CFA files.

35. In the congressional record, as in virtually all records related to the memorial, the near absence of the words *North Korea, South Korea, communism, Cold War,* and *containment* is remarkable.

36. *Extension of Remarks, Korean War Veterans Memorial,* 99th Cong., 1st sess., *Congressional Record* 131, no. 68 (May 22, 1985).

37. The financial mismanagement of the earlier Korean memorial effort was also a factor here. In his testimony before the Committee on Energy and Natural Resources (Report, October 29, 1985), John Kenny, president of the National Korean War Memorial, Inc., suggested setting up a fund with the American Battle Monuments Commission to avoid further trouble.

38. See Scruggs and Swerdlow, *To Heal a Nation.*

39. Highsmith and Landphair, *Forgotten No More,* p. 51.

40. These veterans were graybeards because they did not feel compelled to come together as an organization until thirty years after the end of the war, when their beards were turning gray.

41. "As a Result of Questions Asked Last July 27th at Reunion," *Graybeards* (April 1991), www.kwva.org/graybeards/index.html.

42. The appointees were Edward R. Borcherdt, U.S. Marine Corps; Col. Fred V. Cherry, U.S. Air Force; John B. Curcio, U.S. Navy; Gen. Raymond G. Davis, U.S. Marine Corps; Thomas G. Dehne, Disabled American Veterans; Col. Conrad Hausman, U.S. Army; Col. Rosemary T. McCarthy, U.S. Army Nurse Corps; James D. McKevitt, U.S. Air Force; Carlos Rodriguez, Eastern Paralyzed Veterans Association; William F. McSweeny, U.S. Army; Gen. Richard Giles Stilwell, U.S. Army; and Col. William E. Weber, U.S. Army. More than one party to the process has mentioned to me a lack of respect demonstrated for Col. McCarthy in meetings.

43. The Stilwells were of patrician stock. The family first came to the United States in the 1600s, and the first General Stilwell had to call on presidential assistance to get himself into West Point. Barbara Tuchman's *Stilwell and the American Experience in China, 1911–1945* includes some interesting family history.

44. U.S. Commission of Fine Arts website, www.cfa.gov.

45. National Capital Planning Commission website, www.ncpc.gov.

46. *Commemorative Works Act,* Public Law 99–652 (Nov. 14, 1986).

47. "The Korean War Veterans Memorial National Design Competition," November 1988, CFA files, CFA minutes, 26/JUL/89–1.

48. Ibid.

49. The language of the call for designs for the Vietnam Veterans Memorial was also quite prescriptive, but the terms prescribed were quite distinct: "The Memorial Fund set four major criteria for the design: (1) that it be reflective and contemplative in character, (2) that it harmonize with its surroundings, especially the neighboring national memorials, (3) that it contain the names of all who died or remain missing, and (4) that it make no political statement about the war." Vietnam Veterans Memorial Fund website, www.vvmf.org.

50. "The Korean War Veterans Memorial National Design Competition," November 1988, CFA files, CFA minutes 26/JUL/89–1.

51. Ibid.

52. In a question and answer section of the document that anticipates questions that might come from competition entrants, a question about major battles fought during the war is answered with a list of the ten campaigns. Ibid.

53. Burns Lucas, Leon, and Lucas design statement, personal papers of Don Leon, p. 1.

54. V. Burns Lucas, D. A. Leon, J. P. Lucas, and E. Pennypacker Oberholtzen, Design statement of the Korean War Veterans Memorial (n.d.), State College: Pennsylvania State University. CFA files, CFA minutes 26/JUL/89–1.

55. The initial proposal for figures nine feet tall was eventually reduced to seven feet, but this was hardly the most dramatic change made to the proposed design.

56. Burns Lucas, quoted in "Korean War Memorial," *Washington Post,* June 15, 1989.

57. David Douglas Duncan, *This Is War!,* p. 23.

58. "Korean War Memorial," *Washington Post,* June 15, 1989.

59. Forgey, "War Memorial Revisions Decried," D11.

60. Lucas Burns quoted in the CFA files, CFA minutes 26/JUL/89–1. .

61. V. Burns Lucas, D. A. Leon, J. P. Lucas, and E. Pennypacker Oberholtzen, "Design Statement of the Korean War Veterans Memorial," State College: Pennsylvania State University. n.d., CFA files., CFA minutes 26/JUL/89–1. They also wanted them in granite. Frank Gaylord is still irate about this; he mentioned it repeatedly. For him, it represents the design team's failure to think through the details of how their design might be realized. Gaylord said it was an indication that they knew nothing about sculpting, because the kind of movement they wanted from these figures would not have been possible in granite. Frank Gaylord interview, April 10, 2007.

62. Inclusion in this context meant not only racial representation, but also representation of various branches of the military.

63. CFA documents contain no mention of race. Barry Schwartz indicates, without documentation, that it was Brown who argued the point. Don Leon says it was absolutely Brown. Don Leon interview, April 10, 2007.

64. Interview with Don Leon, April 10, 2007.

65. Kent Cooper memo, "Some Thoughts from the Designers," June 1, 1993, CFA files, CFA minutes 23/JUN/93–2.

66. Don Leon interview, April 10, 2007. Interviewing the parties involved in this memorial was a little like poking a stick into a beehive—everybody comes out stinging in all directions. Leon is still unhappy with Stilwell, Gaylord, and Cooper. He seems to have made peace with Brown. Gaylord talks about Cooper with venom and expresses anger and begrudging respect for Stilwell. His disdain for Brown could be cut with a knife.

67. Schwartz and Bayma, "Commemoration and the Politics of Recognition," p. 953.

68. Ibid.

69. See my *Carried to the Wall* for a more detailed reading of the figures.

70. See Fish, *The Last Firebase,* p. 14.

71. See Savage, *Standing Soldiers, Kneeling Slaves;* Piehler, *Remembering War the American Way;* Blight, *Beyond the Battlefield;* O'Leary, *To Die For;* and others.

72. See Welch, *Killing Custer;* and Kasson, *Buffalo Bill's Wild West,* for a start.

73. In my research, I found uneasiness about this but no one willing to address it explicitly. I will return to this problem with greater specificity in the context of the proposed memorial for black Revolutionary War veterans.

74. Don Leon interview, April 10, 2007.

75. See Linda Witt and Mary Jo Binker's *A Defense Weapon Known to Be of Value,* for more on this.

76. Barbara Gamarekian, "Architects Clash over Korean War Memorial," *New York Times,* Dec. 15, 1990, 17.

77. Forgey, "War Memorial Revisions Decried," D11.

78. Ibid.

79. Gamarekian, "Architects Clash over Korean WAR Memorial."

80. This impulse prefigures the relationship between the National World War II Memorial and the movie *Saving Private Ryan.* See chapter 5 for more on this.

81. Forgey, "War Memorial Revisions Decried."

82. Susan Chira, "American's Battle over How to Remember Its Forgotten War," *New York Times,* Nov. 18, 1990, E18.

83. This is, I think, comic understatement in the face of a larger-than-life live action battle scene but also a misreading of the KWVMAB; they didn't want their memorial to be anything like the Wall. CFA files, CFA minutes, 17/JAN/91.

84. Barbara Gamarekian, "Panel Turns Down Plan for Korean War Shrine," *New York Times,* Jan. 19, 1991, 20.

85. Quoted in Schwartz and Bayma, "Commemoration and the Politics of Recognition," p. 956.

86. William Lecky as quoted in Highsmith and Landphair, *Forgotten No More,* p. 74.

87. Gaylord is convinced that his idea for the ponchos saved the memorial. The special qualities of their movement allowed him to be both impressionistic and precise. Frank Gaylord interview, Apr. 10, 2007.

88. U.S. Army Corps of Engineers, Baltimore District, website, www.nab.usace .army.mil/projects/washingtonDC/Korean.html.

89. The map and chart are posted on the American Battle Monuments Commission website, "Korean War Veterans Memorial," www.abmc.gov/memorials /memorials/kr.php.

90. Lecky as quoted in Schwartz and Bayma, "Commemoration and the Politics of Recognition," p. 956.

91. Walter Benn Michaels, "Autobiographies of the Ex-White Men," in *The Futures of American Studies,* ed. Pease and Wiegman, pp. 233–34.

92. Frank Gaylord interview, April 10, 2007.

93. Cooper-Lecky memo dated July 10, 1992, CFA files, CFA minutes, 21/MAY/92–1.

94. Ad hoc committee memo, Nov. 15, 1994, CFA files, CFA minutes, 23/SEP/93 (italics in original).

95. Frank Gaylord interview, April 10, 2007.

96. Cooper memo, July 27, 1994, CFA files, CFA minutes, 23/SEP/93.

97. Ibid.

98. The limp wrist as a marker of homosexuality would have had a particularly sharp resonance for those thinking about soldiers in 1994. In 1993, Clinton's infamous "Don't Ask, Don't Tell" policy for homosexuality in the military was put in place—clearly defining the military as antigay but allowing the service of those willing to remain silent on the question of their sexuality.

99. Frank Gaylord interview, April 10, 2007.

100. Dean, *Imperial Brotherhood.*

101. Gaylord's trouble with the memorial did not end when the design was completed. In 2006 he sued the United States for copyright infringement over the use of a photograph of the memorial on a thirty-seven-cent stamp. He won the case in 2010 when the federal circuit court ruled in his favor.

102. Schwartz and Bayma, "Commemoration and the Politics of Recognition," p. 946.

103. Bill Clinton to Colonel Homes, Dec. 3, 1969, reproduced in "Bill Clinton's Draft Letter," *Frontline,* www.pbs.org/wgbh/pages/frontline/shows/clinton /etc/draftletter.html.

104. Ibid. For Clinton, as he defended this letter years later, a declaration of war and the implied participation of Congress in waging the war were crucial requirements for calling up a draft and part of the reason for his mixed feelings about a draft for the Korean "Police Action."

105. *Remarks at the Dedication Ceremony for the Korean War Veterans Memorial, Clinton, Bill,* 30 Weekly Comp. Pres. Doc. 1317 (July 31, 1995).

106. Quoted in Reston, "The Monument Glut," 48.

107. Ibid. It is important to note here that Cooper is talking about blind devotion in the context of a memorial trying inspire future service. Blind devotion once you are in the military chain of command is a practical necessity, but blind devotion in the context of putting your body into that chain of command is something entirely different. This is what Cooper and the memorial are speaking to.

108. Christina Klein, *Cold War Orientalism,* p. 9.

CHAPTER 2

1. Robin Shulman, "Sharpton's Ancestor Was Owned by Thurmond's," *Washington Post,* Feb. 26, 2007, A01.

2. Ibid.

3. Pascoe, *What Comes Naturally,* p. 2.

4. See Sollors, ed., *Interracialism.*

5. Maurice Barboza interview, Feb. 26, 2007. He describes thinking, "I guess I could do that," and undertaking a genealogical search.

6. His paternal grandfather came to the United States from the Cape Verde Islands. Ibid.

7. Maurice Barboza, address to Tri-Chapter Dinner, George Washington, Fairfax Resolves, and George Mason Chapters, Virginia Sons of the American Revolution Army-Navy Country Club of Arlington, Virginia, May 7, 2004, www.melungeons.com/articles/dec2004.htm.

8. Ibid.

9. Barboza interview, Feb. 26, 2007.

10. Barboza, address to Tri-Chapter Dinner.

11. Farmer was accepted on the basis of her relationship to William Hood, a white soldier in the Revolutionary War.

12. Ronald Kessler, "Black Unable to Join Local DAR," *Washington Post,* March 12, 1984, A1.

13. Ibid.

14. Maurice Barboza interview, Jan. 24, 2012. Barboza was full of heartfelt praise for Thompson.

15. Kessler, "Black Unable to Join Local DAR," A1.

16. Ibid.

17. Ibid.

18. "Become a Member," DAR National Society website, www.dar.org/natsociety/content.cfm?ID=145.

19. Kessler, "Black Unable to Join Local DAR." The DAR has maintained the requirement for legitimate descent; in 2010 the DAR still requires "documentation for each statement of birth, marriage, and death." "Become a Member," DAR National Society website, www.dar.org/natsociety/content.cfm?ID=145.

20. See Savage, *Standing Soldiers, Kneeling Slaves;* Piehler, *Remembering War the American Way;* Blight, *Beyond the Battlefield;* O'Leary, *To Die For;* Silber and Clinton, *Divided Houses,* and others.

21. Ronald Kessler, "Embattled Head of National DAR Pledges Action against Any Bias," *Washington Post,* Apr. 5, 1985, C3.

22. Ruth Marcus, "DAR Reprimands, Then Suspends Punishment of Two Members," *Washington Post,* Oct. 11, 1985, C1.

23. Ibid.

24. Not long after, the DAR adopted a new rule requiring members to give nine months' notice before filing a lawsuit against the organization. The nine months' wait was supposed to make those filing suit think long and hard about it and was described as being similar to waiting for a baby. Ruth Marcus, "DAR Imposes Delay on Filing Suits," *Washington Post,* Apr. 16, 1986, C3.

25. Kessler, "Embattled Head of National DAR Pledges Action against Any Bias."

26. Ibid.

27. Maurice Barboza interview, Feb. 26, 2007.

28. Testimony of Maurice Barboza before the National Capital Memorial Advisory Commission, June 27, 2006,, National Mall Liberty Fund D.C. website, www.libertyfunddc.org (accessed Feb. 2007) .

29. Sarah King to Joseph Hassett of Hogan and Hartson, May 4, 1984, National Mall Liberty Fund D.C. website, www.libertyfunddc.org (accessed Feb. 2007).

30. Ibid.

31. Repeated efforts to get access to information about African American membership over a period of several years have failed to yield results.

32. Adele Logan Alexander, "Daughters of Revolution and Children of Slavery," *Washington Post,* May 3, 1984, A21.

33. Maurice Barboza interview, Feb. 26, 2007.

34. Barboza describes this as a source of pain and frustration to Lena Santos Ferguson until the end of her life. Ibid.

35. Barboza, Gary Nash, and Henry Louis Gates agree that the 2001 book included the best research produced to date, but it is still short some 2,600 soldiers. The bibliographies on which both editions draw are excellent. And the second edition is quite remarkable.

36. Maurice Barboza and Gary Nash, "We Need to Learn More about Our Colorful Past," *New York Times,* July 31, 2004, A17.

37. Ibid.

38. Maurice Barboza interview, Feb. 26, 2007.

39. The introduction to this edition places the book in a long tradition of DAR research. Editor Eric Grundset writes, "The hope is that this current body of work will not only be of interest to students and scholars interested in the important contributions of African Americans and American Indians in America's fight for independence, but that it will also encourage the female descendants of these patriots to join the important volunteer and educational work of the NSDAR." Grundset, ed. *Forgotten Patriots,* p. i.

40. Jane Leavy, "DAR, in Step with the Times," *Washington Post,* April 19, 1985, C1.

41. Ibid.

42. The DAR was also quite famously and adamantly opposed to the ERA.

43. "Republic of South Africa Threatened," National Society, DAR, 94th Continental Congress, Third Day, Afternoon, quoted in Leavy, "DAR, in Step with the Times."

44. Her 2005 book, *Dear Senator: A Memoir by the Daughter of Strom Thurmond,* tells a fascinating story.

45. *The Tavis Smiley Show,* Jan. 28, 2005, www.pbs.org/kcet/tavissmiley/archive/20050128_transcript.html.

46. Shaila Dewan and Ariel Hart, "Thurmond's Biracial Daughter Seeks to Join Confederacy Group," *New York Times,* July 2, 2004, A13.

47. Quoted in ibid.

48. Testimony of Maurice Barboza before the National Capital Memorial Advisory Commission, June 27, 2006, National Mall Liberty Fund D.C. website, www .libertyfunddc.org (accessed Feb. 2007).

49. Public Law 98–245, 98th Cong. (1984).

50. Maurice Barboza interview, Feb. 26, 2007.

51. Ibid.

52. Ibid. The story of Santos Ferguson and the DAR can be reconstructed from fairly reliable sources. The story of the memorial is a much greater challenge. CFA and NPS documents, and to a lesser degree newspapers and congressional testimony, are useful for the details of the design. But the various iterations of the foundation do not have publicly accessible archives. Barboza had a website packed with key documents—congressional testimony, personal correspondence, etc.—but many of these documents were generated by him, and the website, not surprisingly, contained no detailed financial information. Barboza's most recent website, www .libertyfunddc.org, has little material from the 1984–2005 period.

53. Ed Dwight thinks that Johnston quickly became the driving force behind the memorial. Ed Dwight interview, March 3, 2007. Barboza speaks of Sarah King with some bemusement. He says she reminds him of Lyndon Johnson. The legal agreement between King and Ferguson did not require her to support the memorial. But the spirit of the settlement and its requirement that the DAR work proactively at affirmative action linked King's support of the memorial and the lawsuit. Maurice Barboza interview, Feb. 26, 2007.

54. King and Gore had run against each other in a democratic primary in Tennessee in the 1960s.

55. Strange bedfellows indeed, especially when you consider that, less than a month earlier, King had presided over a meeting of the DAR at which the organization had voted to support apartheid in South Africa.

56. Quoted in Patrice Gaines-Carter, "Drive Launched for Memorial for Black Patriots," *Washington Post*, May 28, 1985, B2.

57. Quoted in "Memorial for Blacks Is Sought for Capital," *New York Times*, May 28, 1985, D17.

58. Public Law 99–558, 99th Cong., 2d sess. (1986).

59. Maurice Barboza interview, Feb. 26, 2007.

60. Ibid.

61. "The minutes of the Commission of Fine Arts, for instance, refers consistently to "the memorial to black patriots who fought in the Revolutionary War." CFA files, CFA minutes, 15/MAR/90, 19/SEP/91–2, 19/SEP/96–1.

62. See Frey, *Water from the Rock;* and David and Crane, eds., *The Black Soldier.*

63. See Gary Nash's "The Black Americans' Revolution," in *The Forgotten Fifth*, for an excellent concise version of this history.

64. Frey, *Water from the Rock*, p. 4.

65. Quoted in Saundra Saperstein, "A Monumental Push Rewarded," *Washington Post*, Oct. 29, 1986, B1.

66. J. Carter Brown, "The Mall and the Commission of Fine Arts," in *The Mall in Washington, 1971–1991,* ed. Longstreth, p. 251.

67. Ibid.

68. Public Law 99–625, 99th Cong., 2d sess. (Nov. 11, 1986).

69. *Report of the Committee on Energy and Natural Resources,* 100th Cong., 2d sess., *Congressional Record* S313–2 (Feb. 15, 1988), italics added.

70. Ed Dwight, who would eventually win the design competition, connects the relative ease with which the memorial won its designation and site to the Republican Party's investment in black Republicans in the mid-1980s. He claims Reagan gave Barboza his choice of seven sites. Ed Dwight interview, March 3, 2007.

71. J. Carter Brown to Manus J. Fish, Aug. 12, 1988, CFA files.

72. The only point of agreement about the financial problems seems to be that they were quite serious. Barboza blames Johnston, Dwight blames Barboza, and the record is sketchy.

73. Maurice Barboza interview, Feb. 26, 2007.

74. Ibid.

75. Ibid. Barboza was restrained in this part of our conversation.

76. *Washington Afro-American,* Aug. 9, 1997, A12.

77. Barboza is insistent that the problem was never finding individuals or corporations willing to give. This is likely related to the fact that he is poised to embark on another round of fundraising. Maurice Barboza interview, Feb. 26, 2007.

78. *Statement of Maurice A. Barboza Before the Subcommittee on National Parks, Forests & Public Lands House Committee on Natural Resources H.R. 1693, National Liberty Memorial Act,* March 6, 2008, available at National Mall Liberty Fund D.C. website, www.libertyfundddc.org (accessed July 2009).

79. The Coin Act was sponsored by Senators Moseley-Braun, Chafee, Simon, and Pell in 1985. Moseley-Braun described all members of the Senate as "citizens who enjoy the benefits of their sacrifice."

80. Reed Abelson, "Backers Struggle to Invigorate Black Patriots Memorial Plan," *New York Times,* Feb. 28, 2000, A15.

81. Ibid.

82. While this is obviously not good, it doesn't seem entirely unreasonable or unusual. It breaks down to roughly $200,000 a year raised and spent over a period of twenty years.

83. Barboza is nothing if not tenacious. He continues to fight for the memorial with seemingly unabated passion.

84. CFA files, CFA minutes, 15/MAR/90.

85. Ibid.

86. Ibid.

87. Ibid.

88. Ibid.

89. Ibid.

90. CFA files, CFA minutes, 28/JUL/88–2.

91. Brown to Robert Stanton, April 5, 1990, CFA files, CFA minutes, 15/MAR/90–1.

92. Ibid.

93. Ed Dwight's story is told in the CFA minutes and was often repeated in press coverage of the memorial. Dwight's father played baseball in the Negro League for the Kansas City Monarchs. Dwight himself was the first African American trained as an astronaut. He was trained in the U.S. Air Force and selected during the Kennedy administration, but, facing serious resistance from his fellow astronauts, he resigned in 1966 when it was clear that he would not be supported by subsequent administrations. He then became a sculptor, and is the sculptor for the Martin Luther King Jr. Memorial on the Mall.

94. Ed Dwight interview, March 3, 2007.

95. Ibid.

96. Barboza disagrees with Dwight's account; he does not remember the design competition this way. Barboza interview, Jan. 24, 2012.

97. Ed Dwight interview, March 6, 2007.

98. Ibid.

99. CFA files, CFA minutes, 19/SEP/91–2.

100. Ibid.

101. Ibid. I find this quite baffling; why on earth shouldn't it be a destination?

102. Ibid.

103. Ibid.

104. Ibid. Dwight had arranged the figures so that they would look to Lincoln—a smart, painful, poignant gesture on Dwight's part.

105. Ibid.

106. Brown to Stanton, October 1, 1991, CFA files, CFA minutes, 19/SEP/91–2, exhibit B. Stanton would go on to become the first African American director of the National Park Service.

107. Roxanne Roberts, "Out and About," *Washington Post,* January 17, 2005.

108. Ed Dwight interview, March 6, 2007.

109. Ibid.

110. Maurice Barboza interview, Feb. 26, 2007. He calls Dwight's claim preposterous.

111. Ed Dwight interview, March 3, 2007.

112. Maurice Barboza interview, Feb. 26, 2007.

113. This is part of the push on the Mall in this period—away from the tragic into the terrain of the heroic. But Barboza must be referring to the stories told in the bas-relief wall. The figures are not injured, bloodied, or defeated looking but stand tall with arms.

114. Maurice Barboza interview, Feb. 26, 2007.

115. Ibid.

116. Ibid.

117. National Mall Liberty Fund D.C. website, www.libertyfunddc.org.

118. Ibid.

119. Ibid. Members of the fund board included Maurice Barboza; C. Fred Klienknecht, former grand commander of the Scottish Rite Masons; sculptor Michael Curtis; Joseph Dooley, president of the Virginia Society SAR; Henry Louis Gates, Harvard historian; and the late Major General Lucius Theus, former Tuskegee airman.

120. Ibid.

121. Maurice Barboza, "Questions and Answers about the National Liberty Memorial," Aug. 16, 2006, National Mall Liberty Fund D.C. website, www.liberty funddc.org (accessed Feb. 2007),

122. Senate Bill 2495, 109th Cong., 2d sess.

123. Maurice Barboza interview, Feb. 26, 2007.

124. Shaun Bishop, "Two Charles City Youths Go to Washington in Support of Black Patriots Memorial," *Richmond Times-Dispatch,* July 19, 2006.

125. Senator Christopher Dodd, *Statement before the National Capital Memorial Advisory Commission,* June 27, 2006, National Mall Liberty Fund D.C. website, www.libertyfunddc.org (accessed Feb. 2007).

126. Gates and Nash to Stevens, June 27, 2006, available at National Mall Liberty Fund D.C. website, www.libertyfunddc.org (accessed Feb. 2007).

127. In this it recalls Thomas Ball's 1876 Emancipation Memorial. Both emphasize allegiance to Lincoln rather than freedom or autonomy.

128. Thanks to Dell Upton for talking about this memorial and showing photographs of it in his January 2006 lecture, "Memorials to the Second Civil War: Commemorating the Civil Rights Movement," at the University of Michigan.

CHAPTER 3

1. Anne McClintock, "No Longer a Future Heaven," in *Becoming National,* ed. Eley and Suny, p. 271.

2. *Third Infantry Division Memorial,* S. 1107, 99th Cong., 1st sess. (1985).

3. *Monument Celebrating U.S.-Moroccan Relations,* S. 1379, 99th Cong., 1st sess. (1985).

4. Wilma Vaught interview, April 19, 2007.

5. Ibid.

6. Interview with Marilla Cushman, April 13, 2007.

7. Women in Military Service for America Memorial website, www.womens memorial.org/About/facts.html.

8. See Bond and Freeman, *America's First Woman Warrior.*

9. See Daniel Cohen, *The Female Marine and Related Works.*

10. See Blanton and Cook, *They Fought like Demons.*

11. Segal, *Recruiting for Uncle Sam,* p. 115.

12. Binkin and Bach, *Women and the Military,* p. 5.

13. Segal, *Recruiting for Uncle Sam,* p. 117.

14. The Coast Guard equivalent—the SPARs—were not segregated along race lines. This may have been because they only admitted five African Americans (Olivia Hooker, D. Winifred Byrd, Julia Mosely, Yvonne Cumberbatch, and Aileen Cooke). U.S. Coast Guard website, www.uscg.mil/history/uscghist/WomenChronology .asp.

15. Binkin and Bach, *Women and the Military*, p. 7.

16. Ibid., p. 13. There is now an effort to acknowledge the mistreatment of women in the military who became pregnant in this period and were involuntarily removed form service. The Tyler-Bender Mandatory Discharge Relief Act was introduced in Congress in 2002. It sought to provide an apology to these women and to give them access to military benefits, like burial at Arlington.

17. See Holm, *Women in the Military;* and Miller, *Feminism and the Exclusion of Army Women from Combat.*

18. For arguments against women in the military, see Brian Mitchell's chilling *Weak Link* and *Women in the Military.* He argues that women are "destroying the military's body and soul."

19. Bray was an MP and led an attack on what was either a dog kennel or a Panamanian Defense Forces arms storage site, according to differing reports.

20. *National Defense Authorization Act,* H.R. 2100, 102nd Cong., 2d sess. (Dec. 15, 1991).

21. For example, see James Ridgeway and Nicole Duarte, "'No Women in Combat'? Tell It to the Kids," *Village Voice,* Jan. 4, 2005.

22. For a compelling exploration of the Lynch story, see Conroy and Hanson, eds., *Constructing America's War Culture.*

23. See Bragg, *I Am a Soldier Too.*

24. Piestewa did eventually get some attention, but mostly as a result of a home makeover show on television that remodeled her mother's house to accommodate Piestewa's two young, orphaned children.

25. Brown quoted in Steven Lee Myers, "Living and Fighting alongside Men, and Fitting In," *New York Times,* Aug. 17, 2009, A1. It is also important to note that even as women have become a regular part of military life in Iraq and Afghanistan, the number of rapes and sexual assaults on women in the U.S. military have risen dramatically—it has been said that women soldiers are more likely to be raped than to be hit by enemy fire. Nancy Gibbs, "Sexual Assaults on Female Soldiers: Don't Ask, Don't Tell," *Time,* March 8, 2010.

26. *Women in Military Service of America Memorial,* H.J. Res 36, 98th Cong., 1st sess. (1985).

27. Ibid., Oakar testimony.

28. Hodel was a controversial figure. He followed his career in government with a career as a political consultant. He is credited with inventing the now infamous campaign tactic of "push-polling" and has served as the president of both Focus on the Family and the Christian Coalition.

29. Department of the Interior, *Hearing Before the Subcommittee on Public Lands, Reserved Water and Resource Conservation of the Committee on Energy and*

Natural Resources, United States Senate, 99th Cong, 1st sess. (Oct. 29, 1985) (statement of Denis P. Gavin, Deputy Director of the National Parks Service).

30. Ibid.

31. Ibid.

32. Wilma Vaught interview, April 19, 2007.

33. Public Law 99–610, 99th Cong., 2nd sess. (1986).

34. Ann Herold, "Women Fight for War Memorial," *Los Angeles Times,* Nov. 11, 1985, C2.

35. Ibid.

36. "Wilma L. Vaught," National Women's Hall of Fame website, www.great women.org.

37. Ibid., p. 21.

38. Quoted in Ashabranner, *A Date with Destiny,* p. 20. It is worth noting that the title of this book is not intended to evoke any kind of irony.

39. Ibid., p. 24.

40. Vaught interview, April 19, 2007.

41. Ibid.

42. Ashabranner, *A Date with Destiny,* p. 24.

43. See Ben White, "Arlington National Cemetery: How a Royal Land Grant Became One of America's Landmarks," *Washington Post,* Nov. 10, 1999. The Arlington National Cemetery website also includes a useful short history of the cemetery.

44. Ashabranner, *A Date with Destiny,* p. 26.

45. Ibid.

46. CFA files, CFA minutes, 28/JUL/88.

47. Ibid.

48. Ibid.

49. Ibid.

50. Ibid.

51. Brown to Fish, Aug. 12, 1988, CFA files, CFA minutes, 28/JUL/88–3, exhibit C.

52. "History," WIMSAM website, www.womensmemorial.org.

53. Wilma Vaught interview, April 19, 2007.

54. Ibid.

55. Ben Forgey, "4 Finalists for Memorial," *Washington Post,* June 13, 1989, C2.

56. Wilma Vaught interview, April 19, 2007.

57. Ibid.

58. CFA files, CFA minutes, 20/OCT/94–1.

59. Ibid.

60. Ibid.

61. Ibid.

62. Ibid.

63. The original design had called for the lindens to be placed closer to the road, marking the memorial space as a distinct space, but the commission disliked this idea. By 1994, the trees had been pushed back.

64. Ibid., p. 5. There is a faint echo of memorial as hostess here: the gendered

function as conduit to the greater male world of heroism and grieving rather than drawing attention to itself as a marker of women's contributions in the military.

65. Ibid.

66. Brown to Robert Stanton, November 2, 1994, p. 1, CFA files, CFA minutes 2/NOV/94, exhibit A.

67. Ibid., p. 2.

68. CFA files, CFA minutes, 16/MAR/95–2.

69. Ibid.

70. Some public reference has been made to Weiss and Manfredi's frustration with this process, but it is useful to remember that they were working on this memorial at the same time that the Korean War Veterans Memorial was struggling to move through the bureaucracy in Washington. The architects of that memorial had resisted dramatic revisions to their design and were removed from the project. This had to be very present in the minds of Weiss and Manfredi as they moved through this process.

71. *Brief History of the Women in Military Service for America Memorial* (promotional brochure published by Women in Military Service for America), p. 3.

72. Wilma Vaught interview, April 19, 2007.

73. Ibid.

74. Ibid.

75. This is an odd, late twentieth-century twist in Amy Kaplan's thinking about "manifest domesticity." Kaplan reconceptualizes nineteenth-century ideas about white female domestic culture as formed in relation to linked ideas about foreign and U.S. policies in the world. In this twist, U.S. policies in the world, or in Iraq and Kuwait in particular, quite literally enable a small reframing of women's experience as not always domestic. See Kaplan, "Manifest Domesticity."

76. Marilla Cushman interview, April 13, 2007.

77. It is odd that this sign does not read "Women in Military Service for America Memorial." The Park Service sign for Arlington National Cemetery reads "Arlington National Cemetery." The sign for the Vietnam Veterans Memorial reads "Vietnam Veterans Memorial," not "Vietnam Memorial." Of course, these sites also have much more obvious markers of their presence.

78. Marilla Cushman interview, April 13, 2007.

79. The exhibits at the memorial, most notably *Faces of the Fallen,* which includes portraits of all the 1,300 American soldiers killed in Iraq and Afghanistan between October 2001 and November 11, 2004, have been remarkable. It was an extraordinary exhibit and has been at the memorial since March 2005. Featuring the war dead from current wars, it is the only exhibit of its kind in Washington. It has become a site of pilgrimage for families of the dead. The exhibit had to be redesigned to add small platforms under each portrait to accommodate the objects people leave with the portraits.

80. Marilla Cushman interview, April 13, 2007.

81. Ben Forgey, "A Memorial Passes Muster," *Washington Post,* Oct. 18, 1997.

82. Ibid. I have no idea what he could be referring to when he writes "in front of."

83. Weiss and Manfredi, *Site Specific,* p. 29. It is worth noting that, though there are twenty-two photographs of the memorial in their book *Site Specific,* they do not include a single photograph of the front of the memorial.

84. Ibid, p. 32.

85. Ibid, p. 34.

86. Ibid.

87. Anne McClintock, "No Longer a Future Heaven," in *Becoming National,* ed. Eley and Suny, p. 271.

CHAPTER 4

1. This term is borrowed from Ngai, *Impossible Subjects.*

2. Linda Wheeler, "A Memorial to Prevent a Recurrence," *Washington Post,* Nov. 10, 2000, B3. Ben Forgey of the *Washington Post* covered the "grand opening" of the memorial in June 2001, but there was no coverage of the 2000 event. The grand opening was held after the dedication because not all the elements of the memorial were finished in 2000. Ben Forgey, "Imagery Says It All at Japanese American Memorial," *Washington Post,* June 30, 2001, C1.

3. The National Japanese American Memorial Foundation published the coffee-table book *Patriotism, Perseverance, Posterity: The Story of the National Japanese American Memorial,* edited by Bill Hosokawa, in 2001.

4. The lack of interest in the memorial among these scholars is particularly interesting because they are together building a rich literature on the public memory of the internment. They are, more specifically, writing about sites of memory and new practices of pilgrimage and spectacle as responses to the internment. A notable exception is Ingrid Gessner's *From Sites of Memory to Cybersights,* which takes up the camps as sites of memory with interesting comparisons to both the National Japanese American Memorial to Patriotism during World War II in Washington and the Go For Broke Monument in Los Angeles.

5. Quoted in Rudi Williams. "Japanese American Memorial: A Reminder to Future Generations," *American Armed Forces Press Service,* Nov. 21, 2000.

6. "Rejoices at the Fall of Schmitz in 'Frisco,'" *Boston Herald,* June 16, 1907.

7. This is necessarily a truncated version of a complicated history. For more on this, see Ngai, *Impossible Subjects;* Daniels, *Prisoners without Trial;* Yu, *Thinking Orientals;* and others.

8. Ngai, *Impossible Subjects,* p. 5.

9. Ngai, *Impossible Subjects,* p. 42.

10. *National Japanese American Memorial Foundation Report,* p. 2; Mineta to Atherton, April 21, 1992; Inouye to Atherton, April 14, 1992, all in CFA files, National Japanese American Memorial to Patriotism.

11. *National Japanese American Memorial Foundation Report,* p. 2, CFA files, National Japanese American Memorial to Patriotism. Masaoka had been thinking

about a memorial for a long time. He mentioned a memorial at Arlington in a 1944 Japanese Americans Citizens League report and again in a 1954 JACL newspaper. But in 1944 and 1954 there was little interest in memorials. When he brought it up again at a dinner in 1987, times had changed and a fever to build the memorial was ignited. Masaoka, aware of how controversial he was in Japanese American communities, quickly bowed out of the memorial process, but his writing remained a center of great controversy.

12. NCMAC to Mineta, Sept. 26, 1991, CFA files, National Japanese American Memorial to Patriotism.

13. Ibid. The commissioners were likely aware of the Smithsonian's *A More Perfect Union* and may have concluded that it was enough.

14. Ibid.

15. Mineta to Brown, March 6, 1992, CFA files, National Japanese American Memorial to Patriotism.

16. Inouye to Atherton, March 30, 1992, CFA files, National Japanese American Memorial to Patriotism. It is worth noting that Inouye volunteered from Hawaii, where most Japanese Americans were not moved into camps.

17. Ibid.

18. *Testimony of Norman Mineta Before the National Capital Memorial Commission Regarding H.J. Res. 271 to Establish a Memorial to Honor Japanese American Veterans,* April 28, 1992, p. 4, CFA files, National Japanese American Memorial to Patriotism.

19. Mineta would have a more active role in this process; he was an instigator of federal efforts to contain mistreatment of Arab Americans after September 11, 2001. As secretary of transportation, he sent a letter to all U.S. airlines on September 21, 2001, reminding them that racial profiling of passengers was illegal and would be prosecuted. Ann Coulter, "Highjackers Now Eligible for Preboarding," *Human Events,* May 3, 2004. He continued to advocate for Arab Americans during the remainder of his tenure with the Bush administration.

20. Arab Americans don't seem to have connected with the memorial. It has not, as far as I can tell, been used as a site of protest or organization for Arab Americans facing violence and mistreatment after 9/11.

21. Mineta testimony, April 28, 1992, p. 5, CFA files, National Japanese American Memorial to Patriotism.

22. For some compelling accounts of this logic, see the interviews in Erica Harth's *Last Witnesses.*

23. Mineta testimony, April 28, 1992, p. 4, CFA files, National Japanese American Memorial to Patriotism.

24. Ibid., p. 5.

25. Ibid.

26. Again, paraphrasing Nikhil Singh on Martin Luther King Jr. mythologizing in *Black Is a Country.*

27. Ibid.

28. Brown to Mineta, May 4, 1992, CFA files, National Japanese American Memorial to Patriotism.

29. Ibid. Brown's reference to the early years of the war suggests a limited understanding of the internment and maybe an impulse to minimize it as a mistake of the early part of the war.

30. H.J. Res. 271, 102nd Cong., 2d sess. (1992), italics added.

31. It is worth noting here that there was another Japanese American veterans memorial project underway at this point. A different Go For Broke organization, this one in Los Angeles, was working to build a memorial. They did not have to contend with the charged politics of the Mall and their memorial—the Go For Broke Monument—was designed in 1991 and dedicated in 1999. It lists the names of all Japanese American World War II veterans.

32. Quoted in Frances Y. Sogi and Yeiichi Kuwayama, "Japanese Americans Disunited," *Japanese American Voice*, www.javoice.com/pamphlet1.html.

33. *Buckley Report, National Japanese American Memorial Foundation, Davis Buckley Architect*, p. 16, CFA files, CFA minutes, 18/SEP/97, exhibit B.

34. National Capital Memorial Advisory Commission minutes for March 7, 1995, dated May 2, 1995, p. 6, CFA files, National Japanese American Memorial to Patriotism ,

35. Brown to Foley, September 9, 1994, CFA files, National Japanese American Memorial to Patriotism. It is easy disparage the restrictions applied by the CFA and the NCMAC, but the impulse to limit the number of memorials built, especially in the face of the rush to build them in this period, is actually admirable. And these decisions could not have been easy to make.

36. There actually was a competition for the *veterans* memorial. It was conducted by the Go For Broke veterans, and Barney Matsumoto's design won. But this design was abandoned when the memorial became a *patriotism* memorial.

37. Hammatt, "Touchstones of Memory," p. 5. Buckley had consulted on the Vietnam Veterans Memorial and designed the National Law Enforcement Memorial completed just off the Mall in 1991.

38. Hosokawa, ed., *Patriotism, Perseverance, Posterity*, p. 100. He also consulted Asian Americanists at Columbia University and the University of Pennsylvania.

39. *Buckley Report*, p. 8, CFA files, CFA minutes, 18/SEP/97–1, exhibit B.

40. Ibid.

41. For a discussion of these battles, see Hatamiya, *Righting a Wrong.*

42. *Buckley Report*, p. 8, CFA files, CFA minutes, 18/SEP/97–1, exhibit B.

43. Ibid.

44. Ibid.

45. Buckley seems to have been influenced by Dorothea Lange's OWI photographs of the internment. He relies heavily on them as illustrations in his reports and design presentations.

46. CFA files, CFA minutes, 18/SEP/97.

47. Ibid. This material is riddled with errors. In 1976, Ford officially terminated Executive Order 9066; in 1988 the Civil Liberties Act gave compensation and

acknowledged "the fundamental injustice" of the internment; in 1991 George H. W. Bush sent reparation checks and letters of apology to former internees; in 1993 Clinton signed a letter of apology called for in the 1988 Act. Ford's statement may read to some as an apology, but it was troubling to Japanese American activists that while it is apologetic in tone, it does not actually contain an apology. The Civil Liberties Act provides for but does not actually include an apology. (It does appropriate $1.25 billion for reparations.) Given the multifaceted nature of the long process of the internment apologies, it is not surprising that there is some confusion about the details.

48. Ibid.

49. Ibid. This is an interesting idea but it is difficult to know how visitors would get the symbolism of both the islands from which people came and the stones as the different generations.

50. Akamu's grandfather was the first Japanese American to die in the internment; he was being held at Sand Island in Hawaii under suspicion of disloyalty when he had a fatal heart attack.

51. CFA files, CFA minutes, 18/SEP/97.

52. Ibid, p. 6.

53. Ibid.

54. Ibid.

55. Brown to Carlstrom, CFA files, CFA minutes, 21/MAY/98.

56. CFA files, CFA minutes, 15/JUL/99–1.

57. Ibid.

58. CFA files, CFA minutes, 6/OCT/99.

59. Brown to Carlstrom, Oct. 27, 1999, p. 1, CFA files, CFA minutes, 6/OCT/99, exhibit E.

60. Ibid, p. 2.

61. As Larry Hashima describes it, Masaoka wrote what he called the "Creed" to fill space in a Japanese American Citizens League conference program. He did, however, read it on the floor of the Senate on May 9, 1941. Larry Hashima, "Public Memories, Community Discord," paper presented at the annual meeting of the American Studies Association, Washington, D.C., November 10, 2001,

62. Takahashi to Parsons, March 9, 2000, CFA files, CFA minutes, 21/OCT/99–1.

63. CFA files, National Japanese American Memorial to Patriotism, Masaoka Letters.

64. Melvin Chiogioji, "Letters to the Editor: Memorial Foundation Chair Responds to Allegations," *Nichi Bei Times Japanese American Daily*, January 8, 2000. The *Nichi Bei Times* was first published in 1946 by Japanese Americans to help Japanese Americans reacclimate after the internment.

65. Ibid.

66. *Lim Report, Research Prepared for the Presidential Select Committee on JACL resolution #7, 1990.*

67. Masaoka as quoted from Lim interview transcript in Gerald Yamada to

Brown, Jan. 7, 2000, p. 11, CFA files, National Japanese American Memorial to Patriotism, Masaoka Letters.

68. "Controversy over Planned Memorial," *Nichi Bei Times,* May 31, 2000.

69. Ibid.

70. The Japanese American Voice website (www.javoice.org) is full of expressions of this problem.

71. Hashima, "Public Memories, Community Discord," p. 5.

72. Ibid, p. 7.

73. Hosokawa, *Patriotism, Perseverance, and Posterity,* p. 153. Hosokawa includes an eighteen-page chapter on the fundraising for the memorial. It is the best available source regarding money for the memorial.

74. Ibid.

75. Ibid, p. 166. The Korean War Veterans Memorial was partially paid for by donations from Korean corporations, but the politics of Japanese corporations donating to the memorial would have been wildly different—and would have undermined the fundamental argument at the memorial about the American nature of the project.

76. Ibid, p. 154.

77. Ibid.

78. Ibid, p. 164.

79. Ibid, p. 169.

80. Tashima, "Patriotism," p. 2007.

81. Ibid., p. 2008.

82. Ibid., p. 2008, drawing on Muller, *Free to Die for Their Country.*

83. As Tashima points out, not segregating the Nisei when African Americans were segregated would have "drawn attention" to the segregation.

84. The story of those who requested repatriation or expatriation to Japan—three thousand people—is also not well known. Mae Ngai, "'An Ironic Testimony to the Value of American Democracy': Assimilationism and the World War II Internment of Japanese Americans," in *Contested Democracy,* ed. Sinha and Von Eschen, p. 248.

85. Tashima, "Patriotism," p. 2011.

86. Ibid.

87. Quoted in ibid., p. 2014.

88. Okada, *No-No Boy,* p. 4.

89. De Leon remarks, Nov. 9, 2000, reprinted by the *American Forces Press Service,* www.defense.ogv/newsarticle.aspx?id=45581.

90. Ibid.

91. Ibid.

92. Ibid.

93. Ngai, *Impossible Subjects,* p. 238.

CHAPTER 5

1. The number of memorial visitors who understand the significance of the gold star will diminish with time, unless there is a revival of the Service Flag. People born after 1960, for instance, are not likely to know that a gold star in the window meant a dead son or father.

2. There are bas-reliefs that line the main entrance to the memorial, and these do include women, African Americans, and Asian Americans. The figures depicted in the bas-reliefs are not all white and male, but they are so lilliputian in the scale of the memorial that their impact is seriously limited. They seem lovely and ancillary.

3. Art historian Martin Berger's work is useful here. He argues, in *Sight Unseen,* that nineteenth-century landscape paintings without figures need to be understood as racialized images—as emphatic expressions of ideas about whiteness. This memorial without figures can be understood in this same vein.

4. For more on this, see *Carried to the Wall*. Also see Shanken, "Planning Memory" and *194X*. It is worth noting that some colleges and universities and small towns did put lists of their dead on existing memorials or modest plaques or memorials.

5. Hass, *Carried to the Wall,* p. 58.

6. The Iwo Jima Memorial is a complicated exception, and it is for Marines only. This memorial is fascinating, in turns venerated and ignored, dismissed, or reviled as Marine Corps self-promotion by those not associated with the Marine Corps. After 9/11, firefighters at Ground Zero gave new life to the Iwo Jima memorial in the culture.

7. Mills, *Their Last Battle,* p. xxvi.

8. I have also seen this reported as a pancake supper and a town meeting.

9. H.R. 3742, 100th Cong., 2d sess. (July 7, 1988).

10. Earlier versions of the law had included a museum, but, at the urging of the CFA, this requirement was deleted in 1989. Despite the deletion, the ABMC continued to assume that the memorial would include something like a museum—a visitors' center or some other exhibition space.

11. The congressional record is, again, frustratingly devoid of any discussion of this question. This may have had something to do with the average age of the veterans but was likely driven by other reasons.

12. They were Admiral Ming Chang, a rear admiral with thirty-four years of Navy service and a Bronze Star recipient; Dr. Miguel Encinitas, an Army Air Corps and Air Force veteran of World War II, Korea, and Vietnam with two Purple Hearts; Helen Fagin, PhD, holocaust survivor and retired professor of English and Judaic Studies who had helped craft content for the U.S. Holocaust Memorial Museum; Mark Fleming, staff director and chief counsel for the U.S. House of Representatives Committee on Veterans Affairs; Melissa Growden, the granddaughter of Roger Durbin; Jess Hay, chair of the Texas Foundation for Higher Education and member of the boards of directors of SBC Communications, Viad Corporation, and Trinity Industries; Jon Mangis, Virginia's commissioner of veterans affairs; and Bill Murphy, a World War II Marine Corps veteran and longtime activist in veterans' affairs.

13. CFA files, CFA minutes, 27/JUL/95.

14. Ibid.

15. Ibid.

16. Ibid.

17. Ibid.

18. A similar gesture was made at the groundbreaking of the U.S. Holocaust Memorial Museum. Dirt from the sites of the camps was buried in Washington at the museum site. See Ed Linenthal's *Preserving Memory* for more on this.

19. Linenthal and Engelhardt, eds., *History Wars,* p. 2.

20. Harwit, *An Exhibit Denied,* p. 406.

21. *Resolution Relating the "Enola Gay" Exhibit,* S. Res. 257, 103rd Cong., 2d sess. (Sept. 20, 1994).

22. Detweiler to Clinton, Jan. 19, 1995, quoted in "Legion Protests Enola Gay Plan by Smithsonian," *Associated Press,* Jan. 20, 1995.

23. Crouch memo to Martin Harwit, July 21, 1993, available at the Air Force Association website, www.afa.org.

24. "National World War II Memorial Design," PSA#1577, *Commerce Business Daily,* April 19, 1996.

25. Joseph Fishkin, "Monumental Error," *New Republic,* Sept. 25, 2000, 2.

26. Paul D. Spreiregen, "A Democratic Approach for Our World War II Memorial," *Washington Post,* May 5, 1996, C8.

27. Ibid.

28. CFA files, CFA minutes, 27/JUL/96.

29. "National World War II Memorial Design," PSA #1665, *Commerce Business Daily,* Aug. 23, 1996.

30. One detail about the competition is often neglected in discussions of the memorial, but it had a dramatic impact on the final design. The call for designs included a sentence that read, "The design program for the Memorial includes underground space for educational facilities." Kaptur's initial bill for the memorial called for a memorial and a museum. Though the word *museum* was dropped from subsequent bills, the idea that the memorial should include a visitors' center or museum continued to dictate the way people thought about the memorial. All the designs submitted were significantly shaped by the need to accommodate vast interior spaces at the Rainbow Pool. The designs submitted, the jury deliberations, the selected design, and the design approved and built would likely have been quite different if the interior space had been dropped before the design competition rather than after the design had been selected and considerably reworked.

31. Brinkley, ed., *The World War II Memorial,* p. 33.

32. The glass pillars emerging from the Rainbow Pool were designed by Marion Wiess and Michael Manfredi, who had won the competition for the design of the Women in Military Service for America Memorial in 1992.

33. CFA files, CFA minutes, 16/JAN/95.

34. Ibid.

35. CFA files, CFA minutes, 24/JUL/97.

36. Ibid.

37. Ibid.

38. Ibid.

39. Ibid.

40. The Roosevelt Memorial site was in fact selected in 1958, long before the current memorial building frenzy on the Mall. But the Rainbow Pool was not considered. The FDR site does have a pedigree of sorts: the McMillan Plan had suggested that it might be a fitting site for a future presidential memorial.

41. Ibid.

42. CFA files, CFA minutes, 21/MAY/98.

43. Ibid.

44. This includes the $90 million in donated advertisements.

45. Abraham Lincoln to Mrs. Lydia Bixby, Nov. 21, 1864, www.papersofabrahamlincoln.org/Bixby%20Letter.html. Much has been made of the veracity of the letter—did Lincoln write it or did John Hay?—and of the accuracy of the president's grasp of the situation, since Bixby seems only to have lost three sons, and she seems to have supported the Confederacy. None of this comes up in the film.

46. Bodnar, "Saving Private Ryan and Postwar Memory in America." p. 805.

47. Ibid., p. 817.

48. Ibid., p. 811.

49. The impact of this film is remarkable. It has changed how I teach undergraduates about World War II because it is so much how they know the war. Since about 1999, I have had to dedicate time, in courses that include the war, to teaching about *Saving Private Ryan* as a film that can teach us something about American culture in the 1990s rather than the one true story of the war.

50. CFA files, CFA minutes, 20/MAY/99.

51. Archibald MacLeish, "The Young Dead Soldiers Do Not Speak," typewritten copy, 1941, www.loc.gov/teachers/lyrical/poems/dead_soldiers.html.

52. Ibid.

53. Michael Kimmelman, "Ideas and Trends: Turning Memory into Travesty," *New York Times,* March 4, 2001.

54. Thanks to David Winter, University of Michigan.

55. CFA files, CFA minutes, 20/MAY/99.

56. *Philadelphia Press,* 1898. The history of the eagle as an American icon is directly linked to the military and the history of the Mall. L'Enfant first came to George Washington's attention as the designer of the insignia of the Society of Cincinnati, an organization of Revolutionary War officers; L'Enfant's use of the eagle caught Washington's eye and earned his approval. The eagle was also used shortly before this in the Great Seal of the United States.

57. CFA files, CFA minutes, 20/JUL/00.

58. They fell out of favor in the Vietnam War era, but have begun to make something of a return to popularity. They were adopted at roughly the same time as dog tags, another marker of the growing importance of recognizing soldiers as citizens before and after their deaths.

59. *Minutes of the National Capital Planning Commission, Special Open Session on the National World War II Memorial,* Sept. 21, 2000, CFA files, National World War II Memorial.

60. CFA files, CFA minutes, 20/JUL/00.

61. Ibid.

62. Paul Goldberger, "Not in Our Front Yard," *New Yorker,* August 7, 2000.

63. The National World War II Memorial website, www.wwiimemorial.com /default.asp?page=overview.aspsubpage=critics.

64. *To Expedite the Construction of the World War II Memorial in the District of Columbia,* S.B. 580. 107th Cong., 1st sess. (May 20, 2001).

65. *To Expedite the Construction of the World War II Memorial in the District of Columbia,* Public Law 107–11, 107th Cong., 1st sess. (May 28, 2001).

66. The concerns about the Mall that emerge in these debates have taken on a life of their own through continued organizing and a battle for the symbolic life of the Mall.

67. The crowds at President Obama's inauguration were not significantly impeded by the memorial. The crowd demonstrated that an equal number of people gathered at the Lincoln Memorial would still be possible, but the flow of the crowd and the sight lines would be limited.

68. CFA files, CFA minutes, 21/NOV/02.

69. Mills, *Their Last Battle,* p. 218.

70. CFA files, CFA minutes, 21/NOV/02.

71. CFA files, CFA minutes 22/APR/03.

72. Bob Carotka, interview, October 18, 2005. It is perfectly reasonable to take the position that resources are limited, that if every memorial spawns a permanent collection of objects that require facilities, acid-free storage, a curatorial staff, administrative oversight, and so on, it would be very expensive. But the policy at the memorial is not about Park Service resources.

73. Ibid.

74. Because there is no official collection, the information I have about the objects left at the memorial comes from interviews with National Park Service employees, mostly rangers stationed at the memorial. As a result, what I know is fairly general, but, because the answers to my questions were quite consistent, I am confident that I have culled an accurate description. The most common articles left are photographs, an even mix of original snapshots and photocopied snapshots. A few are professional portraits or newspaper photographs. Most are from the period of the war, many of soldiers in uniform. Only a few are more recent photographs. Some are laminated, some come with cards, some include long captions about the photographs and the participants, some are left alone. Some are left at the state columns, others scattered across the memorial.

75. Mills, *Their Last Battle,* p. 219.

76. Ibid., p. xiii.

77. Thomas Keenan, "Questions for Friedrich St. Florian," *New York Times,* July 1, 2001, SM23.

SELECTED BIBLIOGRAPHY

ARCHIVES

Commission of Fine Arts Archives, Commission of Fine Art, Washington, D.C.
National Capital Planning Commission Archives, National Capital Planning Commission, Washington, D.C.
National Parks Service, National Capital Region Offices and the Library of Congress

SCHOLARSHIP AND SECONDARY SOURCES

Anderson, Benedict R. *Imagined Communities: Reflections on the Origin and Spread of Nationalism*. London: Verso, 1991 [1983].

Anthias, Floya, and Nira Yuval-Davis. *Racialized Boundaries: Race, Nation, Gender, Colour and Class and Anti-racist Struggle*. London: Routledge, 1992.

Appadurai, Arjun. "Patriotism and Its Futures." In *Modernity at Large: Cultural Dimensions of Globalization*. Minneapolis: University of Minnesota Press, 1994.

Ashabranner, Brent K. *A Date with Destiny: The Women in Military Service for America Memorial*. Brookfield, CT: Twenty-first Century Books, 2000.

Bacevich, A. J. *The New American Militarism: How Americans Are Seduced by War*. New York: Oxford University Press, 2005.

Bailey, Beth. *America's Army: Making the All-Volunteer Force*. Cambridge, MA: Harvard University Press, 2009.

———. "The Army in the Marketplace: Recruiting an All-Volunteer Military." *Journal of American History,* June 2007.

———. *The First Strange Place: The Alchemy of Race and Sex in World War II Hawaii*. Baltimore, MD: Johns Hopkins University Press, 1992.

Baker, Paul R. "Review of Monumental Washington: The Planning and Development of the Capital Center by John W. Reps." *American Quarterly* 20, no. 2 (Summer 1968): 378–79.

Bal, Mieke, Leo Spitzer, and Jonathan Crewe, eds. *Acts of Memory: Cultural Recall in the Present.* Hanover, NH: University of New England Press, 1999.

Balibar, Etienne, and Immanuel Wallerstein, eds. *Race, Nation, Class: Ambiguous Identities.* New York: Verso, 1991.

Banta, Martha. *Imaging Women: Ideas and Ideals in Cultural History.* New York: Columbia University Press, 1987.

Barber, Lucy. *Marching on Washington: The Forging of an American Political Tradition.* Berkeley: University of California Press, 2004.

Barton, Craig. *Sites of Memory: Perspectives on Architecture and Race.* New York: Princeton Architectural Press, 2001.

Bennett, Tony. *The Birth of the Museum.* New York: Routledge, 1995.

Berger, Martin. *Sight Unseen: Whiteness and American Visual Culture.* Berkeley: University of California Press, 2005.

Berlant, Lauren Gail. *The Queen of America Goes to Washington City: Essays on Sex and Citizenship.* Durham, NC: Duke University Press, 1997.

Berryman, Sue. *Who Serves? The Persistent Myth of the Underclass Army.* Boulder, CO: Westview Press, 1988.

Bhabha, Homi. *The Location of Culture.* New York: Routledge, 1994.

Binkin, Martin, and Shirley Bach. *Women in the Military.* Washington, DC: Brookings Institution, 1977.

Bird, William L. "A Suggestion concerning James Smithson's Concept of 'Increase and Diffusion.'" *Technology and Culture* 24, no. 2 (April 1983): 246–55.

Blair, William. *Cities of the Dead: Contesting the Memory of the Civil War in the South, 1865–1914.* Chapel Hill: University of North Carolina Press, 2004.

Blake, Casey Nelson, ed. *The Arts of Democracy: Art, Public Culture, and the State.* Philadelphia: University of Pennsylvania Press, 2007.

———. "The Modernist Moment in Federal Public Art." In *A Modern Mosaic: Art and Modernism in the United States,* edited by Townsend Ludington, Thomas Fahy, and Sarah P. Reuning. Chapel Hill: University of North Carolina Press, 2000.

Blanton, DeAnne, and Lauren M. Cook. *They Fought like Demons: Women Soldiers in the Civil War.* Baton Rouge: Louisiana University Press, 2002.

Blight, David. *Beyond the Battlefield: Race, Memory, and the American Civil War.* Boston: University of Massachusetts Press, 2002.

———. *Race and Reunion: The Civil War in American Memory.* Boston: Harvard University Press, 2001.

Bodnar, John. *The "Good War" in American Memory.* Baltimore, MD: Johns Hopkins University Press, 2010.

———. "Human Rights and the Legacy of World War II." *International Journal of the Humanities* 2 (2004).

———. "Public Sentiments and the American Remembrance of World War II." In *Public Culture: Diversity, Democracy, and Community in the United States,* edited by M. Shafer. Philadelphia: University of Pennsylvania Press, 2008.

———. *Remaking America: Public Memory, Commemorations, and Patriotism in the Twentieth Century.* Princeton, NJ: Princeton University Press, 1991.

———. "Saving Private Ryan and Postwar Memory in America." *American Historical Review* 106 (June 2001): 805–17.

Bogart, Michele. *Public Sculpture and the Civic Ideal in New York City, 1890–1930.* Chicago: University of Chicago Press, 1989.

Bond, Alma, and Lucy Freeman. *America's First Woman Warrior: The Courage of Deborah Sampson.* New York: Paragon House, 1992.

Borklund, Carl W. *U.S. Defense and Military Fact Book.* Santa Barbara, CA: ABC-CLIO, 1991.

Boswell, David, and Jessica Evans. *Representing the Nation: History, Heritage and Museums.* New York: Routledge, 1999.

Bourke, Joanna. "Remembering War." *Journal of Contemporary History* 39, no. 4 (October 2004): 473–85.

Bragg, Rick. *I Am a Soldier Too: The Jessica Lynch Story.* New York: Knopf, 2003.

Brechin, Gray. *Imperial San Francisco: Urban Power, Earthly Ruin.* Berkeley: University of California Press, 1999.

Brinkley, Douglas, ed. *The World War II Memorial: A Grateful Nation Remembers.* Washington, DC: Smithsonian Press, 2006.

Brown, Thomas J. "Review of Memory in Black and White: Race, Commemoration, and the Post-Bellum Landscape." *Public Historian* 26, no. 2 (May 2004): 90–92.

Buddin, Richard J., U.S. Army., and Arroyo Center. *Success of First-Term Soldiers: The Effects of Recruiting Practices and Recruit Characteristics.* Santa Monica, CA: Rand, 2005.

Buell, Frederick. "Nationalist Postnationalism: Global Discourses in Contemporary American Culture." *American Quarterly* 50, no. 3 (1998): 548–91.

Burgett, Bruce, and Glenn Hendler, eds. *Keywords in American Studies.* New York: New York University Press, 2007.

Butler, Judith. *Precarious Life: The Powers of Mourning and Violence.* London: Verso, 2003.

Butler, Sara A. "The Monument as Manifesto: The Pierre Charles L'Enfant Memorial, 1909–1911." *Journal of Planning History* 6, no. 4 (November 2007): 283–310.

Chase, Robert T. "Class Resurrection: The Poor People's Campaign of 1968 and Resurrection City." *Essays in History: Corcoran Department of History at the University of Virginia* 40 (1998).

Chatterjee, Partha. "Beyond the Nation? Or Within?" *Social Text* 56, no. 3 (Fall 1998).

Chung, Tan, ed. *In the Footsteps of Xuanzang: Tan Yun-Shan and India.* New Delhi: Gyan Publishing, 1999.

Cohen, Daniel. *The Female Marine and Related Works: Narratives of Cross-Dressing and Urban Vice in America's Early Republic.* Amherst: University of Massachusetts Press, 1997.

Cohen, Eliot A. *Citizens and Soldiers: The Dilemmas of Military Service.* Cornell Studies in Security Affairs. Ithaca, NY: Cornell University Press, 1985.

Conn, Steven. *Museums and American Intellectual Life, 1876–1926.* Chicago: University of Chicago Press, 1998.

Conroy, Thomas, and Jarice Hanson, eds., *Constructing America's War Culture: Iraq, Media, and Images at Home.* Lanham, MD: Rowman and Littlefield, 2008.

Cook, James. *The Arts of Deception: Playing with Fraud in the Age of Barnum.* Cambridge, MA: Harvard University Press, 2001.

———. "Seeing the Visual in U.S. History." *Journal of American History* 95, no. 2 (September 2008).

Crawford, John. *The Last True Story I'll Ever Tell: An Accidental Soldier's Account of the War in Iraq.* New York: Penguin Books, 2005.

Creef, Elana Tajima. *Imaging Japanese America: The Visual Construction of Citizenship, Nation, and the Body.* New York: New York University Press, 2004.

Cunliffe, Marcus. *George Washington: Man and Monument.* Boston: Little, Brown, 1958.

———. *Soldiers and Civilians: The Martial Spirit in America, 1775–1865.* Boston: Little, Brown, 1968.

D'Amico, Francine, and Laurie Weinstein. *Gender Camouflage: Women in the U.S. Military.* New York: New York University Press, 1999.

Daniels, Roger. *Prisoners without Trial: Japanese Americans in World War II.* New York: Hill and Wang, 2004.

David, Jay, and Elaine Crane, eds. *The Black Soldier: From the American Revolution to Vietnam.* New York: Morrow, 1971.

Davis, Nancy E. "Review of Making Washington City: Proprietors, Dreamers, Builders, by Margaret N. Burri; Melinda Young Frye; Keith Melder; Chester Design Associates and Washington History by Kenneth R. Bowling." *Public Historian* 14, no. 2 (Spring 1992): 107–9.

Dean, Robert. *Imperial Brotherhood: Gender and the Making of Cold War Foreign Policy.* Amherst: University of Massachusetts Press, 2001.

Deloria, Phil. *Playing Indian.* New Haven, CT: Yale University Press, 1999.

Denkler, Ann. *Sustaining Identity, Recapturing Heritage: Exploring Issues of Public History, Tourism, and Race in a Southern Town.* Lanham, MD: Lexington Books, 2007.

Denning, Michael. *Culture in the Age of Three Worlds.* New York: Verso, 2004.

Doss, Erika. *Memorial Mania: Public Feeling in America.* Chicago: University of Chicago Press, 2010.

———. "War, Memory, and the Public Mediation of Affect: The National World War II Memorial and American Imperialism." *Memory Studies* 1 (2008): 227–50.

Dougherty, J. P. "Baroque and Picturesque Motifs in L'Enfant's Design for the Federal Capital." *American Quarterly* 26, no. 1 (March 1974): 23–36.

Duncan, David Douglas. *This is War! A Photo-Narrative of the Korean War.* Boston: Little, Brown, 1990.

Edkins, Jenny. *Trauma and the Memory of Politics.* Cambridge: Cambridge University Press, 2003.

Egerton, Douglas R. *Death or Liberty: African Americans and Revolutionary America*. Oxford: Oxford University Press, 2009.

Eley, Geoff, and Ronald Grigor Suny, eds. *Becoming National: A Reader*. Oxford: Oxford University Press, 2004.

Engelhardt, Tom. *The End of Victory Culture: Cold War America and the Disillusioning of a Generation*. New York: Basic Books, 1995.

Ensign, Tod. *America's Military Today: The Challenge of Militarism*. New York: New Press, 2004.

Evans, Thomas. "The All-Volunteer Army after Twenty Years: Recruiting in the Modern Era." *Army History: The Professional Bulletin of Army History* 27 (Summer 1993): 40–46.

Fairclough, Adam. "Civil Rights and the Lincoln Memorial: The Censored Speeches of Robert R. Moton (1922) and John Lewis (1963)." *Journal of Negro History* 82, no. 4 (Autumn 1997): 408–16.

Fanning, Kay. "National Mall and Memorial Parks: Union Square." *National Park Service Cultural Landscape Inventory*. National Park Service, March 2006.

Faust, Drew Gilpin. *This Republic of Suffering: Death and the American Civil War*. New York: Knopf, 2008.

Field, Cynthia R. "Review of a Plan Wholly New: Pierre Charles L'Enfant's Plan of the City of Washington by Richard W. Stephenson and A Quest for Grandeur by Charles Moore and the Federal Triangle by Sally Kress Tompkins." *Public Historian* 17, no. 3 (Summer 1995): 132–35.

Field, Cynthia R., and Jeffrey T. Tilman. "Creating a Model for the National Mall: The Design of the National Museum of Natural History." *Journal of the Society of Architectural Historians* 63, no. 1 (March 2004): 52–73.

Fish, Lydia. *The Last Firebase: A Guide to the Vietnam Veterans Memorial*. Shippensburg, PA: White Mane, 1987.

Fiske, John. *Media Matters: Everyday Culture and Political Change*. Minneapolis: University of Minnesota Press, 1994.

Fredland, J. Eric, Curtis Gilroy, Roger D. Little, and W. S. Sellman, eds. *Professionals on the Front Line: Two Decades of the All-Volunteer Forces*. Washington, DC: Brassey's, 1996.

Frey, Silvia. *Water from the Rock: Black Resistance in a Revolutionary Age*. Princeton, NJ: Princeton University Press, 1991.

Friedland, Roger, and Deirdre Boden. *NowHere: Space, Time and Modernity*. Berkeley: University of California Press, 1994.

Fussell, Paul. *The Great War and Modern Memory*. New York: Oxford University Press, 1975.

———. *Wartime: Understanding and Behavior in the Second World War*. Oxford: Oxford University Press, 1989.

Geraghty, Tony. *Guns for Hire: The Inside Story of Freelance Soldiering*. London: Portrait Books, 2007.

Gerstle, Gary. "In the Shadow of Vietnam: Liberal Nationalism and the Problem of War." In *Americanisms: New Perspectives on the History of an Ideal*, edited by

Micheal Kazin and Joseph McCartin. Chapel Hill: University of North Carolina Press, 2006.

Gessner, Ingrid. *From Sites of Memory to Cybersights: (Re)Framing Japanese American Experiences.* Heidelberg: Universitatsverlag Winter Heidelberg, 2005.

Gillette, Howard. "Washington: Symbol and City." *Journal of American History* 79, no. 1 (June 1992): 208–12.

Gillis, John R. *Commemorations: The Politics of National Identity.* Princeton, NJ: Princeton University Press, 1994.

———. *A World of Their Own Making: Myth, Ritual, and the Quest for Family Values.* New York: Basic Books, 1996.

Glassberg, David. *Sense of History: The Place of the Past in American life.* Amherst: University of Massachusetts Press, 2001.

Glazer, Nathan, and Cynthia Field, eds. *The National Mall: Rethinking Washington's Monumental Core.* Baltimore, MD: Johns Hopkins University Press, 2008.

Gordon, Linda, and Gary Y. Okihiro. *Impounded: Dorothea Lange and the Censored Images of Japanese American Internment.* New York: W. W. Norton, 2006.

Green, Mark, and New Democracy Project. *What We Stand For: A Program for Progressive Patriotism.* New York: New Market Press, 2004.

Griffith, Robert K. *Men Wanted for the U.S. Army: America's Experience with an All-Volunteer Army between the World Wars.* Contributions in Military History 27. Westport, CT: Greenwood Press, 1982.

Grinker, Roy Richard. *Korea and Its Futures: Unification and the Unfinished War.* New York: St. Martin's Press, 1998.

Groth, Paul, and Todd Bressi. *Understanding Ordinary Landscapes.* New Haven, CT: Yale University Press, 1997.

Grundset, Eric, ed. *Forgotten Patriots: African American and American Indian Patriots in the Revolutionary War: A Guide to Service, Sources, and Studies.* Washington, DC: Daughters of the American Revolution, 2008.

Hagopian, Patrick. *The Vietnam War in American Memory: Veterans, Memorials, and the Politics of Healing.* Amherst: University of Massachusetts Press, 2009.

Halbwach, Maurice. *On Collective Memory.* Edited by Lewis Coser. Chicago: University of Chicago Press, 1992.

Hammatt, Heather. "Touchstones of Memory." *Landscape Architecture,* June 2002.

Haraway, Donna. "Teddy Bear Patriarchy: Taxidermy in the Garden of Eden, New York City." *Social Text* 11 (Winter 1984–85): 20–64.

Harris, C. M. "Washington's Gamble, L'Enfant's Dream: Politics, Design, and the Founding of the National Capital." *William and Mary Quarterly* 56, no. 3 (July 1999): 527–64.

Harris, Neil. *Cultural Excursions: Marketing Appetites and Cultural Tastes in Modern America.* Chicago: University of Chicago Press, 1990.

Harth, Erica. *Last Witnesses: Reflections on the Wartime Internment of Japanese Americans.* New York: Palgrave, 2001.

Harwit, Martin. *An Exhibit Denied: Lobbying the History of the Enola Gay.* New York: Copernicus, 1996.

Hashima, Lawrence. "Public Memories, Community Discord: The Battle over the 'Japanese American Creed.'" *Multiple Publics/Civic Voices: Online Panel Discussions,* 2001, http://epsilon3.georgetown.edu/~coventrm/asa2001/panel11/hashima.html.

Hass, Kristin. *Carried to the Wall: The Vietnam Veterans Memorial and American Memory.* Berkeley: University of California Press, 1998.

Hatamiya, Leslie. *Righting a Wrong: Japanese Americans and the Passage of the Civil Liberties Act of 1988.* Stanford, CA: Stanford University Press, 1993.

Henderson, William Darryl. *The Hollow Army: How the U.S. Army Is Oversold and Undermanned.* New York: Greenwood Press, 1990.

Hendrickson, Paul. *The Living and the Dead: Robert McNamara and Five Lives of a Lost War.* New York: Alfred A. Knopf, 1996.

Henson, Pamela M. "'Objects of Curious Research': The History of Science and Technology at the Smithsonian." *Isis* 90 (1999): S249–69.

Herrera, Richard. "Self-Governance and the American Citizen as Soldier, 1775–1861." *Journal of Military History* 65, no. 1 (January 2001): 21–52.

Highsmith, Carol M., and Ted Landphair. *Forgotten No More: The Korean War Veterans Memorial Story.* Washington, DC: Chelsea, 1995.

Hill, Mike. *Whiteness: A Critical Reader.* New York: New York University Press, 1997.

Hillier, Amy. "Redlining and the Homeowners' Loan Corporation." *Journal of Urban History* 29, no. 4 (2003).

Hines, Thomas S. "The Imperial Facade: Daniel H. Burnham and American Architectural Planning in the Philippines." *Pacific Historical Review* 41, no. 1 (February 1972): 33–53.

———. "No Little Plans: The Achievement of Daniel Burnham," *Museum Studies* 2 (1988): 96–105.

Hobsbawm, Eric. *Nations and Nationalism since 1780: Programme, Myth and Reality.* Cambridge: Cambridge University Press, 1990.

———. *On History.* New York: New Press, 1997.

Hobsbawm, Eric, and Terence Ranger, eds. *The Invention of Tradition.* Cambridge: Cambridge University Press, 1983.

Holm, Jeanne. *Women in the Military: An Unfinished Revolution.* Novato: Presidio Press, 1982.

Hosokawa, Bill, ed. *Patriotism, Perseverance, and Posterity: The Story of the Japanese American Memorial.* Washington, DC: National Japanese American Memorial Foundation, 2001.

Howard, John. *Concentration Camps on the Home Front: Japanese Americans in the House of Jim Crow.* Chicago: University of Chicago Press, 2008.

Huebner, Andrew. *The Warrior Image: Soldiers in American Culture from World War II to Vietnam.* Chapel Hill: University of North Carolina Press, 2008.

Huyssen, Andreas. *Present Pasts: Urban Palimpsests and the Politics of Memory.* Stanford, CA: Stanford University Press, 2003.

Iwamura, Jane Naomi. "Critical Faith: Japanese Americans and the Birth of a New Civil Religion," *American Quarterly* 59, no. 4 (March 2007): 937–68.

Jager, Shelia Miyoshi. *Narratives of Nation Building in Korea: A Genealogy of Patriotism.* London: M. E. Sharpe, 2003.

Janz, Wesley. "Theaters of Power: Architectural and Cultural Productions." *Journal of Architectural Education* 50, no. 4 (1997): 230.

Jay, Gregory. "White Out: Race and Nationalism in American Studies." *American Quarterly* 55, no. 4 (December 2003): 781–95.

Kammen, Michael G. *Mystic Chords of Memory: The Transformation of Tradition in American Culture.* New York: Knopf, 1991.

———. *Visual Shock: A History of Art Controversies in American Culture.* New York: Knopf, 2006

Kaplan, Amy. "Manifest Domesticity." *American Literature* 70, no. 3 (1998): 581–606.

Kasson, Joy. *Buffalo Bill's Wild West: Celebrity, Memory and Popular History.* New York: Hill and Wang, 2000.

Kazin, Michael, and Joseph A. McCartin, eds., *Americanism: New Perspectives on the History of an Ideal.* Chapel Hill: University of North Carolina Press, 2006.

Kerin, James R. *The Korean War and American Memory.* Philadelphia: University of Pennsylvania, 1994.

Kiernan, V. G. *America, the New Imperialism: From White Settlement to World Hegemony.* London: Zed Press, 1978.

King, Desmond. *The Liberty of Strangers: Making the American Nation.* New York: Oxford University Press, 2005.

Klein, Christina. *Cold War Orientalism: Asia and the Middlebrow Imagination, 1945–1961.* Berkeley: University of California Press, 2003.

Klein, Kerwin. "On the Emergence of Memory in Historical Discourse." *Representations* 69 (2000): 127.

Kodat, Catherine Gunther. "Saving Private Property: Steven Spielberg's American DreamWorks." *Representations* 71 (Summer 2000): 77–105.

Kohlstedt, Sally Gregory. "History in a Natural History Museum: George Brown Goode and the Smithsonian Institution." *Public Historian* 10, no. 2 (Spring 1988): 7–26.

Landsberg, Allison. *Prosthetic Memory: The Transformation of American Remembrance.* New York: Columbia University Press, 2004.

Laqueur, Thomas. "Among the Graves." *London Review of Books,* December 18, 2008, p. 6.

———. "The Places of the Dead in Modernity." In *The Age of Cultural Revolutions: Britain and France, 1750–1820,* edited by Colin Jones and Drod Wahman. Berkeley: University of California Press, 2002.

Leckie, Robert. *Conflict: The History of the Korean War, 1950–1953.* New York: De Capo, 1996.

Lembcke, Jerry. *The Spitting Image: Myth, Memory, and the Legacy of Vietnam.* New York: New York University Press, 1998.

Levinson, Sanford. *Written in Stone: Public Monuments in Changing Societies*. Durham, NC: Duke University Press, 1998.

Lieven, Anatol. *America Right or Wrong: An Anatomy of American Nationalism*. New York: Oxford University Press, 2004.

Lightfoot, Mary Ann, Peter F. Ramsberger, and Peter Greenston. *Matching Recruits to Jobs: The Enlisted Personnel Allocation System*. Alexandria, VA: U.S. Army Research Institute for the Behavioral and Social Sciences, 2000.

Linenthal, Edward. *Preserving Memory: The Struggle to Create America's Holocaust Museum*. New York: Columbia University Press, 2001.

———. *Sacred Ground: Americans and Their Battlefields*. Chicago: University of Illinois Press, 1991.

———. "Struggling with History and Memory." *Journal of American History* 82, no. 3 (December 1995): 1094–1101.

———. *The Unfinished Bombing: Oklahoma City in American Memory*. New York: Oxford University Press, 2003.

Linenthal, Edward, and Tom Engelhardt, eds. *History Wars: The Enola Gay and Other Battles for the American Past*. New York: Henry Holt, 1996.

Lipsitz, George. "The Possessive Investment in Whiteness: Racialized Social Democracy and the 'White' Problem in American Studies." *American Quarterly* 47, no. 3 (September 1995): 369–87.

———. *Time Passages: Collective Memory and American Popular Culture*. Minneapolis: University of Minnesota Press, 1990.

Loewen, James. *Lies across America: What Our Historic Sites Get Wrong*. New York: New Press, 1999.

Longstreth, Richard, ed. *The Mall in Washington, 1791–1991*. Washington, DC: National Gallery of Art, 1991.

Lowenthal, David. "Fabricating Heritage." *History and Memory* 10, no. 1 (March 1998): 5.

———. *The Past Is a Foreign Country*. Cambridge: Cambridge University Press, 1985.

MacLeish, Archibald. *The Collected Poems of Archibald MacLeish*. New York: Houghton Mifflin, 1962.

Madsen, David. "James Smithson and His Legacy: The Chronicle of an Historic Bequest." *Journal of Higher Education* 36, no. 2 (February 1965): 97–104.

Maki, Mitchell T., Harry H. L. Kitano, and S. Megan Berthold, eds. *Achieving the Impossible Dream: How Japanese Americans Obtained Redress*. Urbana: University of Illinois Press, 1999.

Marling, Karal Ann, and John Wetenhall. *Iwo Jima: Monuments, Memories, and the American Hero*. Cambridge, MA: Harvard University Press, 1991.

Mauss, Marcel. *The Gift: Forms and Functions of Exchange in Archaic Societies*. New York: Norton, 1967.

Mauss, Marcel, and Hubert Henri. *Sacrifice: Its Nature and Function*. Chicago: University of Chicago Press, 1964.

McGregor, James. *Washington from the Ground Up*. Cambridge, MA: Harvard University Press, 2007.

Miller, Laura. *Feminism and the Exclusion of Army Women from Combat.* Cambridge, MA: Harvard University Press, 1995.

Mills, Nicolaus. *Their Last Battle: The Fight for the National World War II Memorial.* New York: Basic Books, 2004.

Mirzoeff, Nicolaus. *The Visual Culture Reader.* London: Routledge, 1998.

Mitchell, Brian. *Weak Link: The Feminization of the Military.* Washington, DC: Regnery, 1989.

———. *Women in the Military: Flirting with Disaster.* Washington, DC: Regnery, 1998.

Mosse, George. *Fallen Soldiers: Reshaping the Memory of the World Wars.* New York: Oxford University Press, 1990.

Muller, Eric. *Free to Die for Their Country: The Story of Japanese American Draft Resisters in World War II.* Chicago: University of Chicago Press, 2001.

Murray, Alice Yang. *Historical Memories of the Japanese American Interment and the Struggle for Redress.* Stanford, CA: Stanford University Press, 2008.

Nash, Gary. *The Forgotten Fifth: African Americans in the Age of Revolution.* Cambridge, MA: Harvard University Press, 2006.

———. *The Unknown American Revolution: The Unruly Birth of Democracy and the Struggle to Create America.* New York: Viking, 2005.

Nelson, Carey. "Martial Lyrics: The Vexed History of the Wartime Poem Card." *American Literary History* 16, no. 2 (2004).

Ngai, Mae. *Impossible Subjects: Illegal Aliens and the Making of Modern America.* Princeton, NJ: Princeton University Press, 2004.

Nobel, Philip. *Sixteen Acres: Architecture and the Outrageous Struggle for the Future of Ground Zero.* New York: Henry Holt, 2005.

Nora, Pierre. "Between Memory and History: *Les Lieux de Memoire.*" *Representations* 26 (Spring 1989): 1–21.

Okada, John. *No-No Boy.* Seattle: University of Washington Press, 1977.

O'Leary, Cecilia Elizabeth. *To Die For: The Paradox of American Patriotism.* Princeton, NJ: Princeton University Press, 1999.

Olick, Jeffery. "'Collective Memory;' A Memoir and Prospect," *Memory Studies* 1, no. 1 (2008): 23–29.

———. *The Politics of Regret: On Collective Memory and Historical Responsibility.* New York: Routledge, 2007.

———. "Social Memory Studies: From 'Collective Memory' to the Historical Sociology of Mnemonic Practices." *Annual Review of Sociology* 24 (1998): 105–40.

———, ed. *States of Memory: Continuities, Conflicts, and Transformations in National Retrospection.* Durham, NC: Duke University Press, 2003.

O'Malley, Therese. "'Your Garden Must Be a Museum to You': Early American Botanical Gardens." *Huntington Library Quarterly,* 59, nos. 2–3 (1997): 207.

Orr, David W. *The Last Refuge.* Washington, DC: Island Press, 2004.

Orvis, Bruce R., Beth J. Asch, U.S Army, U.S. Dept. of Defense, Office of the Secretary of Defense, Arroyo Center, and National Defense Research Institute. *Mili-*

tary Recruiting: Trends, Outlook, and Implications. Santa Monica, CA: Rand, 2001.

Pascoe, Peggy. *What Comes Naturally: Miscegenation Law and the Making of Race in America.* New York: Oxford University Press, 2009.

Pease, Donald. "National Narratives, Postnational Narration." *Modern Fiction Studies* 43, no. 1 (March 1997): 1–23.

Pease, Donald, and Robyn Wiegman. *The Futures of American Studies.* Durham, NC: Duke University Press, 2002.

Peets, Elbert. "The Genealogy of the Plan of Washington." *Journal of the Society of Architectural Historians* 10, no. 2 (May 1951): 3–4.

Penczer, Peter. *The Washington Mall.* Arlington: Oneonta Press, 2007.

Phillips, Kenneth, ed. *Framing Public Memory.* Tuscaloosa: University of Alabama Press, 2004.

Piehler, G. Kurt. *Remembering War the American Way.* Washington, DC: Smithsonian Press, 1995.

Pinsky, Robert. *Gulf Music.* New York: Farrar, Straus, and Giroux, 2008.

Polan, Annette, and Anne Murphy. *Faces of the Fallen: America's Artists Honor America's Heroes, March 23–September 5, 2005.* Washington, DC: Women in Military Service for America Memorial Foundation, 2006.

Portolano, Marlana. "Increase and Diffusion of Knowledge: Ethos of Science and Education in the Smithsonian's Inception." *Rhetoric Review* 18, no. 1 (Autumn 1999): 65–81.

Rodin, Judith, and Stephen P. Steinberg. *Public Discourse in America: Conversation and Community in the Twenty-First Century.* Philadelphia: University of Pennsylvania Press, 2003.

Rosenbaum, Alan. "Opposing Views: Rediscovering America at the 1893 World's Columbian Exposition: Adapted from USONLA, Frank Lloyd Wright's Design for America by Alvin Rosenbaum." *Blueprints: The Journal of the National Building Museum* 11, no. 1 (Winter 1993): 2–7.

Rowe, John. *Post-Nationalist American Studies.* Berkeley: University of California Press, 2000.

Roxworthy, Emily. *The Spectacle of Japanese American Trauma: Racial Performativity and World War II.* Honolulu: University of Hawaii Press, 2008.

Rustad, Michael. *Women in Khaki: The American Enlisted Woman.* New York: Praeger Books, 1982.

Rydell, Robert W. *All the World's a Fair: Visions of Empire at American International Expositions, 1876–1916.* Chicago: University of Chicago Press, 1984.

Sadler, Kim Martin, ed. *Atonement: The Million Man March.* Cleveland: Pilgrim Press, 1996.

Sandage, Scott A. "A Marble House Divided: The Lincoln Memorial, the Civil Rights Movement, and the Politics of Memory, 1939–1963." *Journal of American History* 80, no. 1 (June 1993): 135–67.

Savage, Kirk. "History, Memory, and Monuments: An Overview of Scholarly Literature on Commemoration," online essay commissioned by the Organization

of American Historians and the National Park Service, 2005, www.cr.nps.gov/
history/resedu/savage.htm.

———. *Monument Wars: Washington, D.C., the National Mall and the Transformation the Memorial Landscape.* Berkeley: University of California Press, 2009.

———. "The Past in the Present: The Life of Memorials." *Harvard Design Magazine,* no. 9 (Fall 1999): 19–23.

———. "The Self-Made Monument: George Washington and the Fight to Erect a
National Monument." *Winterthur Portfolio* 22, no. 4 (Winter 1987): 225–42.

———. *Standing Soldiers, Kneeling Slaves: Race, War, and Monument in Nineteenth-Century America.* Princeton, NJ: Princeton University Press, 1997.

Schwartz, Barry. *Lincoln and the Forge of National Memory.* Chicago: University of
Chicago Press, 2000.

———. "Memory as a Cultural System: Abraham Lincoln in World War II." *American Sociological Review* 61, no. 5 (1996): 908.

Schwartz, Barry, and Todd Bayma. "Commemoration and the Politics of Recognition: The Korean War Veterans Memorial." *American Behavioral Scientist* 42,
no. 6 (March 1999): 946–67.

Scobey, David M. *Empire City: The Making and Meaning of the New York City
Landscape.* Philadelphia: Temple University Press, 2002.

Scott-Childress, Reynolds. *Race and the Production of Modern American Nationalism.* New York: Garland, 1999.

Scruggs, Jan, "Twenty-Fifth Anniversary of the Wall," *CNN,* November 11, 2007.

Scruggs, Jan, and Joel L. Swerdlow. *To Heal a Nation: The Vietnam Veterans Memorial.* New York: Harper and Row, 1985.

Scruggs, Jan, and Vietnam Veterans Memorial Fund. *The Wall That Heals.* Washington, DC: Vietnam Veterans Memorial Fund, 1992.

———. *The War and the Wall: Service, Sacrifice and Honor.* Washington, DC: Vietnam Veterans Memorial Fund, 2002.

Segal, David R. *Recruiting for Uncle Sam: Citizenship and Military Manpower Policy.* Lawrence: University of Kansas Press, 1989.

Segrue, Thomas. *The Origins of the Urban Crisis.* Princeton, NJ: Princeton University Press, 1996.

Shanken, Andrew. *194X: Architecture, Planning, and Consumer Culture on the
American Homefront.* Minneapolis: University of Minnesota Press, 2009.

———. "Planning Memory: Living Memorials in the United States during World
War II." *Art Bulletin* 84, no. 1 (March 2002): 130–47.

Sherman, Daniel J. "Bodies and Names: The Emergence of Commemoration in
Interwar France." *American Historical Review* 103, no. 2 (April 1998): 443–66.

Shy, John. *A People Numerous and Armed: Reflections on the Military Struggle for
American Independence.* Ann Arbor: University of Michigan Press, 1990.

Silber, Nina, and Catherine Clinton. *Divided Houses: Gender and the Civil War.*
New York: Oxford University Press, 1992.

Simpson, David. *9/11: The Culture of Commemorations.* Chicago: University of Chicago Press, 2006.

Singh, Nikhil Pal. *Black Is a Country: Race and the Unfinished Struggle for Democracy.* Cambridge, MA: Harvard University Press, 2005.

———. "Culture/Wars: Recoding Empire in an Age of Democracy," *American Quarterly* 50, no. 3 (1998): 471–522.

Sinha, Manisha, and Penny Von Eschen, eds. *Contested Democracy: Freedom, Race and Power in American History.* New York: Columbia University Press, 2007.

Smith-Rosenberg, Carol. "Dis-Covering the Subject of the 'Great Constitutional Discussion,' 1786–1789." *Journal of American History* 79, no. 3 (December 1992): 841–73.

Snyder, Claire R. *Citizen-Soldiers and Manly Warriors: Military Service and Gender in the Civic Republic Tradition.* New York: Rowman and Littlefield, 1999.

Sollors, Werner, ed., *Interracialism: Black-White Intermarriage in American History, Literature, and Law.* New York: Oxford University Press, 2000.

Sonne, Wolfgang. *Representing the State: Capital City Planning in the Early Twentieth Century.* Berlin: Prestel, 2003.

Sontag, Susan. *Regarding Others in Pain.* New York: Farrar, Straus and Giroux, 2003.

Sorkin, Michael. *Starting from Zero: Reconstructing Downtown New York.* New York: Routledge, 2003.

Sturken, Marita. *Tangled Memories: The Vietnam War, the AIDS Epidemic, and the Politics of Remembering.* Berkeley: University of California Press, 1997.

Tashima, A. Wallace. "Patriotism: Do We Know It When We See It?" *Michigan Law Review* 101, no. 6 (May 2003): 2007–15.

Thelen, David, ed. *Memory and American History.* Bloomington: University of Indiana Press, 1990.

Thomas, Christopher. *The Lincoln Memorial and American Life.* Princeton, NJ: Princeton University Press, 2002.

Torgovnick, Marianna. *The War Complex: World War II in Our Time.* Chicago: University of Chicago Press, 2005.

Trachtenberg, Alan. *The Incorporation of America.* New York: Hill and Wang, 2007.

Tracy, James. *The Military Draft Handbook: A Brief History and Practical Advice for the Curious and Concerned.* San Francisco: Manic D Press, 2006.

Tuchman, Barbara. *Stilwell and the American Experience in China, 1911–1945.* New York: Grove Press, 1970.

Tucker, Spencer, and Jinwung Kim. *Encyclopedia of the Korean War: A Political, Social, and Military History.* Santa Barbara, CA: ABC-CLIO, 2000.

Vasquez, Joseph Paul III. "Shouldering the Soldiering: Democracy, Conscription, and Military Casualties." *Journal of Conflict Resolution* 49, no. 4 (December 2005): 849–73.

Vincent, Andrew. *Nationalism and Particularity.* Cambridge: Cambridge University Press, 2002.

Von Eschen, Penny. "Enduring Public Diplomacy." *American Quarterly* 57, no. 2 (June 2005): 335–43.

————. *Satchmo Blows Up the World: Jazz Ambassadors Play the Cold War.* Cambridge, MA: Harvard University Press, 2004.

Wallis, Brian, Marianne Weems, and Phillip Yanawine, eds. *Art Matters: How Culture Wars Changed America.* New York: New York University Press, 1999.

Warner, Michael. "Publics and Counterpublics." *Public Culture* 14, no. 1 (Winter 2002): 49–90.

Washington-Williams, Essie Mae. *Dear Senator: A Memoir by the Daughter of Strom Thurmond.* New York: Harper Collins, 2005.

Weiss, Marion, and Michael Manfredi. *Site Specific: The Work of Weiss/Manfredi Architects.* Princeton, NJ: Princeton Architectural Press, 2005.

Welch, James. *Killing Custer: The Battle of Little Big Horn and the Fate of the Plains Indians.* New York: Penguin Books, 1995.

Westbrook, Robert. *Why We Fought: Forging American Obligations in World War II.* Washington, DC: Smithsonian Books, 2004.

Williams, Cindy, ed. *Filling the Ranks: Transforming the U.S. Military Personnel System.* Cambridge, MA: MIT Press, 2004.

Winter, Jay. *Remembering War: The Great War between Memory and History in the Twentieth Century.* New Haven, CT: Yale University Press, 2006.

————. *Sites of Memory, Sites of Mourning: The Great War in European Cultural History.* Cambridge: Cambridge University Press, 1995.

Witt, Linda, and Mary Jo Binker. *A Defense Weapon Known to Be of Value: Service Women of the Korean War Era.* Lebanon, NY: University Press of New England, 2005.

Yerushalmi, Yosef, ed. *Jewish History and Jewish Memory.* Hanover, NH: Brandeis University Press, 1998.

Young, James E. *At Memory's Edge: After-Images of the Holocaust in Contemporary Art and Architecture.* New Haven, CT: Yale University Press, 2000.

————. "Memory and Counter-Memory: The End of the Monument in Germany." *Harvard Design Magazine,* no. 9 (Fall 1999).

————. *The Texture of Memory: Holocaust Memorials and Meaning.* New Haven, CT: Yale University Press, 1993.

Yu, Henry. *Thinking Orientals: Margin, Contact, and Exoticism in Modern America.* New York; Oxford University Press, 2001.

INDEX

Page numbers in italics refer to figures, illustrations, and tables.

Abelson, Reed, 78–79
abstraction, 197; and Black Revolutionary War Patriots Memorial, 82, 86; and Korean War Veterans Memorial, 29–30, 40, 50; and National World War II Memorial, 167–69, 195; and Vietnam Veterans Memorial, 29–30, 99, 168; and Vietnam Women's Memorial, 99; and Women in Military Service for America Memorial, 99
Ad Council, 176
Afghanistan War, 89, 190–91; women in, 101, 216n25, 218n79
African American churches, 201n39
African American neighborhoods, 8, 76
African Americans, 8, 12, 100, 213n70, 214n106, 216n14; and civil rights activism, 14–15, 185, 203nn55–56; in Civil War, 18, 60, 76; and Korean War Veterans Memorial, 17, 38, 46–47, 51–52, *51*; and National World War II Memorial, 224n2; and Vietnam Veterans Memorial, 7, 47. *See also* Black Revolutionary War Patriots Memorial; *names of African Americans*
Akamu, Nina, 138, 222n50
Alexander, Adele Logan, 67, 69–70
Alien Land Law (1913), 126
all-volunteer military, 2–3, 8; and Korean War Veterans Memorial, 21, 26, 29, 40,

56; and National World War II Memorial, 156, 161, 195; and Women in Military Service for America Memorial, 99, 100–101
Amache internment camp, 122
American Battle Monuments Commission (ABMC), 21, 202n50; archives of, 201n40; and Black Revolutionary War Patriots Memorial, 61, 92; and Korean War Veterans Memorial, 31, 36, 39–41, 45, 49–52, *50, 51,* 55–56, 205n20, 206n37; and National World War II Memorial, 158–161, 163–170, 172–73, 176, 184, 187–191, 195
American Indians, 7; and Daughters of the American Revolution, 68–69, 211n39; and Korean War Veterans Memorial, 17, 46–47, 51–52, *51;* and National Liberty Memorial, 90; in Revolutionary War, 68–69, 211n39; and Women in Military Service for America Memorial, 101–2, 216n24
American Legion, 99, 104, 162, 175
American Revolution Bicentennial Administration, 75
American Veterans Committee (AVC), 99, 104
Anderson, Benedict, 4, 40
Anderson, Marian, 14–15, 70, 203n55
apartheid, 70, 212n55

Arab Americans, 99, 130, 151, 220nn19–20
Aratani, George T. and Sakaye, 146
architects, 12, 39; and Black Revolutionary
    War Patriots Memorial, 79; and Hemi-
    cycle, 106; and Korean War Veterans
    Memorial, 32, 37, 45–46, 49, 55, 218n70;
    and National Japanese American
    Memorial to Patriotism during World
    War II, 134, 136; and National World
    War II Memorial, 165, 167, 169–171, 173,
    185; and Vietnam Veterans Memorial,
    37, 185; and Women in Military Service
    for America Memorial, 110, 113–14, 119,
    218n70. See also names of architects and
    architectural firms
Arlington House, 106–7
Arlington National Cemetery, 12, 34, 49,
    106–9, 217n43; and National Japanese
    American Memorial to Patriotism dur-
    ing World War II, 122, 128, 130, 219n11;
    and National World War II Memo-
    rial, 160, 173, 186; and Third Infantry
    Memorial, 97; and Women in Military
    Service for America Memorial, 106–9,
    111–13, 115, 117–121, 216n16, 218n77
Army Corps of Engineers, U.S., 51
Army Nurses Corps, 100
Ashabranner, Brent, 105–7, 217n38
Ash Woods, 24, 41–43
Asian Americans, 144, 205n22; and Korean
    War Veterans Memorial, 17, 46–47,
    51–52, 51; and National World War II
    Memorial, 224n2
Asian immigrants, 126–27, 133, 136, 144, 150
assimilation, 144–45
astronauts, 214n93
AT&T, 114
atomic bomb, 161–63, 194

Bailey, Beth, 8
Baker, George. See Brewer, Lucy
Baker, Hal, 205n20
Balibar, Etienne, 200n17
Ball, Thomas, 215n127
Barboza, Maurice, 61–62, 210nn5–6; and
    Black Revolutionary War Patriots
    Foundation, 77–79, 213n72, 213n75,
    213n77; and Black Revolutionary War

Patriots Memorial, 17–18, 61, 71–76,
    79–83, 85, 87–89, 93–95, 127, 212nn52–
    53, 213n70, 213n83, 214n96, 214n113;
    and Daughters of the American Revo-
    lution, 62, 67–68, 70, 88, 211nn34–35;
    and National Liberty Memorial, 89–92,
    215n119; website of, 212n52
Bayma, Todd, 26
Beaux Arts style, 16, 168
Belil, Eli, 31–32, 204n18
belonging, national, 19–20, 68, 125, 128
Berger, Martin, 224n3
Berlant, Lauren, 200n18
Berlin, Ira, 68
Bethune, Mary McLeod, 14
bicentennial, U.S., 14, 75
Bismarck (N.D.) internment camp, 141
Bixby, Lydia, 176–77, 226n45
Black Genealogy (Blockson), 62
Black History Month, 61–62
Black Revolutionary War Patriots Com-
    memorative Coin Act, 78, 213n79
Black Revolutionary War Patriots Founda-
    tion (BRWPF), 72, 74–75, 77–79, 81,
    83, 85, 88–89, 92, 213n82
Black Revolutionary War Patriots Memo-
    rial, 2, 17–19, 27, 36, 58–61, 70–96, 103,
    205n30, 212n52; and American flag,
    92; background of, 59–62; corporate
    sponsors for, 77–78, 92; and Daughters
    of the American Revolution, 59, 62–
    75, 77–78, 88, 92–93, 210n11, 212n53,
    212n55; design competition for, 81–82,
    214n96; and figures of black family, 83–
    88, 84, 85, 92; and figures of black sol-
    diers, 17–18, 20, 60–61, 81–87, 84, 85,
    92, 95; first design of, 79–81; fundrais-
    ing for, 36, 72–73, 77–79, 88, 92, 212n52,
    213n72, 213n77, 213n82; hidden behind
    berms, 83, 86–87, 93; and landscape
    solution, 80–83, 86, 95; as legitimation
    project, 17–18, 60–61, 74, 83, 86–87,
    93–95; National Japanese American
    Memorial to Patriotism during World
    War II compared to, 127–29, 132; and
    National Liberty Memorial, 89–92,
    215n119; National World War II Memo-
    rial compared to, 153, 156; second design

of, 81–89, *84, 85,* 214n101, 214n104; site
of, 75–76, 91, 213n70; third design of,
91–92, *93;* unbuilt status of, 2, 17–19,
88, 92–95; visitors to, 80, 83; Women in
Military Service for America Memorial
compared to, 98

blacks. *See* African Americans

Blake, Casey Nelson, 33

Blight, David, 5, 7, 10, 47

Blockson, Charles, 61–62

Bodnar, John, 177–78

Bonus Army (1932), 203n55

Borcherdt, Edward R., 206n42

Bourke, Joanna, 9

Brandston, Howard, 111

Bray, Linda, 101, 216n19

Brewer, Lucy, 99–100

Brimmer, Andrew, 77

Brody, Carolyn S., 141

Brown, Heidi V., 102, 216n25

Brown, J. Carter: and Black Revolutionary
War Patriots Memorial, 75–76, 80–81,
83–85; death of, 191; and Korean War
Veterans Memorial, 38, 45, 49–50, 53,
205n34, 207n63, 207n66; and National
Japanese American Memorial to Patriotism during World War II, 132–33, 135–
36, 140, 143, 221n29; and National World
War II Memorial, 160, 163, 169–170,
172–73, 186, 191; and Women in Military
Service for America Memorial, 108–13

Brown, Willie, 78

Brown University, 38

Buckley, Davis, 134–38, 141, 221n45,
222n49

Buddhist temples, 146

Burnham, Daniel, 12, 15, 159, 166

Burns Lucas, Veronica, 42–43, 45, 49,
207n61

Bush, George H. W., 44, 134, 221n47

Bush, George W., 101, 187–88, 220n19

Butler, Carrie, 70

Byrd, D. Winifred, 216n14

Calloway, Colin, 68

Capitol, 11–12, 201n45; and civil rights
activists, 15, 203n55; and National Japanese American Memorial to Patrio-

tism during World War II, 122, 135–36;
and National World War II Memorial,
166, 170

Capra, Frank, 19, 157, 203n56

Carlstrom, Terry, 140

Carotka, Bob, 191–92, 227n72

*Carried to the Wall: American Memory
and the Vietnam Veterans Memorial*
(Hass), 7

Catholics, 7

Caucasians. *See* whites

Cayton, Andrew, 68

cemeteries, 106, 154–55, 160, 202n50. *See
also names of cemeteries*

Chang, Ming, 224n12

Chase, John, 167

Cherry, Fred V., 206n42

Chicago World's Fair, 12, 107, 202n49

Children of the Revolution, 65

Childs, David, 167, 175

Chinese Exclusion Act (1882), 126

Chiogioji, Melvin H., 144

Christian, Daysha, 90–91

Christian Coalition, 216n28

Christian Science Monitor, 34

citizenship: and Black Revolutionary War
Patriots Memorial, 87, 127; and Gulf
War, 130; and Korean War Veterans
Memorial, 32, 46; and National Japanese American Memorial to Patriotism
during World War II, 18, 122, 124, 127,
130, 144, 147, 150; and National Liberty
Memorial, 89–91; naturalized citizens,
32, 127, 144

City Beautiful Movement, 202n49

Civil Liberties Act (1988), 136, 142, 221n47

civil rights activists, 14–15, 33, 128, 172–
73, 185, 187–88, 193–94, 203nn55–56,
203n60, 221n47

Civil War, 2–3, 7–8, 10, 18, 199n5; and
Black Revolutionary War Patriots Memorial, 60, 67, 70; Bull Run,
106; deserters from, 10; as "good war,"
3, 199n8; memorials of, 47, 76; and
National Liberty Memorial, 89; Union
Army, 76, 129, 157; and war dead, 2, 18,
70, 89, 106, 129, 155, 157, 176–77; women
in, 100

Clarke, David A., 66, 72–73, 77
class, social, 8, 200n20
Clinton, Bill: and apology for Japanese
American internment, 221n47; "Don't
Ask, Don't Tell" policy of, 209n98; and
Enola Gay fight, 162; and Korean War
Veterans Memorial, 56–57; letter on
Vietnam War draft, 55–57, 209n104;
and National World War II Memorial,
158, 160, 169
Coast Guard, 216n14
Cold War, 3, 17, 21–24, 26, 29, 33–35, 41, 54,
156, 161
colonialism, 22–23, 26, 29
commemoration, 9, 198; and Black Revolutionary War Patriots Memorial, 76, 78,
213n79; and Civil War, 7; commemorative aesthetic, 38; commemorative coins,
78, 213n79; commemorative quotas, 46;
and Korean War Veterans Memorial, 27,
35–36, 46; and National Japanese American Memorial to Patriotism during
World War II, 129, 138; and National
World War II Memorial, 155, 158, 167,
170, 174; and Vietnam Veterans Memorial, 15–16; and Women in Military Service for America Memorial, 103, 118
Commemorative Works Act (1986), 39, 76,
128–29, 133, 186
Commemorative Works Clarification and
Revision Act (2003), 90–91
Commerce Business Daily, 164
Commission of Fine Arts (CFA), 13,
202nn51–52; archives of, 201n40; and
Black Revolutionary War Patriots
Memorial, 75–76, 79–86, 88, 92, 212n52,
212n61, 214n93; and Korean War Vet-
erans Memorial, 36, 38–39, 45, 48–50,
52, 207n63; and National Japanese
American Memorial to Patriotism dur-
ing World War II, 129, 132, 138, 140–41,
143, 221n35; and National World War
II Memorial, 159–161, 163, 166, 169–
175, 178–182, 185–191, 195, 224n10; and
Women in Military Service for America
Memorial, 108, 110–13, 120, 217n63
Committee of 100 on the Federal City, 186
communism, 22–23, 26, 30, 35, 41, 206n35

Confederacy, 226n45; United Daughters of
the Confederacy, 65, 70
Congress, U.S., 11–13, 38–39, 201n45,
202n50; and Black Revolutionary War
Patriots Memorial, 2, 18, 27, 36, 66, 71–
77, 79, 89, 92, 96, 156, 205n30, 212n52,
213n79; and Civil War, 76; and *Enola
Gay* fight, 161–62, 194; and Korean
War, 22–23, 204n5; and Korean War
Veterans Memorial, 18, 27, 29, 33–39, 96,
156, 205n30, 205n34, 206n35, 206n37,
209n104; and Moroccan Monument,
96–97; and National Japanese American Memorial to Patriotism during
World War II, 126, 128–130, 133–36; and
National Liberty Memorial, 90–91;
and National World War II Memorial,
152, 157–59, 161–62, 164, 167, 171–72,
187–88, 224nn10–11, 225n30; and Navy
Memorial, 103; Ninety-Ninth Congress,
27, 35–36, 96–97; and service flags, 184;
and Third Infantry Memorial, 96–97;
and Vietnam Women's Memorial, 99,
103; and Women in Military Service for
America Memorial, 18, 27, 36, 96–97,
99, 102, 104, 114, 156, 205n30, 216n16
Constitution, USS, 99
Constitution Gardens, 14; and Black Rev-
olutionary War Patriots Memorial,
75–76, 80–81, 83, 85, 91; and National
World War II Memorial, 159–160, 163,
187
Constitution Hall, 14, 70, 75, 94
Cooke, Aileen, 216n14
Cooper, Kent, 45–46, 48, 51–53, 57,
185–86, 207n66, 209n107. *See also*
Cooper-Lecky
Cooper-Lecky, 46, 49, 52
Corcoran Gallery of Art, 45–46
Costner, Doris Strom, 60
courage: and Black Revolutionary War
Patriots Memorial, 73, 82; and Korean
War Veterans Memorial, 30–31, 56; and
National Japanese American Memo-
rial to Patriotism during World War II,
125–27, 133, 148; and National World
War II Memorial, 166; of those who
refused to serve, 127

Courtenay, Roger, 83
Coxey's Army (1894), 203n55
Creef, Elena Tajima, 125, 219n4
Crouch, Tom, 163
Crystal City (Tex.) internment camp, 141
Cumberbatch, Yvonne, 216n14
Curcio, John B., 206n42
Curtis, Michael, 215n119
Cushman, Marilla, 115
Custer, George Armstrong, 47
Custis, George Washington Parke, 106
Custis, Mary Anna Randolph, 106
Custis-Lee Mansion, 106, 111

Dachau concentration camp, 149
A Date with Destiny (Ashabranner), 105–7, 217n38
Daughters of the American Revolution (DAR), 59, 62–71, 92, 210n11; and affirmative action program, 66, 212n53; and Black Revolutionary War Patriots Memorial, 59, 62, 70, 72–75, 77–78, 88, 92–93, 210n11, 212nn52–53, 212n55; bylaws of, 66, 70; Constitution Hall, 14, 70, 75, 94; and discrimination, 14, 65–67, 70; Elizabeth Jackson chapter, 63, 66; Forgotten Patriots Symposium, 68; and genealogical research, 66–70, 211n39, 211nn34–35; and lawsuits, 66, 210n24, 212n53; and legitimacy requirement, 63–64, 67–68, 210n19; and Marian Anderson concert, 14, 70; Mary Washington chapter, 62–63; and miscegenation, 64, 67–68, 74; National Congress, 63, 65; Ninety-Fourth Continental Congress of the National Society, 69–70; opposition to ERA, 211n42; and sponsorship requirement, 62–64, 77–78; support of South African apartheid, 70, 212n55; tax-exempt status of, 65–66
Davis, Raymond G., 206n42
D.C. Preservation League, 186
Dean, Robert, 54
Declaration of Independence, 14, 75, 81, 89, 150
decolonization, 26, 29, 57
The Deer Hunter (film), 30

Defense Department, U.S., 29, 100, 104, 160
Dehne, Thomas G., 206n42
De Leon, Rudy, 149–150
democracy, 1, 3, 6–8; and civil rights activists, 14, 203n55; and draft, 56; and National Japanese American Memorial to Patriotism during World War II, 124, 131, 142, 147; and National Mall design, 12, 107; and National World War II Memorial, 160–61, 169–173, 177, 180
Denver Post, 142
Detweiler, William, 162
Diamonstein-Spielvogel, Barbaralee, 140
Dietsch, Deborah, 173
discrimination, 14, 65–67, 70. *See also* prejudice
diversity. *See* race/ethnicity
Dodd, Christopher, 90–91
dog tags, 2, 6, 226n58
Dole, Bob, 175
Dooley, Joseph, 215n119
Dowd, Greg, 68
draft, 2, 8, 28; and Clinton letter, 55–56, 209n104; and draft resisters, 147–49, 223n83, 223n85; and National Japanese American Memorial to Patriotism during World War II, 147–48, 223n83, 223n85; and National World War II Memorial, 156; and Women in Military Service for America Memorial, 99, 101
Duara, Prasenjit, 200n17
Duchamp, Marcel, 139
Duncan, David Douglas, 42–43
Durbin, Roger, 157–58, 160; granddaughter of, 158–59, 224n12
Dwight, Ed, 81–92, *84,* 212n53, 213n70, 213n72, 214n93, 214n96, 214n104

eagles: and National Japanese American Memorial to Patriotism during World War II, 138–39; and National World War II Memorial, 152, 179–180, 182–84, 186, 226n56; in political cartoon (1898), 183–84
Edkins, Jenny, 5
Ehrlich, Akemi Dawn Matsumoto, 142
Eley, Goeff, 199n9

Ellison, Ralph, 47
Emancipation Memorial, 215n127
Encinitas, Miguel, 224n12
Engelhardt, Tom, 161
Enola Gay, 161–63, 194
ERA (Equal Rights Amendment), 101, 211n42
ethnicity. *See* race/ethnicity
exceptionalism, American, 19

Fagin, Helen, 170–71, 185, 224n12
family, 3, 6; and Black Revolutionary War Patriots Memorial, 60–61, 79, 83–88, *84, 85*, 92–93, *93*, 98; and Daughters of the American Revolution, 64–65, 67, 69, 78; and Lincoln's Bixby letter, 176–77, 226n45; and National Japanese American Memorial to Patriotism during World War II, 18, 122, 126–27; and National World War II Memorial, 172, 176–77, 196; and *Saving Private Ryan* (film), 175–77, 226n45
Farmer, Karen, 62–63, 210n11
Faust, Drew Gilpin, 2
Federal Advisory Committee Act, 186
Federal Bureau of Investigation, 130
Federal Housing Authority, 8
Feldman, Judith, 186
feminists, 101
Ferguson, William C. Sr., 158
Finley, Joyce, 65
Fish, Jack, 109
Fishkin, Joseph, 165
Fleming, Mark, 224n12
Focus on the Family, 216n28
Foley, Thomas, 135
Ford, Gerald, 221n47
forgetting, 4–5; and Korean War Veterans Memorial, 21–22, 24, 34, 45, 204n2
Forgey, Ben, 117–18, 218n82, 219n2
Forgotten Patriots (DAR), 68–69, 211n39
freedom, 3, 15, 28; and Black Revolutionary War Patriots Memorial, 72–74, 80, 83, 87, 215n127; and civil rights activists, 15, 203n56; and Korean War Veterans Memorial, 17, 23, 25–27, 31, 36, 39–41, 204n18; and National Japanese American Memorial to Patriotism dur-

ing World War II, 124, 126, 150; and National Liberty Memorial, 89; and National World War II Memorial, 152–53, 171–74, 177–180, 184–85, 190
Freedom Plaza, 159
Frey, Sylvia, 68, 74

Garrigus, John, 68
Gates, Henry Louis, 91, 211n35, 215n119
Gavin, Dennis P., 103–4
Gay, Jonah, 61
Gaylord, Frank, 45–46, 52–55, 207n61, 207n66, 208n87, 209n101
gay rights movement, 15
gender: and Korean War Veterans Memorial, 17, 26, 38, 47–48, 54, 57, 206n42; and nationalism, 4–5, 20, 197, 200n20; and National World War II Memorial, 153, 224n2; and Women in Military Service for America Memorial, 18, 97–98, 102, 116, 120, 217n64
genealogy, 17–18, 59–63, 67–68, 92, 210nn5–6, 211nn34–35; and census records, 68
General Motors, 62, 77–78, 92, 115
General Services Administration, 165–66; Knoxville, 33
Gentleman's Agreement (1907), 126
George Washington Memorial Parkway, 120–21
Gerstle, Gary, 193, 199n8
Gessner, Ingrid, 219n4
Gettysburg, battle of, 2, 6, 155, 199n5
Gettysburg Address, 2, 6, 31, 34, 156–57, 203n56
Ghana, 78
Gingrich, Newt, 161
Go For Broke Monument (Los Angeles), 219n4, 221n31
Go For Broke National Veterans Association, 128, 132–34, 221n36
gold stars, 152–53, 155, 180, 184–86, 188, 190–91, *192*
Goodman, Louis E., 148
Gore, Al, 72, 212n54
Grant Memorial, 170, 172
The Graybeards newsletter, 37, 206n40
grief, 4; and Black Revolutionary War

Patriots Memorial, 88, 214n113; and
Korean War Veterans Memorial, 30, 40;
and National World War II Memorial,
177, 192; and Vietnam Veterans Memo-
rial, 7, 29–30, 56, 191; and Women in
Military Service for America Memo-
rial, 217n64
Ground Zero, 165, 224n6
Growden, Melissa, 158–59, 224n12
Grundset, Eric, 211n39
Gulf War, 49, 89, 130; women in, 97, 101,
114

Haapala, Ken, 172
Haley, Alex, 17, 61, 66
Hall, Gwendolyn Midlo, 68
Ham, Debra Newman, 68
Hammerschmidt, John, 35
Hanks, Tom, 175–78
Hardy, Hugh, 167–68, 171
Hart, Frederick, 37, 47, 160
Hashima, Larry, 145, 147, 222n61
Hausman, Conrad, 206n42
Hawaii, 136, 144, 220n16, 222n50
Hay, Jess, 224n12
Hay, John, 177
Heart Mountain Relocation Center (Wy.),
122, 128, 142, 147–48
Hemicycle, 106–16, 118–19
heroism, 2–3, 5, 196–97; and Black Revo-
lutionary War Patriots Memorial, 80,
88, 214n113; and Korean War Veterans
Memorial, 17, 21, 34, 43, 45, 48, 52–53,
55–56, 58, 61; and National Japanese
American Memorial to Patriotism dur-
ing World War II, 125, 127, 129–130, 136,
149–150; and National Liberty Memo-
rial, 90–91; and National World War II
Memorial, 152, 156, 160, 166, 174, 177–
79, 192, 194, 196; and Vietnam Veterans Memorial, 16–17, 34, 37–38; and
Women in Military Service for America
Memorial, 97, 101–2, 105, 120, 217n64
Herrington, Herman, 175
Heyman, Michael, 162–63
highways as memorials, 6, 8, 155
Hines, Thomas, 202n49
Hispanics, 46, 51, 51

Hitler, Adolf, 173, 182
Hobsbawm, Eric, 4, 40
Hodel, Donald Paul, 76, 103–4, 216n28;
and "push-polling," 216n28
Hofstra, Warren, 68
Hogan and Hartson law firm, 66, 69–70
Holcomb, G., 30–32, 34, 41
Holm, Jeanne, 108
Holocaust: Dachau concentration camp,
149; survivors of, 224n12; and witness-
ing, 201n39
Holocaust Memorial Museum, U.S.,
224n12, 225n18
Holton, Woody, 68
homosexuality, 209n98
Hood, William, 210n11
Hooker, Olivia, 216n14
Hosokawa, Bill, 142, 223n73
Hutchison, Tim, 187
Huxtable, Ada Louise, 167
Hyundai Motors of America, 37

"I Have a Dream" (King), 15
Immigration Act (1924), 126
imperial power, 26, 29, 54, 57, 119–120, 154,
182
inclusion, national, 19–20, 197; and Black
Revolutionary War Patriots Memorial,
17–18, 59; and Korean War Veterans
Memorial, 45, 207n62; and National
Japanese American Memorial to Patrio-
tism during World War II, 127–28, 131;
and National Liberty Memorial, 91; and
National World War II Memorial, 153
Indian wars, 202n48
Inouye, Daniel, 128–130, 132, 142, 148–49,
220n16
Interior Department, U.S., 185–86
The Invention of Tradition (Hobsbawm), 4
Iraq War, 89, 190–91; and war dead, 101–2;
women in, 101–2, 216nn24–25, 218n75,
218n79
Iraq War, first. See Gulf War
Iwamura, Jane Naomi, 125, 219n4
Iwo Jima Memorial, 30, 157, 224n6

Japanese American Citizens League
(JACL), 143–48, 219n11, 222n61

Japanese Americans: denial of civil rights, 129, 136–38; and draft resisters, 147–49, 223n83, 223n85; 522nd Field Artillery Battalion, 149; 442nd Infantry Combat Team, 125, 128, 134, 136, 141–42, 149; as "impossible subjects," 124, 126–27, 150, 219n1; internment of, 18–19, 122–29, 131, 133–142, 144–45, 147–150, 219n4, 220n16, 221n29, 221n45, 221n47, 222n50; Issei, 144–45; Lange's OWI photographs of, 221n45; and Loyalty Test, 147–48; Military Intelligence Service, 136, 141; and model minority myth, 145; Nikkei, 144; Nisei, 145, 147–48, 223n83; 100th Infantry Battalion, 125, 134, 136, 141–42; and reparations, 221n47; Sansei, 145. *See also* National Japanese American Memorial to Patriotism during World War II

Japanese American Voice, 143; website of, 223n70

Japanese Canadians, 146

Japanese immigrants, 126–27, 133, 136, 144

Japan/Japanese: atomic bomb dropped on, 161–63, 194; and Korean War, 22, 29; Sino-Japanese War, 22. *See also entries beginning with* Japanese

Jefferson, Thomas, 10, 12

Jefferson Memorial, 12, 49, 166, 203n61

Jerusalem (Ohio), 157, 160

Johnson, Lyndon, 212n53

Johnson, Nancy L., 71–72, 74

Johnston, Margaret, 62, 65, 72, 77–78, 92, 212n53, 213n72

Jones, Joanne, 78

Jones, John Paul, 170

Journal of the American Institute of Architects, 32

Jung, Carl, 16

Justice Department, U.S., 141

Kansas City Monarchs, 214n93

Kaplan, Amy, 218n75

Kaptur, Marcy, 157–58, 225n30

Kaskey, Ray, 180, 182–83

Kassebaum, Nancy, 162

Kelley, P. X., 190

Kempthorne, Dirk, 91

Kendall, Donald, 167

Kennedy, John F., 39, 203n64, 214n93; gravesite of, 111

Kenny, John, 206n37

Kerin, James, 204n2

Kerrey, Robert, 171–72

Kidder, Rolland, 172

Kim, Chayon, 32–34, 205n20, 205n22

Kimmelman, Michael, 180

King, Martin Luther Jr., 15, 166, 172–73, 203nn60–61, 220n26; memorial of, 203n61, 214n93

King, Sarah, 63–66, 69–70, 72–73, 77, 212n53, 212nn54–55

Kirken, Rolf, 45

Klein, Christina, 26

Klienknecht, C. Fred, 215n119

Knoxville Flag, 33

Kodak, 115

Kooskia (Idaho) internment camp, 141

Korea/Koreans: Naktong River, 42; North Korea/Koreans, 22–23, 42–43, 206n35; private donations from, 37; and reunification, 22; South Korea/Koreans, 22–23, 43, 204n11, 206n35; and wildlife in DMZ, 23–24. *See also names of Koreans*

Korean Augment to the U.S. Army (KATUSAs), 46

Korean War, 21–24, 29–36, 57; Allied Forces, 35, 205n34; and Clinton letter, 56, 209n104; and demilitarized zone (DMZ), 23–24, 41, 43; as "the Forgotten War," 21–22, 24, 34, 45, 204n2; Korean civilian deaths in, 23, 27, 35; photograph of, 42–43; Pusan Perimeter, 42; as "the 6/25 War," 22; stalemate in, 21, 23, 41–43; and thirty-eighth parallel, 22–23, 41–43, 45, 50; as walking war, 41–42; and war dead, 23, 25, 27, 30, 34–36, 41, 44, 57, 204n7, 204n11; women in, 102. *See also* Korean War Veterans Memorial (KWVM)

Korean War Memorial Advisory Board (KWMAB), 21, 36–41, 45–46, 48–50, 56, 206n42, 208n83

Korean War Memorial coin, 37

Korean War Project website, 205n20

Korean War Veterans Act (1985), 34–35

Korean War Veterans Association (KWVA), 34–35, 37–38; *The Graybeards* newsletter, 37, 206n40

Korean War Veterans Memorial (KWVM), 1, 17, 20, 21–58, *25, 28, 55,* 96; American flag in, 24–26, *25,* 40–42, 44; architects for, 32, 37, 45–46, 49, 55; background of, 21–24; Black Revolutionary War Patriots Memorial compared to, 61, 82, 87–88, 95; and blind devotion, 17, 21, 57, 61, 88, 98, 123, 132, 209n107; blindness of soldiers depicted, 54–55; corporate sponsors not sought for, 37, 223n75; cost of, 36–37; dedication of, 17, 21, 37, 56–57; Delta Scheme design of, 48–49; design competition for, 39–46, 165–66, 206n49, 207n52, 207n61, 207n66; design elements of, 24–27, 36–37, 40–42, 44, *50;* Field of Service, 24–27, *25;* final design of, 49–55; first design of, 39–45, 48–49, 207n55, 207n61, 207n66; "Freedom Is Not Free," 25–27; fundraising for, 31, 36–37, 79, 205n20, 205n23, 206n37, 223n75; as "GI Joe battle scene," 49; history of, 207n52; and impressionistic styling, 50, 52, 54; kiosk providing interactive computer in, 27; larger-than-life figures of soldiers in, 21, 24–29, *25, 28,* 40–58, *50, 51, 55,* 204n17, 207n55; and lawsuits, 49, 209n101; legislation for, 18, 27, 29, 33–39, 205n30, 205n34, 206n35, 206n37; and limp wrists, 53–54, 88, 98, 209n98; Mural Wall, 24–25, *25,* 41, 50–51, *50;* and National Japanese American Memorial to Patriotism during World War II, 123, 128, 132; as national recovery project, 21; National World War II Memorial as response to, 156–160, 163, 165–67, 170, 186, 189; origins of, 30–35, 98, 205n22, 205n30; pattern of mountainous terrain in, *25,* 42; and peace, 44, 48–49, 56; ponchos in, 24, 50, 52, 98, 208n87; Pool of Remembrance, 25–27; questionnaire concerning, 32–33, 37; redesigns of, 45–49; slogan of, 26, 56; on thirty-seven-cent stamp, 209n101; visitors to, 24, 27, 43; and war movies, 48, 208n80; Women in Military Service for America Memorial compared to, 218n70

Kuwait, 114–15, 218n75
Kuwayama, Kelly, 143

Lacy, Bill, 169
Lange, Dorothea, 221n45
Laqueur, Thomas, 2
Latinos, 38, 47
Leavy, Jane, 69
Lecky, William, 50–53, 204n17. *See also* Cooper-Lecky
Lee, Jean, 146
Lee, Robert E., 106
L'Enfant, Pierre, 10–11, *11,* 106, 171, 173, 226n56
Leon, Don, 43, 45–46, 49, 207n61, 207n63, 207n66
liberals, 99, 193–94, 199n8; racial liberalism, 150
liberty: and Black Revolutionary War Patriots Memorial, 71–74, 82, 87–88; and Korean War Veterans Memorial, 44; and National Japanese American Memorial to Patriotism during World War II, 132; and National Liberty Memorial, 89–90, 92; and National World War II Memorial, 174, 189
Lim, Deborah, 144–45
Lim Report, 144–45
Lin, Maya, 16–17, 37–39, 165, 168, 189, 191, 203n66
Lincoln, Abraham, 10, 12, 14–15, 44, 75, 89, 92, 203n55, 215n127; Bixby letter, 176–77, 226n45; Gettysburg Address, 2, 6, 31, 34, 156–57, 203n56
Lincoln Memorial, 12–16, 201n47; and Black Revolutionary War Patriots Memorial, 75, 86, 92, 94, 214n104; and civil rights activists, 14–15, 203nn55–56, 203n61; and defining moments of nineteenth century, 160, 164, 172, 189; and Korean War Veterans Memorial, 24–25, 48; in *Mr. Smith Goes to Washington* (film), 157, 203n56; and National World War II Memorial, 152, 157, 159–160, 164, 166, 168, 170, 174, 176, 187–88, *193,* 227n67; and Obama's inauguration, 227n67; and Women in Military Service for America Memorial, 107–8, 111

Linenthal, Edward, 6–7, 161
Long, Robert, 167
Lordsburg/Santa Fe (N.M.) internment
    camp, 141
Los Angeles Times, 34, 104
loss, 19, 196; and Korean War Veterans
    Memorial, 30, 56–57; and National Jap-
    anese American Memorial to Patriotism
    during World War II, 122–24, 129, 140;
    and National World War II Memorial,
    155–56, 160, 172, 174–180, 184–85, 188,
    191–92; and Vietnam Veterans Memo-
    rial, 6–7, 16, 30, 56–57, 156, 172
loyalty: and Black Revolutionary War
    Patriots Memorial, 87; and Gulf War,
    130; and National Japanese American
    Memorial to Patriotism during World
    War II, 123–24, 127, 130–31, 133, 136–
    38, 140–41, 145, 149–150; and National
    World War II Memorial, 171
Lucas, John Paul, 43, 45, 49, 207n61
Ludtke, Lawrence, 45–46
Lynch, Jessica, 101–2

MacArthur, Douglas, Mrs., 32
MacLeish, Archibald, 1–2, 20, 153, 156, 179–
    180, 184, 190–91, 196
Manfredi, Michael, 110, 112–14, 118–120,
    218n70, 219n83, 225n32. *See also* Weiss/
    Manfredi
Mangis, Jon, 224n12
Manzanar internment camp, 122
March on Washington (1993), 15
Marine Corps, 157, 224n6, 224n12
Martin Luther King Jr. Memorial, 203n61,
    214n93
Marutani, William, 132
Masaoka, Mike, 128, 142–48, 150, 219n11,
    222n61
masculinity: and Black Revolutionary War
    Patriots Memorial, 18, 87–88; and Cold
    War, 54; "ideology of masculinity," 54;
    and Korean War Veterans Memorial, 21,
    52–55, 58, 61, 88; and National Japanese
    American Memorial to Patriotism dur-
    ing World War II, 127; and Women in
    Military Service for America Memo-
    rial, 120

Matisse, Henri, 139
Matisse, Paul, 139–140
Matsui, Robert T., 142
Matsumoto, Barney, 221n36
Matsunaga, Spark M., 142
Mauldin, Bill, 158
Mayflower, 61
McCarthy, Rosemary T., 206n42
McClendon, Sarah, 158
McClintock, Anne, 4, 96, 120
McKee, Myron, 32, 205n23
McKevitt, James D., 206n42
McKim, Charles Follen, 107. *See also*
    McKim, Mead, and White
McKim, Mead, and White, 106–7, 112, 116
McMillan, James, 12–13, 15, 205n22;
    McMillan Commission, 12–13; McMil-
    lan Commission Report, 13; McMillan
    Plan, 12–13, *13,* 15, 38, 75, 106–7, 136, 166,
    169–171, 173, 202n51, 226n40
McNair, Fort, 128–29
McSweeny, William F., 206n42
Memorial Bridge, 12, 106–9
Memorial Day, 7, 72, 155–56, 180, 187–88
Memorial Drive, 106–8, 112, 115
Memorial Gate, 110
memory, 1–10, 14, 19, 99, 196, 199n9,
    201n39, 219n4; collective memory, 5–6,
    9, 201n37; and Holocaust, 201n39; and
    Korean War Veterans Memorial, 27,
    34–35, 40, 43, 55, 57; memory boom, 5,
    47, 63, 106–7; memory-nation nexus,
    3–4, 6, 15; and National Liberty Memo-
    rial, 91; and National World War II
    Memorial, 153–54, 171, 173, 192; post-
    memory, 5; prosthetic memory, 5; shared
    memory, 5; vernacular memory, 5; and
    Vietnam Veterans Memorial, 191; whit-
    ening of, 2, 7–8, 47, 197; and Women in
    Military Service for America Memo-
    rial, 99, 120
Merck Pharmaceuticals, 115
Mexican Americans, 7, 17, 46, 51–52, *51*
Miami Herald, 205n23
Michaels, Walter Benn, 52
military service, 8, 18–20, 196–97; and 2
    percent cap on women, 100–101; and
    all-volunteer military, 2–3, 8, 21, 26, 29,

40, 56, 99, 101, 156, 161, 195; and ban on pregnant women, 100–101, 216n16; and ban on women with children, 100–101; "Be All You Can Be" advertising campaign, 29; and Black Revolutionary War Patriots Memorial, 60, 74, 82–83, 87; and Clinton letter, 55–56, 209n104; and desegregation, 31, 45, 47; and draft, 2, 8, 28, 55–56, 99, 147–49, 156, 209n104, 223n83, 223n85; and gold stars, 152–53, 155, 180, 184–86, 188, 190–91, *192;* and Korean War Veterans Memorial, 26, 28–29, 34–35, 37, 39–40, 46, *51,* 52, 56–57, 209n107; and militias, 2, 74, 199n3; and National Japanese American Memorial to Patriotism during World War II, 18, 123–24, 127–131, 133–34, 136–37, 145–150; and National World War II Memorial, 153, 156, 158, 162, 164, 194; and post-Vietnam military, 3, 17, 97, 101, 114–15, 156, 190–91, 195, 199n8, 216n19; and recruitment, 26, 29, 40, 74, 156; and service flags, 2, 152, 184, 224n1, 226n58; and standing federal army, 2; and "support our troops" logic, 125, 176, 194; and those who refused to serve, 127; and Vietnam War, 2–3, 8, 16, 19, 55–56, 161, 163, 176, 178; and women in combat units, 100–101, 197; and Women in Military Service for America Memorial, 96–102, 105, 110–11, 113–16, 118–120, 216n19, 217n64. *See also* soldiers; veterans
Miller, Robert, 173
Million Man March, 203n60
Mills, Nicolaus, 155–57, 189–190, 192–94
Mineta, Norman, 128–132, 136, 142, 151
Minidoka (Idaho) Relocation Center, 148
Minneapolis Star Tribune, 205n23
miscegenation, 18, 60, 64, 67–68, 74
Missoula (Mont.) internment camp, 141
Mitchell, Brian, 216n18
modernism: and Korean War Veterans Memorial, 32–33; and National World War II Memorial, 168, 181; and Vietnam Veterans Memorial, 16, 189
Monette, Paul, 15
Monument Wars (Savage), 201n42

moral authority, 14–15, 18, 203n55
Moroccan Monument, 96–97, 104
Mosely, Julia, 216n14
Mount Vernon's Ladies Association, 65
Mr. Smith Goes to Washington (film), 157, 203n56
Murphy, Bill, 224n12
Muschamp, Herbert, 194
Myer, Edward, 29

Nash, Gary, 68, 91, 211n35
National Archives, 25
National Capital Memorial Advisory Commission (NCMAC), 76; and Black Revolutionary War Patriots Memorial, 103; and Moroccan Monument, 104; and National Japanese American Memorial to Patriotism during World War II, 128–132, 135, 220n13, 221n35; and National Liberty Memorial, 90; and Women in Military Service for America Memorial, 103–4, 110
National Capital Park and Planning Commission, 38–39
National Capital Planning Commission (NCPC): archives of, 201n40; and Black Revolutionary War Patriots Memorial, 75–76; and Korean War Veterans Memorial, 36, 38–39, 45; and National World War II Memorial, 160, 163, 166, 173, 181, 185–86, 195; and Women in Military Service for America Memorial, 110
National Coalition to Save Our Mall, 186
National Committee for the Korean War, 32, 205n23
National Defense Authorization Act (1992–93), 101
National Environmental Policy Act, 186
National Gallery of Art, 38, 167; I. M. Pei addition to, 38
National Historical Preservation Act, 186
nationalism, 19, 197, 202n48; and Black Revolutionary War Patriots Memorial, 17–18, 20, 60; and civil rights activists, 14–15; and Civil War, 2, 201n47; and Korean War Veterans Memorial, 17, 40, 57–58; and National Japanese American

nationalism *(continued)*
    Memorial to Patriotism during World
        War II, 19–20, 125, 150; and National
        Mall design, 12, 15–19; and National
        World War II Memorial, 19, 153, 155,
        176, 182, 195; scholarly theories on, 3–6,
        9–10, 40, 199n9, 200nn17–18, 200n20;
        and Vietnam Veterans Memorial, 3, 28,
        132; and Women in Military Service for
        America Memorial, 20, 98–99, 116, 119
National Japanese American Memorial
    Foundation (NJAMF), 125, 133, 135–38,
    140–44, 146
National Japanese American Memorial to
    Patriotism during World War II, 1–2,
    18–19, 58, 122–151, *123, 124;* and apol-
    ogy for internment, 18–19, 122–25, *124,*
    133, 136–38, 146, 221n47; background
    of, 125–28, 219n7; and blind devo-
    tion, 19, 123, 127, 132, 146, 148, 150–51;
    as cautionary tale, 123–24, 129–130,
    133; community meetings for design
    of, 136; corporate sponsors not sought
    for, 146, 223n75; crane memorial in,
    122, *123,* 138–140, *139,* 141, 150; dedica-
    tion of, 125–27, 149–150, 219n2; design
    competition for, 136, 221n36; design ele-
    ments of, 122, 136–38, 222n49; design of,
    136–140; draft resisters missing from,
    147–49, 223n83, 223n85; fundraising
    for, 79, 146–47, 223n73, 223n75; grand
    opening of, 219n2; and haiku, 142–43;
    "Here We Admit a Wrong," 18, 122, *124,*
    142; inscriptions in, 18, 122–24, *124,*
    137–38, 140–43, 145; and internment/
    internment camps, 122–29, *123,* 131, 133–
    142, 144–45, 147–150, 219n4, 220n16,
    221n29, 221n45, 221n47, 222n50; and
    Japanese American Creed, 140, 142–
    47, 150, 222n61; Japanese bell in, 122,
    137–140; names of soldiers killed in
    war, 122, 125, 141–42; as national recov-
    ery project, 131; National World War II
    Memorial compared to, 153; origins of,
    128, 145, 219n11; as redemptive, 122, 131,
    133; resistance to, 147–49; site of, 135–
    36; and tanka, 142–43; and those who
    refused to serve, 127; visitors to, 139, 141,

143, 149, 222n49; water element in, 122,
    135, 137–38, 222n49
National Korean War Memorial, Inc.,
    206n37
National Liberty Memorial (NLM), 89–
    92, *93;* National Liberty Memorial
    Foundation, 91; National Mall Liberty
    Fund D.C., 89–91, 215n119
National Mall (Washington, D.C.), 1–5,
    9–20, 136, 199n2, 201n39, 201n42; and
    civil rights activism, 14–15, 33, 128, 172–
    73, 185, 187–88, 203nn55–56, 203n60,
    221n47; design of, 10–20, 201n45,
    202n54; and effort to "save the Mall,"
    186; gardens on, 10, 14, 75; L'Enfant's
    plan of, 10–11, *11,* 106, 171, 173; and
    McMillan Plan, 12–13, *13,* 15, 38, 75,
    106–7, 136, 166, 169–171, 173, 202n51,
    226n40; military buildings on, 10, 14,
    75, 202n53; museums on, 11, 13; and
    Obama's inauguration, 227n67; peri-
    ods of neglect, 10, 12–13; pilgrimages
    to, 1, 11, 20, 202n48; as sacred national
    ground, 14–15, 173, 185; as symbolic
    space, 10, 12, 14–15, 27, 107–8, 187–88,
    227n66; train station on, 10, 12; what
    was speakable on, 18, 95; and White
    City (Chicago World's Fair), 12, 107,
    202n49. *See also names of war memori-
    als and other structures on the Mall*
National Park Service (NPS), 13; archives
    of, 201n40; and Black Revolution-
    ary War Patriots Memorial, 76, 81, 83–
    84, 86, 88, 92, 212n52, 214n106; and
    National Japanese American Memorial
    to Patriotism during World War II, 135–
    36, 138, 140, 143; and National World
    War II Memorial, 173, 186, 190–91,
    227n72, 227n74; and Women in Mili-
    tary Service for America Memorial, 98,
    103–4, 106, 108–10, 113–15
National Women's Hall of Fame, 104–5
National World War II Memorial, 2, 19–
    20, 152–195, *181, 183, 192, 193;* advertise-
    ments for, 175–76; background of, 154–
    56; and beheaded columns (proposed),
    168–171, *169,* 173–74, 179, 182, 184, 191,
    195; bronze wreaths in, 152, 179–181, 183,

186; as "bureaucrat's idea of classical grandeur," 186, 192; and cenotaph (proposed), 179, 182, 184; as "complete architectural recognition of the war," 191–92; corporate sponsors for, 176; dedication of, 19, 155–56, 180, 191; design competition for, 164–68, 225n30; eagles in, 152, 179–180, 182–84, 186; and *Enola Gay* fight, 161–63, 194; and eternal flame (proposed), 174, 178–180, 184–85; and Fascist architecture, 169–170, 173–74, 181–82, 187–88; fiftieth anniversary of, 158, 160; final design of, 180–86, *181, 183;* first design of, 168–174, *169,* 175, 179, 182; fundraising for, 175–78; geographic terms of, 153–54, 174–75, 180, 183, *183;* "Here We Mark the Price of Freedom," 152, 190, 196; inscriptions in, 152, 154, 174, 179–181, 185, 188–191, *193,* 196; and lawsuits, 186–88, 191, 227n66; leaving objects at, 191–92, 227n72, 227n74; legislation for, 152, 158–59, 224nn10–11; and Lincoln's Bixby letter, 176–77, 226n45; and MacLeish's poem, 153–54, 156, 177, 179–180, 184, 190–91, 196; and militarism, 173, 182, 194–95; and museum or visitors' center (proposed), 168, 173–74, 224n10, 225n30; and National Japanese American Memorial to Patriotism during World War II, 128, 132, 140; as national recovery project, 165; origins of, 30, 98, 157, 205n30, 224n8; and peace, 179; pillars in, 152, 154, 180, 190; and power, 157, 173–74, 182–83, 195; and Rainbow Pool, 152, 154, 160, 163–64, 168–69, 172–73, 175–76, 180, 185–87, 225n30, 225n32, 226n40; as reclamation project, 178; as representing defining moment of twentieth century, 159–161, 164, 172, 189; and "sacred soil" at site from cemeteries around world, 160, 225n18; and *Saving Private Ryan* (film), 175–78, 208n80, 226n45, 226n49; second design of, 174–75; site of, 159–164, 166–67, 170, 173, 175, 182, 185–87; steles in, 180–81; third design of, 178–180; triumphal arches in, 152, 174, 178–181, 184, 186, 190; visitors to,

152, 170–71, 184–85, 189, 191, 196, 224n1; Wall of Freedom in, 180, 184; wall of gold stars in, 152–54, 184–86, 188, 190–91, *192;* water elements in, 152, 154, 174, 180–81, *193;* website of, 186–87

National World War II Memorial Advisory Board, 158–59, 161, 170, 185, 224nn11–12

Native Americans. *See* American Indians

Navy Memorial, 103, 203n64

Navy Nurses Corps, 100

Nazis, 173–74, 181–82, 187–88

Negro League, 214n93

neoclassical architecture, 12, 16, 92, 106–7; and National World War II Memorial, 168, 170–71, 173–75, 180–82, 189

newspapers: Dear Abby letter, 37; editorial pages of, 173; letters to the editor, 30–31, 33–34, 155, 182. *See also names of newspapers*

Newton, David, 91–92

New York Times: on Black Revolutionary War Patriots Memorial, 78–79; on Daughters of the American Revolution, 67–68, 71; on Korean War Veterans Memorial, 34, 49; on National World War II Memorial, 180; on women in military, 216n25

Ngai, Mae, 126–27, 150, 219n1

Nichi Bei Times (San Francisco), 144–45

9/11 memorial, 167

9/11 terrorist attacks, 191, 193, 220nn19–20, 224n6

Nixon, Richard M., 8, 14, 75

No-No Boy (Okada), 148–49

Norris, Bill, 34

Norton, Eleanor Holmes, 172, 185

Oakar, Mary Rose, 99, 102, 104

Obama, Barack, 227n67

O'Brien, Greg, 68

Occidental International Corporation, 38

Office for the National Mall and Memorial Parks, 191

Okada, John, 148–49

O'Leary, Cecelia, 7, 47

Olick, Jeffery, 3

Olin, Laurie, 167

Owenby, Barry, 190

Page Law (1875), 126
Panama, invasion of (1989), 101, 216n19
parks as memorials, 6, 155
Parris, Stan, 33, 36
Parsons, John, 138, 140, 143
Pascoe, Peggy, 60
patriots/patriotism, 3, 12, 33, 75, 196; and
    Black Revolutionary War Patriots
    Memorial, 71–74, 87–88, 212n61; and
    Daughters of the American Revolution,
    65, 67–69, 211n39; and Japanese Ameri-
    can soldiers killed in war, 221n36; and
    Korean War Veterans Memorial, 33, 40,
    43; and National Japanese American
    Memorial to Patriotism during World
    War II, 18, 127, 130, 133–37, 145–150; and
    National Liberty Memorial, 89–90; and
    National World War II Memorial, 157,
    161, 164–65, 167, 177–78, 193; and Viet-
    nam Veterans Memorial, 33, 193
PBS, 70
Peck, Robert, 49, 111–12, 174
Pei, I. M., 38
Pennsylvania State University, 42, 207n61
Pennypacker Oberholtzen, E., 43, 207n61
Pentagon, 101, 128
Penthouse magazine, 31
Pepper, Claude, 35
Perot, Ross, 114
Phelan, James, 126–27
Phillip Morris, 78
Piestewa, Lori, 101–2, 216n24
Poor People's March, 203n60
Poston internment camp, 122, 147
Potomac River, 107, 121, 187
Powell, Colin, 77
Powell, Earl, 167
prejudice, 67, 122, 124, 140, 149. See also
    discrimination
Public Works Administration, 180
Puerto Ricans, 7, 46
Purnell, Marshall, 79–83, 85

Quakers, 65
Queissner, Robert, 184

race/ethnicity, 6–7, 33; and apartheid, 70,

212n55; and Black Revolutionary War
    Patriots Memorial, 60, 74, 83, 87–88,
    94–95; and black/white dichotomy, 68,
    74; and Coast Guard SPARs, 216n14;
    and Daughters of the American Revo-
    lution, 14, 62–70; and Korean War
    Veterans Memorial, 17, 30–31, 45–46,
    48, 50–53, 51, 56–58, 61, 95, 204n17,
    207nn62–63, 208n73; and miscege-
    nation, 18, 60, 64, 67–68, 74; multi-
    racial color guards, 47; and national-
    ism, 4–5, 20, 200n17, 200n20; and
    National Japanese American Memorial
    to Patriotism during World War II, 18–
    19, 124, 126–134, 138–39, 144–45, 147,
    150–51, 220n19; and National Liberty
    Memorial, 89–91; and National World
    War II Memorial, 153, 171, 224nn2–3;
    racial logic, 18, 88, 150; racial profiling,
    220n19; racial purity, 18; and skin color,
    67–69; "traces of race," 51–53, 56, 58,
    83; and Vietnam Veterans Memorial,
    46–47; and whitening of memory, 2, 7–
    8; and Women in Military Service for
    America Memorial, 100, 216n14; and
    Women's Army Corps (WACs), 100.
    See also names of racial and ethnic groups
racism, 69, 74, 124, 130, 145, 151
Rainbow Pool, 152, 154, 160, 163–64, 168–
    69, 172–73, 175–76, 180, 185–87, 225n30,
    225n32, 226n40
rape, 101, 216n25
Reagan, Ronald: and Black Revolutionary
    War Patriots Memorial, 71, 73, 213n70;
    and Daughters of the American Revo-
    lution, 69; and Korean War Veterans
    Memorial, 36–39, 158; and National Jap-
    anese American Memorial to Patriotism
    during World War II, 142; and Viet-
    nam Veterans Memorial, 16, 37–38; and
    Women in Military Service for America
    Memorial, 104
Reflecting Pool (Capitol), 159
Reflecting Pool (Mall), 14, 24, 159, 164,
    166–67
Reich Chancellery, 182
remembering/remembrance, 4–9, 197;

and Black Revolutionary War Patriots Memorial, 98; and Korean War Veterans Memorial, 22, 26–27, 31, 34–35, 42, 45–46, 48–49, 54, 58; in MacLeish poem, 1, 20; and National Japanese American Memorial to Patriotism during World War II, 18, 134, 137–38, 147; and National World War II Memorial, 153, 156, 178, 205n30; and Vietnam Veterans Memorial, 16

Renan, Ernest, 3–4, 40

Republican Party, 213n70

Revolutionary War, 2, 18, 59, 61, 73–74, 199n3, 203n55; Continental Army, 74; and Daughters of the American Revolution, 63–64, 67–68, 210n11, 211n35, 211n39; Fourth Massachusetts Regiment, 99; and National Liberty Memorial, 90–91; Society of Cincinnati, 226n56; and war dead, 18, 70–71, 89; women in, 99, 102. *See also* Black Revolutionary War Patriots Memorial

rewriting the past, 1–2, 5, 20; and Black Revolutionary War Patriots Memorial, 60–61, 74, 91, 95; and civil rights activists, 14; and Korean War Veterans Memorial, 21, 32–33, 47, 56; and National Japanese American Memorial to Patriotism during World War II, 124, 127; and National World War II Memorial, 170, 190–91, 194–95

Richmond Times-Dispatch, 90–91

Robinson, Harry G., 113–14, 170

Rodriguez, Carlos, 206n42

Roosevelt, Eleanor, 14, 70

Roosevelt, Franklin Delano, 159, 172, 226n40

Roosevelt Memorial, 159, 172, 226n40

Roots (Haley), 17, 61, 66

Roxworthy, Emily, 125, 219n4

sacrifice, 4, 6, 196–98; and Black Revolutionary War Patriots Memorial, 17–18, 59, 94–95, 213n79; in Civil War, 2, 106–7; and Korean War Veterans Memorial, 20, 22, 26, 29, 31–32, 36, 39–41, 43–44, 48, 54–58, 61; and National Japanese

American Memorial to Patriotism during World War II, 122, 124–25, 127, 129–134, 146, 150; and National World War II Memorial, 20, 153, 155–56, 162, 164–65, 167, 169–172, 174–75, 177–78, 180, 184–85, 188–190, 194–95; and Vietnam Veterans Memorial, 16, 72, 131; and Women in Military Service for America Memorial, 102–3, 116, 120. *See also* sacrificing soldiers

sacrificing soldiers, 197–98; and Black Revolutionary War Patriots Memorial, 17, 59, 61, 72, 94–95; and Korean War Veterans Memorial, 20, 22, 32, 44, 58, 61; and National Japanese American Memorial to Patriotism during World War II, 124–25, 127, 131, 133, 150; and National World War II Memorial, 20, 153, 162, 194–95; and Women in Military Service for America Memorial, 98, 107, 120

Sampson, Deborah, 99

Samsung Information Systems, 37

Sandage, Scott, 14

Sand Island (Hawaii) internment camp, 141, 222n50

Santos Ferguson, Lena: and Black Revolutionary War Patriots Memorial, 71–72, 77–79, 88; and Daughters of the American Revolution, 62–71, 77, 88, 92, 211n34, 212nn52–53; and National Liberty Memorial, 91

Saudi Arabia, 114–15

Savage, Kirk, 7, 9, 47, 201n42

Saving Private Ryan (film), 175–78, 208n80, 226n45, 226n49

Schwartz, Barry, 26, 46, 55, 204n17, 207n63

Scottish Rite Masons, 215n119

Scruggs, Jan, 15–16, 30

Secret Service, 130

segregation/desegregation: housing segregation, 8; and Marian Anderson concert, 14; and military service, 31, 45, 47, 153, 216n14, 223n83; and National World War II Memorial, 153; Thurmond as segregationist, 60; and Women's Army Corps (WACs), 100

Selective Service System, 8, 29, 148

Senate, U.S., 72, 91, 158, 162; Committee on Energy and Natural Resources, 96; Subcommittee on Public Lands, 96; Subcommittee on Public Lands, Reserved Water, and Resource Conservation, 96. *See also* Congress, U.S.; *names of U.S. senators*

September 11, 2001, terrorist attacks. *See* 9/11 terrorist attacks

service flags, 2, 152, 184, 224n1, 226n58

Sharpton, Al, 59–60

Shaw Memorial (Boston), 47

Sherman, David, 106, 108

Shurtleff, Robert. *See* Sampson, Deborah

Sight Unseen (Berger), 224n3

Signers Memorial, 14, 75–76, 80–82, 85, 89, 202n54

Simon, Cathy, 167

Singh, Nikhil, 220n26

Sino-Japanese War, 22

Site Specific (Weiss and Manfredi), 219n83

Skidmore, Owings, and Merrill, 75

slaves/slavery, 7; and Black Revolutionary War Patriots Memorial, 73–74, 76, 87; and Daughters of the American Revolution, 64, 67; and genealogy, 59–60; and Mount Vernon's Ladies Association, 65; and National Liberty Memorial, 89–91; in Revolutionary War, 64–65, 67, 73–74, 76, 81; runaway slaves, 73–74, 76, 81, 90; and slaveholders, 81, 106; slave pens on Mall, 10; and slave trade, 10, 38

Smiley, Tavis, 70

Smith, Fred, 175

Smith, Luther, 171

Smith, Wayne, 79

Smithsonian Institution, 10–11, 202n48; "The Crossroads: The End of World War II, the Atomic Bomb, and the Cold War" (exhibition), 161–63, 194; *A More Perfect Union* (exhibit), 128, 220n13; National Air and Space Museum, 161–63, 194; National Museum of American History, 128, 159, 220n13; National Museum of the American Indian, 135

social power/position, 9, 16, 19–20, 197, 201n39; and Daughters of the American

Revolution, 69; and Korean War Veterans Memorial, 21; and National World War II Memorial, 191, 205n30

Society of Cincinnati, 226n56

Society of the Third Infantry Division, 96

Sogi, Francis, 143

soldiers, 2, 6, 196–98; and Black Revolutionary War Patriots Memorial, 17–18, 59–61, 71–76, 81–88, *84, 85,* 92–95, 212n61, 214n113; and blind devotion, 17, 19, 21, 57, 61, 88, 98, 123, 127, 132, 146, 148, 150–51, 209n107; burial in marked graves of, 2, 6, 155, 199n5; citizen soldiers, 2, 6–7, 17, 156, 193, 199n3; in Civil War, 2, 6, 18, 47, 61, 70, 76, 106, 199n8; and Daughters of the American Revolution, 66, 68, 210n11, 211n35, 211n39; and dog tags, 2, 6, 226n58; and *Enola Gay* fight, 161–63; and Korean War Veterans Memorial, 17, 21–29, *25, 28,* 36, 40–58, *50, 51, 55,* 98, 204n7, 204n17, 207n55; and Lincoln's Bixby letter, 176–77, 226n45; and MacLeish's poem, 1–2, 20, 153–54, 156, 177, 179–180, 184; naming of, 6, 16, 25, 41, 48, 69, 122, 125, 137, 141–42, 185–86, 206n49, 218n79, 221n31, 224n4; and National Japanese American Memorial to Patriotism during World War II, 18–19, 122–25, 127–134, 137, 141–42, 146–151, 221n31; and National Liberty Memorial, 89–91; and National World War II Memorial, 19, 152–54, 156, 158, 161–64, 168, 171, 176–180, 194–95, 227n74; in post-Vietnam wars, 3, 17, 97, 101, 114–15, 199n8, 216n19; and *Saving Private Ryan* (film), 175–76, 178, 208n80, 226n49; and service flags, 2, 152, 224n1; and Vietnam Veterans Memorial, 2–3, 6–8, 16–17, 131–32, 199n8; and Women in Military Service for America Memorial, 97–102, 106–7, 114–16, 119–120, 216n19, 216nn24–25, 218n79. *See also* sacrificing soldiers

Sons of the American Revolution, 62

Sontag, Susan, 201n37

Soviet Union, 33; collapse of, 21; invasion of Afghanistan, 29; and Korean War, 22–24

Spanish-American War, 100
SPARs, 216n14
Speer, Albert, 173–74, 181–82
Spielberg, Steven, 175, 178
Spreiregen, Paul, 165–66, 173
Stanton, Robert, 84, 113, 214n106
Stevens, Ted, 91
Stewart, Jimmy, 203n56
St. Florian, Friedrich, 168–69, *169*, 171–74,
    178–182, 184–85, 194–95
Stilwell, Richard Giles, 46–49, 189,
    206nn42–43, 207n66
Stilwell family, 38, 206n43
Strom Thurmond Memorial, 93–94, *94*,
    215n128
Stump, Bob, 187
Sunday Herald (Boston), 126
Suny, Ronald, 199n9
Supreme Court Building, 135

Taggart, Cal, 146–47
Takahasha, Rita, 143, 147
Tashima, A. Wallace, 147–48, 223n83
Teraski, Paul and Hisaka, 146
terrorists, 130, 220n19. *See also* 9/11 terror-
    ist attacks
*Their Last Battle: The Fight for the National
    World War II Memorial* (Mills), 155–57,
    189–190, 192–94
Theus, Lucius, 215n119
Third Infantry Memorial, 96–97
Thompson, Elizabeth, 62–63
Thurmond, Strom, 59–60, 70, 158, 211n44;
    memorial of, 93–94, *94*, 215n128
Tiberio, Faith K., 65
Tidal Basin, 159, 172, 187, 203n61
To Heal a Nation (Scruggs), 16
traditional art, 32–33, 168. *See also* neoclas-
    sical architecture
tragedy, 7; and Black Revolutionary War
    Patriots Memorial, 88; and Korean
    War Veterans Memorial, 17, 25, 30, 57;
    and National World War II Memorial,
    177, 179, 195–96; and Vietnam Veterans
    Memorial, 17, 25, 30, 57, 189
trauma, 5, 16, 145, 178, 200n18
triumph, 1, 13, 16, 47, 196; and Black Revo-
    lutionary War Patriots Memorial, 82,

88; and civil rights activists, 14; and
    Korean War Veterans Memorial, 26,
    34; and National Japanese American
    Memorial to Patriotism during World
    War II, 129, 137, 139, 149–150; and
    National World War II Memorial, 152,
    154, 160–61, 171, 174, 178, 180, 182, 184–
    85, 188, 191–92, 194–95; and Vietnam
    Veterans Memorial, 16
Truman, Harry, 22–23, 142
Tsutsumida, Cherry, 125–27, 138, 145
Tuchman, Barbara, 206n43
Tule Lake (Calif.) Relocation Center, 122,
    142, 148
Twenty-Fifth Infantry Division Associa-
    tion reunion, 34
Tyler-Bender Mandatory Discharge Relief
    Act (2002), 216n16

Union Station, 122, 136
United Daughters of the Confederacy, 65,
    70
United Farm Workers, 193
United Nations, 23, 27, 30–31, 35, 41, 57,
    204n11, 205n34; Security Council Reso-
    lution 82, 23
United States: Great Seal of, 226n56; and
    imperial power, 26, 29, 54, 57, 119–120,
    154, 182; and Korean War, 22–24, 26,
    204n7
Upton, Dell, 16, 203n66, 215n128

Vaught, Wilma, 98, 104–6, 108–10, 112,
    114–15, 118, 120–21, 217n38
Vessey, John W., 167–68
veterans, 196–97; African American, 36,
    61, 71, 79, 92, 98, 103; of Civil War, 7;
    Japanese American, 79, 125–133, 145–
    46, 149, 221n31, 221n36; of Korean War,
    17, 21, 30–38, 41–42, 45–46, 50, 55, 57,
    79, 98, 102, 205n20, 206n40, 206n42;
    of Revolutionary War, 36, 61, 71, 79, 92,
    98, 103, 203n55; of Vietnam War, 15–16,
    30–34, 37, 46–47, 102–3, 131, 163, 172,
    175, 191; women as, 36, 97, 99, 103–4,
    110, 116–17; of World War II, 18, 45–46,
    79, 98–99, 102, 125–133, 145–46, 149,
    152–58, 161–63, 167–68, 170–71, 175–76,

veterans *(continued)*
    186, 191, 194, 205n30, 221n31, 221n36,
    224nn11–12. *See also names of veterans
    and veterans' groups*
Veterans Day (1995), 160
Veterans of Foreign Wars, 99, 104, 191
Vietnam Veterans Memorial (VVM), 6–
    7, 16, 46, 197; and Black Revolutionary
    War Patriots Memorial, 72, 75; call for
    designs for, 50, 165, 206n49; dedica-
    tion of, 1, 14, 32–34, 37, 167, 205n30;
    designed by Maya Lin, 16, 37–39, 165,
    168, 189, 191, 203n66; fundraising for,
    36; Korean War Veterans Memorial as
    response to, 17, 21, 24–25, 27–34, 36–
    41, 45, 48–50, 57–58, 98, 131, 206n49,
    208n83; leaving objects at, 6–7, 17, 191;
    National Japanese American Memo-
    rial to Patriotism during World War
    II compared to, 128, 131–32; National
    World War II Memorial as response
    to, 131, 156–57, 159–160, 163, 165, 167,
    170, 172, 174, 178, 185–86, 188–190,
    193, 226n58; origins of, 15–16, 30; pro-
    posed by Jan Scruggs, 15–16, 30; reac-
    tions to, 16–17; as redemptive, 131; *The
    Three Servicemen* sculpture, 16, 37–38,
    46–47, 50, 160; visitors to, 6–7, 16–17;
    Women in Military Service for Amer-
    ica Memorial compared to, 98–99, 102,
    114, 218n77
Vietnam War, 2–3, 8, 19, 28, 57, 197, 199n8;
    and anti-war movement, 15, 166, 193–94;
    and Clinton letter, 55–56; and military
    service, 2–3, 8, 16, 19, 55–56, 161, 163, 176,
    178; and National Liberty Memorial,
    89; and war dead, 6–7, 16, 34, 41, 186,
    191, 226n58; women in, 102
Vietnam Women's Memorial, 99, 103
Von Eschen, Penny, 23

WACs (Women's Army Corps), 99–100,
    158
Wade, Yolanda, 90–91
Walker, James Dent, 67
Wall Street Journal, 67, 71
Walton, William, 38
War Department, 147

war memorials, 6–9; avoidance of violence
    in, 48–49; history of, 1, 6–10, 15–17,
    199n2, 201n40, 201n42, 203n66; living
    memorials, 6, 8, 31, 106, 155–56, 202n53;
    memorial-building frenzy on Mall,
    27, 39, 76, 135–36, 196, 205n30, 221n35,
    226n40; and nationalism, 3–4, 6, 15–17;
    private donations for, 36–37; resistance
    to, 155; traditions of scale for, 45, 48, 76,
    81, 85, 97, 152, 159–160, 170–73, 182; visi-
    tors to, 1, 16–17, 20. *See also names of
    war memorials*
war movies, 48, 175–76, 208n80, 226n45
War of 1812, 201n45; women in, 99–100
Washington, George, 2, 10, 75, 89, 106,
    226n56
Washington, Martha, 106
Washington Afro-American, 78
Washington Monument, 10–12, 14,
    201nn46–47; and Black Revolutionary
    War Patriots Memorial, 75; and defin-
    ing moments of eighteenth century, 160,
    164, 172, 189; and Korean War Veterans
    Memorial, 48; and National World War
    II Memorial, 160, 164, 166, 168, 170,
    187–88
Washington Monument Society, 10
Washington Post: on Black Revolution-
    ary War Patriots Memorial, 71, 86; on
    Daughters of the American Revolution,
    62–63, 65–67, 69, 71; on Korean War
    Veterans Memorial, 33; on National
    Japanese American Memorial to Patrio-
    tism during World War II, 125, 219n2;
    on National World War II Memorial,
    165; on Women in Military Service for
    America Memorial, 110, 117–18, 218n82
Washington Post and Times Herald, 30
Washington-Williams, Essie Mae, 70–71,
    93–94, 211n44
Watt, James, 37–38
WAVES, 100
Weak Link (Mitchell), 216n18
Weber, William E., 206n42
Weiss, Marion, 110–14, 118–120, 218n70,
    219n83, 225n32. *See also* Weiss/Manfredi
Weiss/Manfredi, 110–14, 118–120, 218n70,
    219n83

Wheeler, Peter, 158
White City (Chicago World's Fair), 12, 107, 202n49
White House, 12, 201n45
whites: and Black Revolutionary War Patriots Memorial, 60–61, 72, 74, 83, 88, 94–95; and Chinese immigrants, 126; and civil rights activists, 14; and Daughters of the American Revolution, 64–65, 67–69, 210n11; and Korean War Veterans Memorial, 17, 46–47, 51–53, 51, 55, 88; and National Japanese American Memorial to Patriotism during World War II, 127; and National Liberty Memorial, 89–90; and National World War II Memorial, 224n3; and Vietnam Veterans Memorial, 46–47; White City (Chicago World's Fair), 12, 107, 202n49; whiteness, study of, 47, 52; whitening of memory, 2, 7–8, 47, 197; whitening of Washington, D.C., 12; white supremacy, 60, 69; and Women in Military Service for America Memorial, 97, 102; and Women's Army Corps (WACs), 100
Willenz, June, 104
Williams, F. Haydn, 159–160, 171, 178–79, 184
"Willie and Joe" (cartoon), 158
Winch, Julie, 68
Windchy, E. G., 33–34
Winter, David, 226n54
Winter, Jay, 5–6, 9, 200n20
witnessing, 9–10, 197, 201nn39–40
women: Asian women prohibited from immigration, 126; in combat units, 100–101, 197; gold-star mothers, 155, 176–77, 226n45; Japanese American women in internment camps, 126; and Korean War Veterans Memorial, 38, 47–48, 206n42; and "manifest domesticity," 218n75; and National World War II Memorial, 181; as nurses during war, 100; passing for men in military, 99–100; pregnant women in military, 100, 216n16; Woman Suffrage Procession (1913), 203n55; women with children in military, 100. See also Daughters of the American Revolution (DAR);

gender; Women in Military Service for America Memorial (WIMSAM); names of women
Women in Military Service for America Memorial (WIMSAM), 1, 18–19, 27, 36, 96–121, 107, 116, 117, 119, 205n30; background of, 98–105; corporate sponsors for, 97, 114–15; dedication of, 97, 116–17, 120; design competition for, 108–10, 118, 225n32; design of, 109–14, 217nn63–64; Education Center in, 114; exhibition space in, 110, 117–18, 218n79; Faces of the Fallen exhibit, 218n79; fundraising for, 36, 97, 104–5, 110, 114–15, 218n75; Grove design for, 110; hall of honor in, 111, 119; and Hemicycle, 106–16, 118–19; invisibility of, 96–99, 103, 105, 110–18, 120–21, 132; leaving objects at, 218n79; museum in, 98; and National Japanese American Memorial to Patriotism during World War II, 128, 132; National World War II Memorial compared to, 153, 156; night lighting for, 110–11; online registry for, 98, 108, 110, 114, 117, 119; origins of, 98–99; and peace, 102; and pleached lindens, 112–14, 217n63; Pylons design for, 110–11; raffle to raise funds for, 114; resistance encountered by, 18, 97–98, 101, 216n18; Saudi and Kuwaiti funds for, 114–15, 218n75; signage for, 18–19, 98, 115–16, 117, 120–21, 218n77; site of, 105–9, 113, 120; Spiral design for, 110; theater in, 98, 108, 110, 119; underground construction of, 18–19, 98, 108–11, 114; visitors' center in, 108; visitors to, 104, 115–17, 218n79; water feature in courtyard of, 112–13, 118
Women in Military Service for America Memorial Foundation, 98–99, 102, 104, 109–11, 113–15; website of, 109
Women in the Military (Mitchell), 216n18
Women's Armed Services Integration Act (1948), 100
Women's Army Auxiliary Corps, 100
Workingman's Party, 126
World Columbian Exposition (Chicago, 1893), 12, 107, 202n49

World War I: and dog tags, 2, 6, 226n58; and living memorials, 155; and military buildings on Mall, 10, 14, 202n53; and service flags, 184, 226n58; and war dead, 6, 184, 226n58; World War I Memorial, 170, 199n2, 203n64

World War II, 3, 6, 8; Allied Forces, 179–180; Battle of the Bulge, 157, 181; fiftieth anniversary of, 157; and GI Bill, 155; as "good war," 3, 161, 163, 194, 199n8; and greatest generation, 19, 149–150, 152, 158, 176; and Iwo Jima Memorial, 30, 157, 224n6; and living memorials, 6, 8, 31, 106, 155–56, 202n53; Pearl Harbor, 180, 193; and war dead, 124–25, 130, 137, 152–57, 160, 168, 170, 177, 179–180, 184–86, 195; women in, 100, 102, 181, 184, 224n2. *See also* National Japanese American Memorial to Patriotism during World War II; National World War II Memorial

World War II Veterans to Save the Mall, 186

Yoda, Steve, 145

Young, James, 9

"The Young Dead Soldiers Do Not Speak" (MacLeish), 1–2, 20, 153–54, 156, 177, 179–180, 184, 190–91, 196